THE MUR

Greg King's biography of the Tsarina Alexandra, *The Last Empress*, was critically acclaimed. A devoted Russophile from youth, King has visited Russia frequently and has been invited to attend the re-burial of the late Royal family scheduled for 2 years ago, but postponed because of Russia's military involvement in Chechnya. Mr King lives in Washington State.

To Laura

with my sincere thanks for
her generous sacrifices, which
helped make this book possible

And to Gabe

for his invaluable friendship
and ability to make me believe

The Murder of Rasputin

The Truth about Prince Felix Youssoupov and the Mad Monk who Helped Bring Down the Romanovs

GREG KING

ARROW

First published by Arrow in 1997

1 3 5 7 9 10 8 6 4 2

Copyright © Greg King 1997

The right of Greg King to be identified as the author
of this work has been asserted by him in accordance
with the Copyright, Designs and Patents Act, 1988

First published in the United Kingdom in 1996 by
Century, 20 Vauxhall Bridge Road, London SW1V 2SA

PUBLISHED BY ARRANGEMENT WITH CAROL PUBLISHING
GROUP INC, 600 MADISON AVENUE, NEW YORK, NY, USA

Arrow Books Limited
Random House, 20 Vauxhall Bridge Road, London SW1V 2SA

Random House Australia (Pty) Limited
16 Dalmore Drive, Scoresby, Victoria 3179, Australia

Random House New Zealand Limited
18 Poland Road, Glenfield
Auckland 10, New Zealand

Random House South Africa (Pty) Limited
Endulini, 5a Jubilee Road, Parktown 2193, South Africa

Random House UK Limited Reg. No. 954009

A CIP catalogue record for this book
is available from the British Library

Papers used by Random House UK Limited
are natural, recyclable products made from wood grown in
sustainable forests. The manufacturing processes conform to
the environmental regulations of the country of origin

ISBN 0 09 965921 9

Printed and bound in Great Britain by
Cox & Wyman Ltd, Reading, Berkshire

Contents

Part Four   The Aftermath

Preface

FEW NAMES CONNECTED with the fall of the Romanov dynasty are as evocative and infamous as that of Gregory Efimovich Rasputin, the legendary Siberian peasant who had such a devastating influence on Tsar Nicholas II and his government. Less well known but forever linked to the peasant is Felix Felixovich Youssoupov, the prince who plotted and eventually carried out his murder. These two men were intimate players in the drama of the Russian Revolution; according to history, Rasputin's scandalous behavior and corrupting influence helped bring it about, while Youssoupov's heroic, if misguided, assassination signaled the beginning of the end of the imperial regime.

Dozens of books have been written about Rasputin and his malignant influence over Nicholas II and his wife, Alexandra. Felix Youssoupov himself is the subject of a copious body of literature. He figures to some degree in every book about Nicholas II, the fall of the Romanov monarchy, the Russian Revolution, and Rasputin. The prince left three autobiographical works. What more, the reader might reasonably ask, could there possibly be left to say about Felix Youssoupov?

There are several answers to this question. First, Prince Felix Youssoupov remains a controversial figure. Among some Russian émigrés he is still regarded as a misguided patriot who tried bravely to save the crumbling Romanov dynasty. Nearly three decades after his death, many still recall him—from personal experience—as a generous benefactor who tirelessly worked on behalf of the impoverished Russian exiles. This image of the prince contrasts violently with his recorded role in history as Rasputin's assassin. Indeed, Youssoupov's life is filled with contrasts: a man who hated the sport of shooting so much that he gave away all his guns, yet was later able to cold-bloodedly plot the murder of Rasputin; the wealthiest man in Russia, who, for a time after the Revolution, was reduced to selling off pieces of his wife's jewelry collection to survive; a man who protested that he did not wish to be remembered for only having killed Rasputin but who, in the end, firmly latched on to the assassination as his key to fame. Before the Revolution he was rich, young, and handsome—regarded as the most eligible prince in all of Russia, a golden youth blessed with all of life's bounty; he was also a notorious transvestite, a homosexual, and a drug addict, hopelessly attracted to the darker pleasures which flourished in imperial Russia.

I first encountered the multifaceted life of Prince Felix Youssoupov while writing my biography of the wife of the last tsar of Russia, Empress Alexandra Feodorovna. The prince naturally proved a central figure in the life of Gregory Rasputin. A study of Empress Alexandra restricted any further exploration into the life of Felix Youssoupov; yet the more I read, the more convinced I became that the prince deserved a biography in his own right. With this in mind I carefully began taking notes for future use.

Considering that the prince himself recorded his life in three separate books—*Rasputin*, in 1927; *Lost Splendour*, in 1952; and *En Exil*, in 1953—it may appear that there was little left to be said. But Felix wrote for posterity; he himself had a clearly defined vision of his life and his place in history and was careful to present only the most flattering portrait of his extraordinary existence. At times he was incredibly candid, describing his transvestite activities and feelings toward women, but it was also a candor tempered by the times in which he wrote. Felix played with the truth to best suit his own ends. There is no clearer example of this than in his description of Rasputin's murder.

Rasputin's murder ensured Felix's place in history. Only a handful of twentieth-century crimes are as well known as the peasant's assassination in 1916. It was described by two of the participants, Felix and another conspirator, Vladimir Purishkevich, in several books and numerous interviews. The murder has formed the centerpiece of biographies of the peasant and has been dramatized on both film and stage. The story of the poisoned peasant, beaten and shot, who refuses to die and eventually succumbs to the icy waters of the Neva River is the stuff of legend. Rasputin's death, like his life, has become a modern myth.

Felix's version of Rasputin's death is not the only account available to historians and Russian scholars; it is, however, the most widely read and repeated version, cited endlessly in the numerous works in which Felix figures. Unfortunately for history, it is filled with inaccuracies, evasion, and lies. Although few historians have questioned the prince's veracity, evidence exists which at the very least challenges many of his assertions concerning the crime. Felix wrote that Rasputin's murder was a political and patriotic act; but was there another, more intimate, personal motive for the crime? Several of those who knew Felix well believed there was and that the prince had carefully concealed the truth of that night to protect his reputation and salvage his place in history. And official documents which contradict the prince's version of the crime have largely been ignored. The truth of Rasputin's murder, therefore, becomes an integral element in the story of Felix's life, a mystery whose tangled threads have, I believe, been brought together for the first time in their entirety.

This book presents relevant, contradictory, and often overlooked evidence concerning Rasputin's murder. But it is more than a simple reinterpretation of that crime. Born into incredible wealth and privilege, Felix finally ended his days as one of the many dispossessed exiles living in France after the Russian Revolution. These two worlds—imperial Russia and the émigré Europe of the 1920s and 1930s—shaped the way in which Felix viewed himself and determined the way he responded to his curious life. Above all else, the picture that emerges is of a man of immense charm, style, and wit. Felix Youssoupov was accustomed to the finest things money could buy, but even when he counted himself among the dispossessed exiles living in France, he managed to live his life with great sophistication and elegance.

Perhaps the most astonishing aspect of the story is the utter banality of Youssoupov's life. He ensured his place in history by killing Rasputin. But he remains little more than a historical footnote. Had he not struck out against the peasant, Felix would undoubtedly have become one of the countless exiles following the Revolution who sank into obscurity, unremembered and ignored. Precisely because he killed Rasputin, however, Felix was able to maintain a certain celebrity status; he was not above using the murder for his own ends, whether social or financial.

At times it has been difficult to piece together the various threads of Felix's life. Twenty-six volumes of Youssoupov papers and documents are held in the Central State Archives in Moscow; but most of this material deals not with the prince but with his ancestors and their relations with members of the Romanov dynasty. When Felix fled Russia, he took some documents with him; but following his death in 1967, his daughter Irina Sheremetiev burned or destroyed most of his personal papers. It is impossible to say whether this was done to protect her father's reputation from any indiscretions he may have confided to paper or if it was simply a misguided act of housecleaning. The destruction of these documents, however, means that the greatest concentration of information on Felix and his life is to be found in his three books. Whenever possible, therefore, I have tried to supplement and confirm the prince's own accounts with the letters, memoirs, and diaries of his contemporaries. In cases where some question of Felix's truthfulness may exist, such as Rasputin's murder, I have been careful to present all the available evidence.

In the end, the picture of Prince Felix Youssoupov which emerges is at times amusing, at times highly tragic. He himself acknowledged his darker side, and it is worth recalling that in this he accurately reflected the self-indulgent world of imperial Russia in which he was raised. He was also capable of great good; the man who killed Rasputin freely gave his own money away to needy exiles when he himself was in dire financial circumstances. This life of contrasts is, in the end, far more interesting than the portrait left to us by the prince himself or that recorded by history and is also more flattering to his enigmatic memory.

Author's Note

I<small>N THIS BOOK</small> I have followed the accepted custom of mixing the Russian titles *Tsar* and *Tsarina* with the Western Emperor and Empress. Until 1721 all Romanov rulers used *Tsar*, a title replaced by Peter the Great with the more Western *Gosudar Imperator* (Sovereign Emperor). The strict etiquette of the Russian court demanded the use of the Western titles; however, Nicholas II himself preferred the more Russian *Tsar*, and the older title was commonly used by his subjects until the Revolution.

The transliteration of Russian names conforms to the Library of Congress method, with certain exceptions. For the sake of clarity and recognition all proper names have been rendered in Western fashion: thus, "Paul" for "Pavel" and "Serge" for "Sergei." I have yet to come across a satisfactory and recognizable transliteration of the name Youssoupov. The Russian transliteration "Iusupov" would be virtually unknown among Western readers; I have therefore chosen the form "Youssoupov," which I believe closest to correct.

Until 1918 the Russians used the Julian rather than the Gregorian calendar. As a result, in the nineteenth century, dates were twelve days behind those in the West; in the twentieth century, the discrepancy was thirteen days. For all events in Russia until the change to the Gregorian calendar in 1918, I have used the Julian calendar; thus, Rasputin's murder, which, according to the Western calendar, took place on 29 December 1916, is here described as having occurred on 16 December 1916. All dates after 1918 are rendered according to the Gregorian system.

The Murder of
Rasputin

Prologue:
St. Petersburg, 1909

P RINCE FELIX YOUSSOUPOV stood at the tall drawing-room windows of the Golovine Mansion, staring out across the thawing ice which choked the Winter Canal in St. Petersburg. Spring had come late to this great northern city, perched at the edge of the Gulf of Finland. Trees reached their leafless fingers toward the expansive sky, spreading above the ugly slush which covered the elaborate gardens and broad avenues. In the late-afternoon sunshine, the windows of the pastel palaces along the Winter Canal blazed like fires, their golden reflections shimmering in the dark waters which spilled into the Neva River.

The Russian capital was filled with handsome, privileged aristocrats, but none was as wealthy or as attractive as Felix Youssoupov. The scion of an ancient noble house, Prince Youssoupov was tall and thin, beautiful rather than handsome, with golden hair, deep blue eyes, and long, almost feminine lashes. He was, as always, impeccably turned out, dressed this afternoon in one of his many suits imported from the best tailors in London and Paris. The clothes were a mark not only of his exquisite, meticulous tastes but also of his vast wealth. Prince Felix Youssoupov, twenty-three years old, cultivated and arrogant, was sole heir to the single largest private fortune in all of Russia.

He had come to this imposing stone mansion on the Winter Canal at the invitation of Maria Golovine. The Golovines were aristocrats who had often served in tsarist governments as advisers and ministers. Maria's late father had been a state councillor, and his widow still commanded great respect among the capital's élite.

Felix Youssoupov had known Maria Golovine for several years. Called Munya by her friends, she was an attractive young woman, popular in St. Petersburg's upper-class circles. Felix later described her as "exceptionally pure minded, good-natured and responsive, and unusually impressionable." He continued.

> But there was much nervous exaltation in her character; and, thanks to this, her spiritual impulses always predominated over her reason. Religion played the chief part in her life, but her religious feelings were tinged with an unhealthy mysticism. Truthful to excess, she was totally incapable of judging either people or facts. When anything surprised her she blindly yielded to the impression which it made on her. She remained wholly under the influence of those in whom she believed and she did not readily distinguish good from evil.[1]

Munya Golovine was deeply in love with Felix. In an effort to capture his attention, she had told him about a new pilgrim then making the rounds of the capital. She described him as "a man of rare spiritual strength, filled with God's blessing, who had been sent to the world to cleanse our hearts and guide our wills, thoughts and conduct."[2] She asked Felix to come to her house to meet him, and the prince agreed, perhaps out of curiosity. Thus, the first meeting between Prince Felix Youssoupov and Gregory Rasputin took place.

Both Munya and her mother waited expectantly for Rasputin. According to Felix, their faces were filled with "the solemn expression of persons awaiting the arrival of a miraculous icon which was to bring a divine blessing on the house." The trio remained silent; suddenly, the drawing-room door opened, and Rasputin entered. The prince later wrote that "there was something repugnant about him."[3]

Youssoupov prided himself on his epicene beauty; not surprisingly, he found Rasputin coarse and common. The peasant was of medium height, strongly built, with long arms and wide shoulders. Thin strands of long hair, parted in the middle, framed his oval face. No one would ever describe Rasputin as a handsome man. Youssoupov found his large nose and thin lips "of the most ordinary peasant type."[4] His long, unkempt beard reached down to his chest. Above all, his narrow eyes, blue gray and piercing in their intensity, commanded attention. "His whole being attracted attention," Youssoupov wrote. "He appeared uncontrained in his movements and yet there seemed to be something dissembled about him, something suspicious, cowardly, searching."[5]

The Golovines invited both Felix and Rasputin to take tea. During the meal, Rasputin spoke on a variety of subjects. Rasputin, according to Felix, "apparently wishing to maintain the tone of one inspired from above, held forth in a dictatorial manner. His speech was quick, voluble, yet often faltering. He quoted scripture texts which had no connection with each other, and his words gave the impression of something involved, if not chaotic."[6]

When tea finished, Rasputin rose to leave. Pointing toward Munya but directing his remarks to Felix, he said, "What a faithful friend you have in her. You should listen to her, she will be your spiritual spouse. Yes, she has spoken very well of you, and I too now see that both of you are good and well suited to each other. As for you, my dear boy, you will go far, very far."[7] With this, Rasputin left.

Contrary to what he would later write in his books, Felix was intrigued by Rasputin. He left the Golovine house "filled with the strange impression" that Rasputin had made on him. A few days later, Munya told him that Rasputin again wished to see him and that he had enjoyed his meeting with the prince. Youssoupov, however, soon left Russia to finish his education at Oxford. A second meeting between prince and peasant did not take place until 1916, when Felix Youssoupov was actively plotting Rasputin's murder.

PART ONE

The Victim

1

Father Gregory of the Street of Peas

THE SUN HUNG LOW in the northern sky, a soft, luminescent halo glowing through the mist of a late autumn afternoon in Petrograd, capital of imperial Russia. Ice choked the Neva River, which cleaved the city in half, mirroring in its fast-flowing waters the grim stone bastions of the Fortress of Saints Peter and Paul and its cathedral's golden spire. The sidewalks along the city's famous Nevsky Prospect bustled with late-afternoon strollers, carefully skirting the gray slush to take their regular promenades. Fat doormen in silk top hats and tight-fitting red-and-black coats bowed as beautiful women rushed from doorway to curb, stepped into their Renault and Delanay-Belleville motorcars, and sped away to keep appointments with hairdressers, jewelers, and couturiers. The food stalls at Yelisievs' Store overflowed with fresh sturgeon, caviar on ice, exotic, out-of-season fruits, and delicate French pastries, luxuries to grace the tables of those who could afford them. These aristocrats adorned themselves with imported British and French fashions and dazzling gems from Fabergé, Bolin, Cartier, and Bulgari. As darkness crept over the city, the black windows of the baroque and classical palaces filled with light, burning through the fog and casting long shadows over the granite quays and winding canals. Smart carriages and brightly painted troikas raced along the streets, carrying refined women and handsome officers to midnight parties and discreet, romantic rendezvous.

It was the fall of 1916, an autumn of delusions. The Great War was two years old, a bitter struggle in which the Russian empire, already ill prepared to navigate the turbulent waters of the twentieth century, suffered greater and more devastating losses than any of the other Allied nations. Petrograd, however, showed little sign of the terrible conflict. Officers lounged in the smoking rooms of their fashionable clubs, sipping champagne and puffing cigars as thousands of their recruits were slaughtered in the trenches.

There were two worlds in Petrograd, each living beside the other, seemingly oblivious to either's existence. At the very apex stood Russian society. In the capital, as elsewhere in the empire, their lavish parties, dinners, and balls continued with the opulence of the prewar years. At the theater, Mathilde Kschessinska, onetime mistress to Tsar Nicholas II, enchanted audiences as she danced *The Pharoah's Daughter*; the basso Feodor Chaliapin sang *Boris Godunov* and *Don Quixote*; and at the Mariinsky Theatre, Tamara Karsavina danced in *Sylvia* and *The Water Lily*. The French ambassador in Petrograd, Maurice Paléologue, recalled: "From the stalls to the back row of the highest circle I could see nothing but a sea of cheery, smiling faces. In the interval the boxes came to life with the irresponsible chatter which made the bright eyes of the women sparkle with merriment. Irksome thoughts of the present, sinister visions of war and the melancholy prospects of the future vanished as if by magic the moment the orchestra struck up. An air of pleasant unreality was in every face."[1]

The reality of the war told more heavily on those unfortunate enough to serve in the front lines or their families left behind who went hungry every night, unable to pay the ever-increasing prices. Buried deep within the shadows, hidden by the factory gates and shielded from the refined sensibilities of many aristocrats, were the working poor, hundreds of thousands of men, women, and children who considered themselves fortunate to have a bed of straw and a bowl of soup each night. The war devastated these workers, deprived them of their young men, made widows and orphans, and broke their spirits. Every day, they rose, trudged through the snow to their factories, toiled for up to sixteen hours, and then, exhausted, stumbled back to the barracks in which they lived.

After two years of the war, Russia somehow staggered on, its economy near collapse, shortages in food and fuel supplies growing every day. Hopes for an early and decisive victory had vanished, replaced with an air of grim indifference. It no longer seemed to be a great patriotic adventure, but a slow, fruitless exercise in humiliation for the Russian troops. When hundreds of thousands of soldiers were lost in the 1916 Austrian campaign, dissent spread across the country. "It was about this time that I first heard people speaking of the Emperor and Empress with open animosity and contempt," remembered Grand Duchess Marie Pavlovna. "The word 'revolution' was uttered more openly and more often; soon, it could be heard everywhere. The war seemed to recede into the background. All attention was riveted on interior events."[2]

Public attention no longer focused on the immense hulk of the Winter Palace, the chief residence of the Romanov tsars. Its deep red quarter-mile length, once brilliantly aglow with golden light from the windows which pierced its façade, was now cloaked in darkness. Hundreds of bureaucrats shuffled along the busy Nevsky on their way to offices and government ministries. But the real center of power in Petrograd that autumn was believed to lie in a simple flat located in the working district of the capital. Here, in a third-floor apartment, lived Gregory Efimovich Rasputin.

Gorokhavaia Ulitsiia—"the Street of Peas"—was very much lower middle class territory. With the money at his disposal, Rasputin could easily have afforded to live at a more fashionable address. But he liked the air of solidarity there, the comfort and the lack of pretension. He first moved into an apartment there in 1914; it would remain his home until his death two years later.[3]

An archway led from the street to the courtyard. The main foyer, with a tiled floor and twisting staircase decorated with an elaborate wrought-iron banister, was not the only means of entrance: Hidden away in a corner of the yard was a small door which opened to a narrow staircase leading to the back door of Rasputin's flat. Rasputin found this an asset; it enabled him to come and go unobserved.

Rasputin's flat, no. 20, was located on the third floor. There were five rooms: a drawing room, a dining room, a study, and two bedrooms, along with a bathroom and kitchen. The flat reflected Rasputin's bourgeois tastes. Massive oak furniture dec-

orated most of the rooms. In the dining room a sideboard filled
with crockery stood next to the table, on which sat a steaming
samovar. Rasputin's bedroom was simply furnished, with a narrow bed covered in a red fox spread, a large chest, and walls
hung with icons and cheap lithographs of Tsar Nicholas II and
Tsarina Alexandra. In the drawing room, chairs lined the walls;
this is where the expectant waited to meet the peasant. His study
was decorated with crude oil paintings, some undoubtedly gifts
from admirers. On a small stand in the anteroom, near the front
door, stood a telephone—Rasputin's link to the Alexander Palace at Tsarskoe Selo, the imperial family's principal residence.

At all hours of the day and night, lines of visitors awaiting
an interview with the peasant stretched up the inside staircase.
All believed that behind these doors lay great power. Visitors
who struck Rasputin's fancy often received a card with a
scrawled "My dear and valued friend: Do this for me. Gregory."[4]
Rasputin wrote slowly and usually did not bother to name the
favor requested or even the correct recipient. "All were drawn
up the same way," wrote Alexander Mossolov, head of the court
chancellery, "a little cross at the top of the page, then one or two
lines giving a recommendation from the *starets*. They opened all
doors in Petrograd."[5]

Rasputin received his petitioners in the large dining room.
Walking through a set of double doors, they finally came face-
to-face with the most infamous man in all of Petrograd. Rasputin
was scarcely an imposing figure. But it was his eyes that struck
most visitors, as they had Prince Felix Youssoupov. "They were
pale blue," wrote one man, "of exceptional brilliance, depth and
attraction. His gaze was at once piercing and caressing, naïve
and cunning, far-off and intent. When he was in earnest conversation, his pupils seemed to radiate magnetism."[6]

Many of the visitors were female. Women seemed fascinated by the man they called Father Gregory. His crude language
and rough demeanor stood in stark contrast to many of their
dilettantish husbands and lovers. Rasputin delighted in humiliating and embarrassing these cultivated members of society,
with their fashionable Parisian dresses and foppish manners. He
described to them the sexual relations of horses in detail, laughing at their downcast eyes and condemning stares. "Yes, yes, my

dears, you are all much too pampered," he would declare. "Follow me in the summer to Pokrovskoe, to the great freedom of Siberia. We will catch fish and work in the fields and then you will really learn to understand God."[7]

Favored visitors often stayed for tea. Rasputin presided at the head of the table, passing cups from the steaming samovar to his eager devotees. His table manners apparently left much to be desired: Aaron Simanovich, who acted as his secretary, later described the peasant "plunging his dirty hands into his favourite fish soup."[8] He would take a bite out of a sandwich or pickled cucumber, then offer the remaining portion to his guests, who begged to be so favored. He loved to test his disciples, dipping his fingers into a pot of jam, then offering his hand to one of his female guests, saying, "Humble yourself! Lick it clean, lick it clean!"[9]

Such peculiar displays formed part of the gospel according to Father Gregory. Rasputin's religious teachings were a curious mixture of sin and salvation, and many women eagerly acceded to his advances. "As, in the eyes of his disciples, Rasputin was a reincarnation of the Lord," wrote one biographer, "intercourse with him, in particular, could not possibly be a sin, and these women found for the first time in their lives a pure happiness, untroubled by the gnawings of conscience."[10] While this is of questionable accuracy, there is little doubt that Rasputin found dozens of willing partners. When one took his fancy, he would rise from the table and lead his choice away, whispering, "You think that I am polluting you, but I am not. I am purifying you." Together, the pair would disappear into his bedroom, described by his followers as "the Holy of Holies."[11]

A number of police detectives stood guard at the main entrance to Rasputin's flat. They were there to protect the peasant as well as to take notes on his activities. Each kept a small book detailing Rasputin's days:

Anastasia Shapovalenkova, the wife of a doctor, has given Rasputin a carpet.[12]

An unknown woman visited Rasputin in order to try to prevent her husband, a lieutenant at present in the hospital, from being transferred from St. Petersburg. . . . [She said] "A servant opened the door to me and showed me to a room where Rasputin, whom I had never seen before, appeared immediately. He told me to take off my clothes. I complied with his wish and went with him into an adjoining room. He hardly listened to my request but kept on touching my face and breasts and asking me to kiss him. Then he wrote a note but did not give it to me, saying that he was displeased with me and bidding me to come back next day."[13]

Madame Likhart visited Rasputin . . . to ask him to intervene on her husband's behalf. Rasputin proposed that she should kiss him; she refused, however, and departed. The mistress of Senator Mamontov arrived. Rasputin asked her to return at 1 A.M.[14]

During the visit of the Pistolkors family Rasputin took the prostitute Gregubova on his knee and murmured something to himself.[15]

As he [Rasputin] went up to his flat he inquired if there were any visitors for him. On hearing that there were two ladies he asked: "Are they pretty? Very pretty? That's good. I need pretty ones."[16]

Rasputin came home in an intoxicated state . . . but left again immediately . . . and did not come back til about 2 A.M., very drunk.[17]

Rasputin came home at 7:30 A.M. with two men and a woman; he was dead drunk, and sang songs on the public street. The unknown persons accompanied him up to his flat and then departed.[18]

The wife of Colonel Tatarinov visited Rasputin and . . . the *starets* embraced and kissed a young girl in her presence; she found the incident so painful that she decided never to visit Rasputin again.[19]

Maria Gill, the wife of a Captain in the 145th Regiment, slept at Rasputin's.[20]

Rasputin came back with Varvarova at 9:50 A.M.; he must have spent the night with her.[21]

Rasputin sent the concierge's wife for the masseuse but she refused to come. He then went himself to Katia, the seamstress who lives in the house, and asked her to "keep him company." The seamstress refused. . . . Rasputin said, "Come next week and I will give you fifty rubles."[22]

Rasputin sent the porter's wife to fetch the masseuse, Utilia, but she was not at home. . . . He then went to the seamstress Katia in her flat. He was apparently refused admittance for he came down the stairs again and asked the porter's wife to kiss him. She, however, disengaged herself from his embrace, and rang his flat bell, whereupon the servant appeared and put Rasputin to bed.[23]

The police kept track of all Rasputin's movements, following him about the capital. When the public learned of the existence of these notes, there was a black market for them, and soon Petrograd wallowed in page after page of Rasputin's sexual exploits. The rumors soon reached a deafening crescendo. "Rasputin's apartments are the scene of the wildest orgies," the American ambassador reported. "They beggar all descriptions and from the current accounts of them which pass freely from mouth to mouth, the storied infamies of the Emperor Tiberius on the Isle of Capri are made to seem moderate and tame."[24]

Such scandalous tales, rumor, and speculation passed from person to person, repeated in newspapers, chalked on walls, and printed in cheap pamphlets, raised the level of animosity to a fever pitch. "Rasputin, Rasputin, Rasputin—it was like a refrain," recalled Grand Duchess Marie Pavlovna; "his mistakes, his shocking personal conduct, his mysterious power. This power was tremendous; it was like dust, enveloping all our

world, eclipsing the sun. How could so pitiful a wretch throw
so vast a shadow? It was inexplicable, baffling, almost incredible."[25] By the fall of 1916, even before his infamous murder,
Gregory Efimovich Rasputin had passed into the realm of legend.

2

Rise to Power

RASPUTIN: HIS VERY NAME has become synonymous with debauchery, sexual licentiousness, evil ambition, and corruption. Little in his life falls into the realm of uncontested fact. The year of his birth has only recently known, and there is next to nothing on record concerning his early life. Even his later, better-documented years in St. Petersburg are open to interpretation: Was he a drunken, barbaric, power-hungry Janus who virtually ran the Russian government during World War I or a simple peasant with spiritual gifts whose enemies did all they could to discredit him? More than any other character in the final drama of the Russian Empire, Rasputin has continued to fascinate. The truth of Rasputin's life lies somewhere between these two diverse views—saint and sinner. Even his name and occupation have disappeared into myth. Rasputin was his family surname, not a nickname given in recognition of his early debaucheries, and he was not a monk; Rasputin had no formal affiliation with any religious order. Yet he is remembered as the "Mad Monk" who almost single-handedly destroyed the Russian Empire.

The acknowledged facts of his life are few. He was born in Pokrovskoe, a small but prosperous Siberian village perched on the banks of the Tura River in Tobolsk Province. Most of Pokrovskoe's citizens lived in little peasant cottages of rough, unpainted logs, with a small barn or pigsty attached at the side. Life on the edge of the Siberian taiga was difficult and shaped the character of the people who lived there. Most of Pokrovskoe's inhabitants were simple, deeply religious, and conservative.

Until recently, the exact date of Rasputin's birth remained a mystery. Various writers and historians speculated that it could have taken place anywhere between 1864 to as late as the mid–1870s. However, the Administrative Records Book of Tobolsk province now reveals that Rasputin was born on 10 January, 1869. There is next to nothing on record of Rasputin's early life. His father, Efimy Rasputin, had at one time been a coachman in the imperial mail, although he was allegedly dismissed for drunkenness and is later said to have turned to horse stealing.[1] By the time of Rasputin's birth, however, Efimy had prospered as a farmer, and his eight-room house was one of the largest in all of Pokrovskoe.

There is little accurate information about Rasputin's childhood. He had an older brother who died by drowning, which seems to have left a vivid impression on the younger boy. One of the earliest stories concerning Rasputin, and one which must be treated with great caution, tells of a gift of prophecy. According to the story, Rasputin, then a small boy, was in bed, ill with a high fever, when his father hosted a group of local peasants, brought together to discuss the theft of a horse. The animal had been owned by one of the poorer peasants, and the villagers were furious. Because the peasants made their living from farming, the theft of a horse was considered a capital crime. As the men spoke, Gregory suddenly sat up in his sickbed and pointed at one of the startled peasants, announcing that he was the thief. Quickly, Rasputin's father stepped in, saying that his son was delirious from his fever and could not be held responsible for his words. But several of the peasants were suspicious of the accused man's reaction. Following him to his house, they saw him lead the stolen horse from his barn and release it into the fields. They beat the peasant severely and recaptured the horse for return to its owner.[2]

If young Rasputin did indeed possess any exceptional powers, he seems not to have cultivated them until he was much older. Whatever religious leanings the boy may have had were soon subjugated to his growing sexuality. It did not take long for Rasputin to acquire a reputation as a local rake. He took a job as a driver for a supply wagon, traveling from village to village within Tobolsk province; on these journeys, he frequently met pretty, voluptuous peasant girls who were not averse to his advances. Rasputin wasted little time on the niceties of the chase, preferring instead to simply grab chests and rip buttons. As a result, he was often kicked and bitten.[3] But many of the girls did not resist, and Rasputin's name soon became notorious among the villages of the province.

On one of his journeys Rasputin traveled to Verkhoturye Monastery. Gregory was so fascinated by what he found there that when he was later sentenced for stealing some fence posts from a neighbor, he asked that as his punishment he be sent to the monastery rather than prison. He stayed for several months. At Verkhoturye, he encountered two heretical sects whose members had found refuge and protection within the Orthodox cloister, the Khlysty and the Skopsty.

The Khlysty believed in masochistic beatings as a form of religious worship; at times, and within certain groups of Khlysty followers, these wild rituals ended in indiscriminate sexual intercourse among the celebrants. Some of the sect members believed that only in this way could they reach God: First, sin had to be committed, then confessed, in order to receive true forgiveness.[4]

This belief in the use of "sin to drive out sin" was not the only heretical philosophy which the young Rasputin encountered at Verkhoturye. The Skopsty held beliefs so influential that Rasputin later came to adopt them as his own. The Skopsty believed that after a period of deprivation, study, penance, and prayer, it was possible to attain the nature and omnipotence of God. They eventually came to interpret this as meaning that whatever sins one might commit, a person who had thus attained this divine nature could not be judged because he had risen above earthly judgment. They also believed that chastity was "the sin of pride" and thus it was wrong to remain chaste only to present a holy image.[5]

Rasputin's own religious beliefs are difficult to delineate. He tended to assimilate the philosophies of others and reinterpret them as his own perverse theology. When Rasputin returned to Pokrovskoe from Verkhoturye, he declared that he had undergone a religious transformation. He was careful to make no claim of special powers, but his aura of holiness certainly attracted the attention of his impressionable friends. He found a woman who was willing to accept the undoubted challenge of being his wife, and the pair were married sometime after 1890.[6] In later years, when she learned of her husband's reputed sexual exploits in the capital, Praskovie Dubrovina never complained, saying, "He has enough for all."[7] Praskovie bore Rasputin four children, two boys and two girls. One son died in infancy, the other was retarded. But the two girls, Maria and Varvara, grew up quite normally and later lived for a time with their father in St. Petersburg.

There is no doubt that Rasputin's religious activities attracted a following in Pokrovskoe. His neighbors believed that he was a member of the Khlysty sect, and there were all sorts of rumors about what really went on in the small cellar which Rasputin had decorated as a chapel. Eventually these tales reached the village priest, who lodged a formal complaint with the archbishop of Tobolsk Province. It was only the first of the many allegations which were to surface about Rasputin's involvement with the sect. The archbishop duly investigated and found that the charges were false; while Rasputin certainly seemed to be fascinated by the sect and eventually borrowed some of their theological ideas as his own, he was never a member of the Khlysty. The allegations, however, were harmful in themselves, no matter what the truth behind them, and they did much to damage Rasputin's already dubious reputation in Pokrovskoe.

One day, while working in the fields, Rasputin claimed to have seen a vision. According to Gregory, the Virgin Mary, dressed in magnificent robes, appeared in the sky and gestured toward the horizon, a sign which he interpreted as an instruction to become a pilgrim. Whether Rasputin actually saw something or merely suffered from a hallucination is irrelevant; the fact is that he seems to have been genuine in his conviction and truly believed that he had been visited by the Virgin Mary. Rasputin staggered home and announced his intention to embark on a journey to find God. His father regarded this suspiciously, saying, "Gregory has turned a pilgrim out of laziness."[8] But there is no reason to believe that Rasputin did not enter on his journey sincerely.

According to Gregory, the Virgin Mary had told him to

walk to the Holy Land. Rasputin left Pokrovskoe and walked some two thousand miles, finally ending his journey in Greece, at a monastery at Mount Athos. He was gone for two years. When he returned to Pokrovskoe, he was certainly a changed man. His entire manner was different. He spoke in riddles, adding bits of theology picked up from the Orthodox Church and from such heretical sects as the Khlysty and the Skopsty and peppering these long, rambling thoughts with half-remembered quotations from the Bible. As a result, his conversation was "desperately hard to follow."[9] Even so, Rasputin was a powerful speaker; he undoubtedly had a gift of persuasive talk and proved to be a charismatic leader among the simple men of Pokrovskoe.

Rasputin eventually left his native village; although it has often been alleged that he was practically driven from Pokrovskoe by villagers angered at his lecherous behavior, the truth appears to be far more mundane. He seems to have left simply on another pilgrimage. Two of the many legends surrounding Rasputin spring from this second journey. The first concerns his name. It has been said that the villagers in Pokrovskoe gave Gregory "Rasputin" as a nickname. In fact, it was his surname, probably derived from the Russian word *raspute*, meaning a fork in the road, and not *rasputstvo*, debauchery, as has often been claimed.[10]

Certainly, the biggest contradiction in Rasputin's character was his sensuality, which he frequently used to achieve his goals. Some of his favorite activities appear to have been sleeping with several naked women or having them wash his sexual organs as a test of his self-control. In the last years of his life, his carnal appetites were enormous, yet there is no reliable evidence that he ever resorted to force to obtain sexual gratification. Apparently, Rasputin never regarded the apparent contradiction between flesh and spirit with any puzzlement.

Equally pervasive misconceptions concern Rasputin's religious affiliations. The Russian Orthodox Church endorsed the belief that God endowed ordinary men with spiritual gifts of healing and foresight. The church contained many wandering holy men rumored to possess divine powers. Called *Stranniki*, many of these holy men spent their lives walking back and forth across the Russian Empire, residing in monasteries or taking advantage of the hospitality offered by local nobility. There were also monks in the church who lived their lives as spiritual guides to the powerful. Such men, given the title of *starets*, were thought not only to heal the spirit but also to interpret the will of God to those seeking answers. Although they operated on the fringes of established Orthodoxy, they were recognized as being if not official representatives of the church, then certainly of their faith.

Rasputin was never a *starets*. A true *starets* lived an austere, religious life, devoid of the sexuality which was a hallmark of Rasputin's later life. Rasputin was simply a wandering peasant in search of adventure and his own salvation. While there is little doubt that he himself believed he had been chosen by God to undertake various journeys, there is no evidence to suggest what Rasputin's genuine religious concerns may have been.

In 1902, Rasputin arrived in Kazan, where he made a favorable impression among the local clergy. Bishop Andrew was so impressed with this new pilgrim that he arranged for Rasputin to visit St. Petersburg, the capital of imperial Russia, so that he could meet with the most important members of the Orthodox Church. In the capital, Gregory met the city's ecclesiastical hierarchy, Father John of Kronstadt and the inspector of the St. Petersburg Theological Academy, Archimandrite Theophan. In turn, Theophan introduced the peasant to Bishop Hermogen of Saratov. It was not unusual for a simple peasant to attract such attention in the Russian capital. Wandering men of God frequently caught the eye of this or that priest, bishop, or prince, who would then promote his new find to his society friends. It was, however, unusual for such an exalted group of church officials to take an interest in an unknown peasant, which gives some indication of the kind of presence which Rasputin must have possessed.

Of the clergy who received Rasputin in St. Petersburg, perhaps none was as influential as Father John of Kronstadt, who presided over St. Andrew's Cathedral at the naval base outside the capital. Father John was one of the most gifted and inspirational of the Orthodox clergy and had served as personal confessor to several members of the imperial family. Many of the Orthodox faithful flocked to him to confess their sins personally, such was his popularity. Their large numbers caused Father John to develop a new form of the sacrament: He gathered his congregation together and listened while they all shouted out their sins at the same time.[11]

Rasputin's introduction to St. Petersburg society brought the two diverse worlds of imperial Russia into a dramatic collision. Rasputin represented the great mass of Russian peasantry, of limited education, narrow-minded and deeply religious. The women of the aristocracy mirrored the world of intense privilege. They were restrained on the exterior, but many longed for something new and daring. In the strange, mysterious peasant, they found their answer. Some women looked to him for rough, sensual pleasures, with which—if the stories about Rasputin are to be believed—he would be only too happy to supply them. Men would look to him for spiritual guidance and, later, power. Others, offended by his crude manner and lack of humility, would openly condemn him as a fake and accuse him of trying to obtain personal power and influence through his contacts in society.

Rasputin left the capital after five months, only to return again two years later. This time he had come to stay. Eventually, Rasputin came to the attention of two members of the imperial family, Grand Duchesses Militza and Anastasia, daughters of King Nicholas of Montenegro. Militza and Anastasia were impressed enough with this new holy man to mention him to the tsar and tsarina. Nicholas and Alexandra were naturally curious and asked Archimandrite Theophan, who also served as their personal confessor, his opinion of the peasant. According to one source, Theophan told the imperial couple the following:

> Gregory Efimovich is a peasant, a man of the people. Your Majesties will do well to hear him, for it is the voice of the Russian soil which speaks through him. . . . I know his sins, which are numberless, and most of them are heinous. But there dwells in him so deep a passion of repentance and so implicit a trust in divine pity that I would all but guarantee his eternal salvation. Every time he repents he is as pure as the child washed in the waters of baptism. Manifestly, God has called him to be one of His Chosen.[12]

Thus, with such an impressive introduction, did Gregory

Rasputin first come into the presence of his sovereigns. On 31 October 1905, Nicholas II recorded in his diary: "Today we have made the acquaintance of Gregory, a man of God, from Tobolsk Province."[13] The reception was brief, but the fateful meeting would change the course of Russian history.

3

The Miracle Worker

IN THE FIRST SIX YEARS of marriage, Empress Alexandra bore her husband Nicholas four daughters, Olga, Tatiana, Marie, and Anastasia. As loved as the four girls were, however, they could not inherit the throne. Paul I, who hated his mother, Catherine the Great, had changed the Romanov laws of succession so that females could inherit only after the legitimate male line in the family had been depleted. At the turn of the century, therefore, if Nicholas and Alexandra failed to produce an heir, the throne would pass to the tsar's brother Michael.

The desire to produce an heir quickly developed into the empress's obsession. Mystics and faith healers, all promising that they could control the sex of an unborn child, found a regular place at court. Both Nicholas and Alexandra believed that the age of miracles had not passed; indeed, the Russian Orthodox Church taught that God endowed certain people with special gifts. The tsar and empress spent many hours receiving various people claiming to be able to help them in their quest for an heir. One of these, known as Matrena the Barefooted, was a retarded peasant woman who wrongly predicted a son would soon be born. Another, Mitia Koliaba, proved a more disagreeable figure. Like Matrena, he was retarded; he was also a cripple, with deformed arms and legs, and suffered from epileptic attacks. When a religious spell came over him, Mitia collapsed on the floor, shrieking and howling, waving his arms and legs wildly in the air while an interpretor translated these cries as divine revelations. Not surprisingly, this spectacle proved so distasteful that he was dismissed.

A third, more influential mystic was Philippe Nazier-

Vachot. He was brought to the Alexander Palace by Grand Duchesses Militza and Anastasia. Nazier-Vachot's credentials were dubious: A former butcher in Lyon, he had turned to faith healing in an attempt to find a more lucrative source of income and had been arrested five times for practicing medicine without a license. He claimed extraordinary powers: once, in the Crimea, Prince Felix Youssoupov met Grand Duchess Militza riding in a carriage with a stranger. He bowed to her, but Militza refused to acknowledge his presence. A few days later, when Felix asked why she had failed to respond, Militza declared that he could not possibly have seen her, since she had been with Nazier-Vachot, "and when he wears a hat he is invisible and so are those who are with him."[1]

Nazier-Vachot first came to Russia in 1901, when the empress was again pregnant. He predicted a son, but the baby turned out to be Grand Duchess Anastasia. In spite of this failure, the Frenchman remained in favor. A year later, the empress was again rumored to be pregnant. Her friend declared that the baby would be a boy. But Alexandra did not give birth, suffering either from a miscarriage or a false pregnancy. Still, Nazier-Vachot continued. In 1903, he announced that the empress was again expecting. The royal doctors were called in and found no sign. By now, Alexandra had had enough and sent the little Frenchman packing. Before he left Russia, he declared that someday God would send the empress another friend who would help her through her troubles.

Alexandra finally gave birth to a son in July 1904. They called him Alexei; instantly he became the center of family attentions. But the joy over his birth quickly gave way to anxiety. At six weeks, Alexei began to bleed from the navel; for three days the blood flowed unchecked. Finally, it stopped. But, with the passing months, as the baby began to crawl about, his skin was covered with horrible dark bruises. Doctors were called in and made the tragic diagnosis: Tsarevich Alexei had hemophilia.

The blow was immediate. Overnight, the lives of the tsar and tsarina changed. Nicholas took the disaster with a fatalistic acceptance of misfortune; Alexandra, however, refused to abandon hope. The terrible knowledge that she herself had transmitted the illness to her only son preyed upon her; doctors were summoned, but each concurred with the original diagnosis. She spent hours praying in her darkened chapel, repeating over and over, "God is just."[2] Her brother-in-law Grand Duke Alexander Michailovich wrote that she "refused to surrender to fate. She talked incessantly of the ignorance of the physicians. She professed an open preference for medicine men. She turned toward religion but her prayers were tainted with a certain hysteria. The stage was ready for the appearance of a miracle worker."[3] It was "the miracle worker" whom Grand Duchess Militza brought with her to the Alexander Palace, in the person of Gregory Rasputin.

This accident of birth ensured Rasputin's privileged position at the Russian court. His influence over the tsarina, and by extension, the tsar, the court, and the Russian government, rested entirely on his ability to control the symptoms of Tsarevich Alexei's hemophilia. Both Nicholas and Alexandra were devastated when they learned of their only son's illness. Rasputin's mysterious powers offered not only comfort but also hope; as long as he remained, the peasant repeatedly assured the imperial couple, Alexei would live.

It is not known when Rasputin first healed the tsarevich. Certainly it could not have been much earlier than 1907, or two years after his introduction to the imperial family. Even so, he did not immediately rise to power; it took several years for the empress's dependency on his powers to reach its peak. But each summons to the palace brought with it success, and the impressionable empress quickly came to believe that Rasputin had been sent by God to save her son's life.

At the time of the tsarevich's birth in 1904, hemophilia remained a terrifying, mysterious disease. Little was known of its causes, even less of its treatment. It first appeared in Alexandra's family half a century earlier when her grandmother Queen Victoria gave birth to a hemophiliac son, Prince Leopold. No previous history had existed; the defective gene simply mutated and spread through Victoria's descendants with devastating results. Passed down from mothers to their sons, hemophilia was unpredictable. Queen Victoria had four sons, but Leopold alone suffered from the disease; of her five daughters, only Alice and Beatrice transmitted the hemophilia genes to their own children. It was through their daughters that hemophilia was passed to the royal houses of Germany, Spain; and Russia.

Princess Alice was Empress Alexandra's mother. When Alexandra married Tsar Nicholas II in 1894, the history of hemophilia within her family was well known. Yet the random nature of the disease meant that unless the tsarina actually gave birth to a hemophiliac son, neither she nor her husband would know if she herself carried the defective gene. It is possible that one or more of Alexandra's daughters would also have transmitted the disease had any of them survived and married. The effects of the disease within the Romanov family were limited to Tsarevich Alexei, but the tragedy of his hemophilia contributed in no small degree to the eventual fall of the dynasty.

Hemophilia first manifested itself in Alexei when he was six weeks old. The tsar wrote in his diary:

> Alix and I have been very much worried. A hemorrhage began this morning without the slightest cause from the navel of our small Alexei. It lasted with but a few interruptions until evening. We had to call . . . the surgeon Fedorov who at seven o'clock applied a bandage. The child was remarkably quiet and even merry; but it was a dreadful thing to have to live through such anxiety.[4]

On the third day, the bleeding abruptly stopped. Alexei recovered, and there were no further incidents for a year. Neither Nicholas nor Alexandra appear to have weighed this first attack against the tsarina's family history, and the imperial physicians made no diagnosis. Alexei quickly grew into a boisterous, chubby little boy whose golden curls and wide smile were the pride of his parents. Then, in July 1905, the young tsarevich suffered a tragic accident which left his parents with no doubt about the disease.

During one of his regular strolls, Alexei managed to climb to the side of his baby carriage and fall to the ground. There was no apparent damage. But within hours, a massive internal swelling formed. This time, when the imperial physicians were consulted, they were forced to admit that there was nothing that they could do. The devastating suspicion was now confirmed: Alexei had hemophilia.[5]

The effect on Nicholas and Alexandra was immediate. The birth of a male heir had occupied their thoughts and filled their prayers for ten years; now their beautiful, precious only son was stricken with an illness which even the doctors admitted they were hopeless to treat. "Your Majesty must realize," Dr. Serge Fedorov sadly told the tsar, "that the heir apparent will never be completely cured of his disease. The attacks of hemophilia will recur now and then. Strenuous measures of protection will have to be taken . . . against falls, cuts and scratches, because the slightest bleeding may prove fatal to persons afflicted with hemophilia."[6]

One of his cousins wrote that the diagnosis of hemophilia aged Nicholas ten years.[7] Alexandra was even more devastated. The knowledge that she herself had passed the disease to her beloved son crushed her spirit. She had never been comfortable with the public responsibilities thrust upon her as empress. Even in the early years of her husband's reign, she had found the endless receptions, dinners, and balls an ordeal. She hated being stared at, felt ill at ease among the critical ladies of St. Petersburg society, and knew herself to be less popular than her mother-in-law, the dowager empress, Marie Feodorovna. Alexei's hemophilia preyed upon her fragile state; when she was away from her son, Alexandra worried constantly over his health, and this preoccupation, along with her forced smile and pervasive shyness, brought first disapproval, then isolation from these aristocratic *grande dames*. Convinced that her son's illness was a sign of divine condemnation, the tsarina gradually withdrew from society, spending endless hours praying for the life of her son.

The parents' worries were intensified by the unpredictability of the disease. No one knew when or where Alexei's hemophilia might strike. One minute he could be playing happily with his sisters; then, after a fall or accidental bump, he and his family would be plunged into a nightmare of uncertainty and fear. A terrible cut or bump might cause little damage, while the slightest bruise could lead to a massive internal hemorrhage which threatened the tsarevich's life. There was no pattern to the disease, no reason, and doctors could do nothing to help the boy.

There is no doubt that Rasputin managed to arrest the tsarevich's bleeding. The simple facts are beyond dispute. Too many instances, too many witnesses, recalled the numerous occasions on which Rasputin appeared and healed the sick boy. Tsar Nicholas II's sister Grand Duchess Olga Alexandrovna, who can scarcely be called one of Rasputin's admirers, later recalled one such incident:

> The poor child lay in pain, dark patches under his eyes and his little body all distorted, and the leg terribly swollen. The doctors were just useless . . . more frightened than any of us . . . whispering among themselves. . . . It was getting late and I was persuaded to go to my rooms. Alicky [the Empress] then sent a message to Rasputin in St. Petersburg. He reached the Palace about midnight or even later. By that time, I had reached my apartments and early in the morning Alicky called me to go to Alexei's room. I just could not believe my eyes. The little boy was not just alive—but well. He was sitting up in bed, the fever gone, the eyes clear and bright, not a sign of any swelling in the leg. Later I learned from Alicky that Rasputin had not even touched the child but merely stood at the foot of the bed and prayed.[8]

And Prof. Serge Fedorov, one of the specialists who regularly treated the tsarevich, readily admitted: "When Alexei was bleeding, I was unable to stop it with any method." Rasputin, however, "would arrive, go up to the sick fellow, look at him without a single worry. After the very briefest time, the bleeding would stop."[9]

Perhaps the most dramatic of Rasputin's interventions occurred in 1912. That autumn, the imperial family traveled to Bielovezh, a hunting lodge in eastern Poland, for their annual shooting holiday. During their stay at Bielovezh, Alexei had an accident. While playing in his bathroom, he slipped at the edge of a large sunken tub and knocked his thigh against the ledge.[10]

When Dr. Eugene Botkin, one of the imperial physicians as-
signed to the tsarevich, examined the boy, he found a large swelling on the inside of his left thigh, just below his groin. In much
pain, Alexei was confined to his bed; within a week, however,
he appeared to have recovered, and Dr. Botkin pronounced him
well enough for the family to keep to their schedule and move
on to another hunting lodge, Spala.

At Spala, the tsarevich appeared to suffer a slight relapse,
and his worried mother kept him confined to the lodge for the
first few days. Finally, however, she agreed to Alexei's request
and took him for a carriage ride in the surrounding forest. The
empress's friend Anna Vyrubova accompanied them. The roads
at Spala were filled with deep ruts, and the ride was a rough
one. After several miles of this bumpy ride, the eight-year-old
boy complained of an uneasy feeling in his lower abdomen and
leg. He was hemorrhaging internally. In a panic, Alexandra ordered the driver to return to the lodge as fast as the carriage
would go. Anna Vyrubova later recalled: "That return drive
stands out in my mind as an experience in horror. Every movement of the carriage, every rough place in the road, caused the
child the most exquisite torture and by the time we reached
home, the boy was almost unconscious with pain."[11]

When doctors examined the boy, they discovered that the
swelling from Bielovezh had dislodged itself and set off a new
hemorrhage in the upper thigh. Both Dr. Botkin and his col-
league Fedorov cabled a number of specialists in the capital, who
rushed to Spala by train and carriage. But after examining the
boy, they decided that there was nothing to be done. There were
no medicines to control the hemorrhage. The blood flowed from
the torn vessels in the leg into the lower abdomen, forming a
dark purple swelling the size of a grapefruit. The left leg drew
up to allow the blood in the swelling a new space to fill and
relieve the pressure. The blood seeped through the little boy's
body, attacking tissue and bones. And although it flowed into
the abdomen, the blood soon reached a point where there was
no more room. Yet it still continued to flow.

The tsarevich's plaintive screams pierced the walls of the
hunting lodge, forcing servants to stuff their ears with cotton in
order to continue their work.[12] From the very beginning of the

crisis, Alexandra never left her son's bedside. Anna Vyrubova wrote: "During the entire time, the Empress never undressed, never went to bed, rarely even laid down for an hour's rest. Hour after hour she sat beside the bed where the half-conscious child lay huddled on one side, his left leg drawn up. . . . His face was absolutely bloodless, drawn and seamed with suffering, while his almost expressionless eyes rolled back in his head."[13] "The poor darling suffered intensely," the tsar wrote to his mother, "the pains came in spasms, and recurred every quarter of an hour. His high temperature made him delirious night and day; and he would sit up in bed and every movement brought the pain on again. He hardly slept at all, had not even the strength to cry, and kept repeating, 'Oh, Lord, have mercy upon me.'"[14] Alexandra sat beside her son, holding his hand, brushing matted hair from his sweat-drenched face, listening impotently as he cried out over and over again, "Mama, help me!"[15] But there was nothing which Alexandra could do except pray, begging God to save the life of her little boy.

The tsarevich was in so much pain that he repeatedly begged to die. "When I am dead, it will not hurt anymore, will it, Mama?" he asked in one heartbreaking moment.[16] In another period of calm, he tearfully begged his parents to build him a little monument of stones in the forest after his death so that they would not forget him.[17] "I was hardly able to stay in the room," wrote a devastated Nicholas to his mother.[18]

On 6 October, Dr. Fedorov announced to the grief-stricken parents that their son's stomach was hemorrhaging. Alexei, he said, might die at any moment. Facing the inevitable, the tsar and tsarina finally consented to the publication of medical bulletins on the state of their son's health. The first bulletin was published on 8 October; it did not, however, describe the nature of the crisis, and there was no mention of hemophilia. On the following day, the boy's condition was such that a priest was summoned to administer last rites to the tsarevich. A medical bulletin, prepared for release on the following day, announced the death of His Imperial Highness the Tsarevich Alexei.[19]

Rasputin was in disfavor with the imperial couple at the time, so they did not turn immediately to the peasant for a cure, as they had for earlier hemophiliac episodes. Only when her son's condition was pronounced desperate by the doctors did the empress ask Anna Vyrubova to cable the peasant, who was at his Siberian home in Pokrovskoe. In the telegram Alexandra asked the peasant to pray for Alexei's life. For the next few hours, she waited anxiously for the answer. Finally, it came: "The Little One will not die. Do not allow the doctors to bother him too much."[20] Within hours, the swelling on the boy's thigh began to disappear, and the internal hemorrhage stopped.

As with all of Rasputin's apparent cures, various theories have been put forth to explain what happened at Spala. It has been suggested that the alleged "miracle" was simply the result of a secret medical treatment. Fedorov told Gen. Alexander Mossolov, the chancellor of the imperial court, at the height of the crisis, "I do not agree with my colleagues. It is most urgently necessary to apply far more drastic measures; but they involve a risk. What do you think—ought I to say so to the Empress? Or would it be better to prescribe without letting her know?"

"I could not possibly give an opinion on so delicate a question," Mossolov replied. Fedorov did not confide to Mossolov what action he was considering. Later, when the tsarevich began to recover, Mossolov asked Fedorov, "Did you apply the remedy you spoke of?"

"If I had done so, I should not have admitted it," the doctor replied in disgust. "You can see for yourself what is going on here."[21] Later, Fedorov admitted that Alexei's recovery was "wholly inexplicable from a medical point of view." This seems to indicate that he was not responsible for the cure.[22]

It has also been argued that the "miracle" was simply a matter of coincidence, Rasputin's cable having arrived at Spala just as the swelling began to recede. Robert K. Massie has suggested that the calming effect of the telegram on the agitated empress was transmitted to her ailing son; because blood vessels are subject to increased pressure during times of stress, Alexei's relaxation might have eased the hemorrhage, thus bringing an end to the crisis.[23] While modern science lends support to this theory, it is unlikely that it is the answer to what happened at Spala in 1912. Alexander Mossolov, who was at the lodge, recorded that during those last days, the tsarevich was delirious and often unconscious. It is doubtful under these circumstances that he would have been aware of what was transpiring around him. The simple facts are beyond dispute. Alexei was dying; the doctors abandoned hope; the last rites were administered; Alexandra sent Rasputin a cable asking him to pray for the life of her son; he replied that the boy would survive; within hours, the hemorrhage ceased. This is powerful, though not conclusive, evidence in favor of Rasputin's ability to heal the tsarevich, even if it fails to explain how or why.

Innumerable theories have been put forward over the years to explain Rasputin's apparent miracles. His "powers" have formed an integral part of the legend surrounding his life. But what was Rasputin's enigmatic secret? How did this simple peasant from Siberia manage to alleviate the suffering of the heir to the Russian throne in the face of medical impotence?

Some have accounted for Rasputin's cures by dismissing his prayers as simply coincidental to each of Alexei's recoveries. Certainly, several of Rasputin's "cures" could have been coincidence, his pronouncements occurring at the same time as a completely natural cessation of the attack. Baroness Sophie Buxhoeveden, the empress's chief lady-in-waiting, believed that Rasputin used "his own sources of information and contrived to come in time for the recovery of the child to be attributed to him."[24] Buxhoéveden seems to implicate Anna Vyrubova, whom she disliked, as Rasputin's accomplice. This was a view championed by the tsar's mother and also by his cousin Grand Duke Alexander Michailovich. But such a theory pushes credulity to its limits. Had Rasputin effected cures of the boy only on one or two occasions, this might have been possible. But after performing this trick over and over again, during an eight-to-ten-year period, certainly his timing would eventually have faltered. The fact is that on no occasion did Rasputin's ability to heal the tsarevich fail him. While coincidence might reasonably have played a part in some of Rasputin's "cures," it cannot explain them all.

It has been argued that Rasputin used potions to drug the tsarevich. Rasputin was known to be friendly with a certain Dr. Peter Badmayev, a Tibetan specialist in herbal remedies. According to Rasputin's virulent enemy Serge Iliodor, Alexei was given "a yellow powder that made him ill without actually endangering his life."[25] These mysterious powders were allegedly administered by Anna Vyrubova. With such an accomplice in the palace, Rasputin would have been able to control not only the timing of the attacks but also his appearances at the tsarevich's side just as the boy began to improve.

Both Buxhoeveden's and Iliodor's theories rely on Anna Vyrubova's complicity for their success. It was Anna who would have had to have informed Rasputin of the boy's progress during his various attacks, and, according to Iliodor, it was she who administered Badmayev's herbal potions to the tsarevich. Such allegations can only be judged on the basis of Anna's loyalty, however, and here, at least, the evidence is overwhelming. Anna Vyrubova, for all of her dedication to Rasputin, was slavishly devoted to the empress. She had known Alexandra for six years prior to meeting Rasputin and remained at her side until the Revolution forced their separation. There is no doubt that her first allegiance was to Alexandra, not Rasputin.

Rasputin has frequently been accused of having used hypnosis to cure the tsarevich. There is some evidence that Rasputin did indeed study hypnosis, but this was not until his later years in the capital. The instruction was minimal, and his teacher was apparently driven from the capital before the lessons could progress.[26] It is doubtful that Rasputin ever mastered the practice. Even so, the idea that the peasant was able to hypnotize the sick tsarevich fails to account for such circumstantial obstacles as the boy's frequent unconsciousness, pain, and even his young age, any of which would likely have presented problems if a deception was involved. Joseph Fuhrmann rightly points out that had Rasputin employed hypnosis to cure the tsarevich, "observers would have realized the reason for Alexei's recovery."[27]

One possible explanation of Rasputin's mysterious powers may lie in his humble origins. Russian peasants were superstitious; they fervently followed the teachings of the Orthodox Church but tempered their devotion with deeply held beliefs in ancient folk remedies and supernatural powers. Certain people claimed to have an ability to control the flow of blood, known as *"zagovarivat' krov."* This was no simple peasant superstition, however; the practice was widely known, and numerous examples of this seemingly inexplicable power were mentioned by members of the imperial court. Baroness Sophie Buxhoeveden discussed this ability in her memoirs. When she was a small girl, one of the horses on her grandfather's estate had suffered a cut on the forelock which penetrated to the bone; the bleeding was such that it was thought that the animal would die. One of the stableboys spoke of a local peasant known as "Alexander the Horse-Leech," said to possess the power to control unchecked bleeding. Alexander was duly sent for, and after he mumbled a few incoherent words and touched the wound, the bleeding suddenly stopped.[28]

"*Zagovarivat' krov*" was apparently also used on human patients with the same results. It is not known if Rasputin himself was privy to this secret, although he would certainly have known of its existence. While such a power might have been employed by Rasputin had he possessed it, it could not account for those documented occasions when, as in Spala, he was nowhere near the tsarevich but worked his cure at a distance.

In the end, Rasputin's mysterious ability to alleviate the symptoms of the tsarevich's illness cannot be reasonably ascribed to deceptive practices, such as intentional medication of the boy, to sheer coincidence, to scientific explanations, or to the learned talents of hypnosis or "*zagovarivat' krov*." The only explanation which can be successfully argued and still be found to fit the facts is that Rasputin did indeed possess certain powers which enabled him to heal the tsarevich. While the Russian Orthodox Church later repudiated Rasputin, at the same time it continued to teach that miracles were real and that certain men had been blessed by God with an ability to heal others. Both Nicholas and Alexandra believed that this was possible, and their acceptance of Rasputin's apparent miracles was merely an extension of official church teaching. This belief in a divine gift further tinged Rasputin with an aura of holiness for the imperial couple, making it easier to dismiss the scandalous stories circulating about him or readily forgive his sins as a true penitent.

After Spala, Rasputin's position at court was finally secure. No matter what temptations he might yield to, no matter how many scandals his private life might hold, the empress would stand by him. Fedorov, disgusted by what he had seen, nevertheless admitted, "And look, Rasputin would come in, walk up to the patient, look at him, and spit. The bleeding would stop in no time. . . . How could the Empress not trust Rasputin after that?"[29]

4

The Fatal Friendship

AT FIRST RASPUTIN moved carefully in the aristocratic world he encountered in St. Petersburg. But the temptations of the capital—drink, women, power—proved too much for him to resist. It would be inaccurate to say that he drank frequently; only during World War I was he known to be drunk with any regularity. His falls stemmed from the nature of the capital— from those women who, out of boredom and craving for excitement, gave themselves freely to him, and the men who, knowing he held the tsar's favor, sought out his influence. Even so, he was never as powerful as his detractors believed; his hold on the imperial family rested solely on his ability to heal the tsarevich. He never understood the political situation in the capital and acted only as a filter for those who wished to communicate their views to the tsar. It was his greatest fault that he not only accepted the overtures made to him, thus promoting the belief that he held great power, but also that he failed to distinguish between his personal desires and those of the Orthodox Church. He did nothing to prevent the women who gave themselves to him from continuing to think that in committing a sin with him, they were growing spiritually. He gradually lost his resistance, and the line between sensual and spiritual pursuits became blurred.

Even at the height of his power and influence, Rasputin never seems to have attracted more than twenty or thirty dedicated followers. Most of them were women, religious devotees who eagerly listened to Rasputin's teachings. The most famous was Anna Vyrubova. She first met Rasputin when the peasant advised against her impending marriage with a young naval officer; Anna ignored Rasputin's dire predictions and married Alexander Vyrubov. Within months, the unconsummated marriage collapsed, and Anna turned to the peasant for spiritual comfort. Along with Rasputin, she was to assume a near-legendary status as one of the evil forces which helped bring about the Revolution.

Anna Vyrubova was the daughter of Alexander Taneyev, a composer of some repute who had been the head of the imperial chancellery, and her mother was a Tolstoy. Her family background, therefore, certainly placed her in court circles. After the Revolution, her numerous enemies described her as an unimportant, unattractive nobody. Yet she was a beautiful young woman when she first met the empress at the turn of the century, somewhat short and with deep blue eyes, full cheeks, thick hair, and an inclination to stoutness. Anna was not a brilliant woman, but she was devoted to the empress and was one of the few trustworthy and loyal people on whom Nicholas and Alexandra could count. The empress appointed her friend a maid of honor, and it was in this position that she unwittingly did the most damage.

Because the public knew so little about the private lives of the imperial family, every gesture, word, or opinion expressed by Anna was taken to be that of the empress. Alexandra tried to keep her relationship with Rasputin a secret, but Anna, who became one of his most vehement supporters, flaunted her friendship with the peasant, and everyone in the capital knew of her role as intermediary between the imperial family and the Siberian holy man. Anna was naïve and failed to realize that her unchecked enthusiasm was damaging the prestige of the monarchy. Newspapers, which were forbidden to couple the names of the empress and Rasputin, freely printed pictures and stories linking Anna and the peasant. Her role in arranging meetings between Rasputin and the empress, most frequently at her little house in the village of Tsarskoe Selo, made Anna the subject of countless intrigues and rumors concerning her loyalty. She was accused of political influence and, in the last days of the imperial regime, was widely believed to have organized orgies at the Alexander Palace, widening the corrupting influence of the peasant over the helpless tsar and tsarina. Wild stories circulated in the capital: that Anna helped Rasputin drug the young tsarevich; that she carried on scandalous affairs with Rasputin, Nicholas II, and Empress Alexandra herself; that she was a German spy. After the Revolution, in an effort to prove her innocence, Anna asked to be examined by a doctor of the provisional government and was medically certified to be a virgin.

Such rumors and intrigues gradually blackened Rasputin's name and reputation as well as those of the tsar and tsarina. As he grew in notoriety, the Orthodox Church did all they could to distance themselves from their former protégé. Over and over again, church officials pleaded with the tsar to send the peasant away from the capital, arguing against his corrupting influence. Archimandrite Theophan, who had initially supported Rasputin and introduced him to powerful clergy in the capital, turned into a virulent enemy. After hearing repeated confessions from women who claimed to have slept with Rasputin, Theophan informed the tsarina of the allegations. Alexandra, in turn, called Rasputin to Tsarskoe Selo; when confronted with Theophan's accusations, the peasant seemed angry and hurt, denying any impropriety.

The empress was not fully convinced; she asked Anna Vyrubova and two ladies from the imperial court to visit Rasputin at his home in Pokrovskoe in 1909. This fact itself demonstrates that Alexandra was fully aware of the rumors concerning her friend and was determined to discover the truth behind them. Anna and one of the women returned from the trip saying that they had observed nothing improper, but the third woman claimed that Rasputin had tried to seduce her maid. It was two against one, and Alexandra, influenced as she was by her need for the peasant, chose to ignore the allegation.

Theophan was convinced that Rasputin must go. He joined forces with Militza and Anastasia, who, by 1910, had become dedicated enemies of the peasant. But, one by one, those who spoke up against the peasant were dismissed, transferred, or fell from imperial favor. The imperial governess, Sophie Tiutcheva, was fired after she objected to Rasputin's presence in the Alexander Palace. Empress Alexandra had virtually cut off all contact with the two Montenegrin sisters, and Theophan himself sealed his own fate by continually objecting to Rasputin's favor: Nicholas II simply dismissed him from his post. On learning of his departure, Rasputin exclaimed, "I have shut his trap!"[1]

Metropolitan Anthony also visited the tsar to protest Rasputin's presence. When he raised objections, Nicholas cut him off, saying that the affairs of the church and those of the imperial family were two different matters. "No, Sire," Anthony replied, "this is not merely a family affair, but the affair of all Russia. The Tsarevich is not only your son but our future sovereign and belongs to all of Russia." But the tsar dismissed the priest without offering any hope.[2]

Alexandra stubbornly refused to believe the stories which circulated about her friend. So convinced was she that he had been sent by God that after the assassination of Prime Minister Peter Stolypin—one of Rasputin's strongest opponents—she informed Grand Duke Dimitri Pavlovich, "Those who have offended God in the person of Our Friend may no longer count on divine protection."[3] Stolypin had conducted a lengthy investigation into Rasputin's activities, much against the wishes of the empress. Her defense of Rasputin was total: "Saints are always calumniated," she told the court doctor.[4] To her friend Anna Vyrubova she exclaimed, "He is hated because we love him."[5] Such protests sound hopelessly naïve; but, in defending Rasputin—with all of his various faults—Alexandra defended the force which she believed kept her only son alive. His sins were of no concern to her; she cared not at all about his private life, only for the undoubted healing powers he possessed.

To the end of his life Rasputin remained a simple peasant, thrust abruptly into an unknown world in which he continued his quest for spiritual goals while at the same time satisfying his carnal appetites. He recognized his sins, repented of them in earnest, but continued to indulge them. Joseph Fuhrmann writes, "He could be a sinner and yet be Chosen. Even a *starets* might be flawed. Everything hinged on how the Imperial couple weighed the evidence. Their all-consuming need for Rasputin set the balance."[6]

The public reacted so violently to Rasputin's presence in the palace because they did not know the reason for which he was there. Nicholas and Alexandra had made a deliberate decision to keep the tsarevich's hemophilia a secret. They feared that the stability of the throne, not to mention the direct succession, might be endangered if the boy's illness became common knowledge. A few members of the Romanov family and court servants were informed of the disease, then sworn to secrecy.

In time the storm of protest surrounding Rasputin's relations with the imperial family erupted into a political crisis. Members of the government rallied against the peasant and angrily denounced him in the Duma, the Russian Parliament. Lurid tales of Rasputin's sexual escapades filled the newspapers along with allegations that he had raped the four young grand duchesses and that he was the empress's lover. The Moscow journal *Golos Moskvy* wrote of "that cunning conspirator against our Holy Church, that fornicator of human souls and bodies— Gregory Rasputin."[7] The tsar warned that any paper mentioning the peasant's name would be fined, but Rasputin proved too valuable a story to drop, and editors paid their fines and printed their stories, anyway.

A young monk named Serge Trufaniev befriended Rasputin in the early days of his relationship with the imperial family. When they first met, Trufaniev, who went by the ecclesiastical name Iliodor, invited Rasputin to visit a religious retreat on the banks of the Volga River. Iliodor was shocked when, on their arrival, Rasputin seized the women present and began to kiss them on the lips.[8] After a few days, the pair traveled on to Pokrovskoe. During the train journey Rasputin bragged of the power he held, the women who had freely given themselves to him, and worst of all, his relationship with the imperial family. "The Tsar thinks I'm Christ incarnate," he told Iliodor. "The Tsar and Tsarina bow down to me, kneel to me, kiss my hands. The Tsarina has sworn that if all turn their backs on Grishka she will not waiver and still always consider him her friend."[9] He added that he frequently kissed the tsarina, often in front of her daughters.[10] Iliodor saw no reason to disbelieve the peasant, but Rasputin was clearly fabricating a story to impress his new friend. Nicholas and Alexandra never acted in the manner that Rasputin claimed; they were still sovereigns, regardless of what Rasputin might have done, and both were too aware of their own royal dignity to bow and scrape before a peasant. But the damage was done. After their final break, Iliodor would repeat such stories

to anyone willing to listen, further blackening the prestige of the
monarchy.

While at Pokrovskoe, Rasputin had shown Iliodor some
personal letters he had received from members of the imperial
family. The peasant allowed his new friend to take several of
them. Two years later, after Iliodor had become convinced of
Rasputin's corrupting influence, he did all he could to sully the
peasant's name. He started by publishing the letters. The most
damaging came from the empress:

> My Beloved, unforgettable teacher, redeemer and mentor,
>
> How tiresome it is without you. My soul is quiet and I re-
> lax only when you, my teacher, are sitting beside me. I
> kiss your hands and lean my head on your blessed shoul-
> der. Oh, how light do I feel then. I only wish one thing: to
> fall asleep forever on your shoulders and in your arms.
> What happiness to feel your presence near me. Where are
> you? Where have you gone? Oh, I am so sad and my
> heart is longing. . . . Will you soon be again close to me?
> Come quickly, I am waiting for you and I am tormenting
> myself for you. I am asking for your Holy Blessing and I
> am kissing your blessed hands. I love you forever.[11]

This brought the crisis to new heights. Suddenly, Rasputin's detractors seemed to have unassailable evidence of his scurrilous
influence over the imperial family. Alexandra had written the
letter in a fit of religious ecstasy, but it seemed to hint at a sexual
relationship with the peasant. Under the best of circumstances,
it would have proved embarrassing; with the public hungry for
any hint of scandal, it undoubtedly compromised both Rasputin's position and the prestige of the Romanov throne. Nicholas
and Alexandra were furious that their private lives were being
violated in this manner, and the empress herself sent an angry
cable to Rasputin, who was in Pokrovskoe at the time, making
it clear that he was in disfavor.

Rasputin's fortunes were low, and it took the apparent miracle at Spala in 1912 to restore him to imperial favor. Two years
later, by the beginning of the World War I, Rasputin stood at the

height of his power and influence. In June of that year—ironically, on the same day that Archduke Franz Ferdinand of Austria and his wife were assassinated in Sarajevo—a religious fanatic stabbed Rasputin. The peasant recovered, but the attack left him an invalid for several months, and his health was never quite the same. Increasingly, he turned to sex and alcohol to relieve his pain. Years later his daughter Maria wrote:

> He became nervous, irritable, subject to continual insomnia, and, in order to forget, to obtain a few minutes of relaxation and calm, he began to drink. Everything pushed him towards it; society in St. Petersburg was notoriously intemperate; and, truly, if there is anything to be astonished at, it is that a simple peasant suddenly implanted into such surroundings of luxury and intemperance should have resisted for so long against the daily temptations of such a life. My father was never addicted to spirits but he abused the use of fine wines, champagne and, above all, muscat and madeira.[12]

This is probably the closest version to the truth of the matter as we are likely to ever have. Maria Rasputin wrote to preserve her father's memory, but all of the available evidence indicates that Rasputin was rarely drunk before the attempt on his life. After 1914, however, his behavior disintegrated rapidly. He spent his nights drinking and then sleeping with a succession of actresses, singers, and prostitutes; by the following afternoon, he had usually recovered enough to put in an appearance at the Alexander Palace. The empress never saw her friend's disintegration first-hand.

The worst incident came in April 1915. Rasputin went to Moscow to pray at the tombs of the saints in the Kremlin's Cathedral of the Assumption. The British ambassador in Moscow, Robert Bruce Lockhart, later wrote:

> I was at Yar, the most luxurious night haunt of Moscow, with some English visitors. As we watched the music hall performance in the main hall, there was a violent fracas in one of the private rooms. Wild shrieks of a woman, a

man's curses, broken glass and the banging of doors. Headwaiters rushed upstairs. The manager sent for the police. . . . But the row and roaring continued. . . . The cause of the disturbance was Rasputin—drunk and lecherous, and neither police nor management dared evict him.[13]

Rasputin had smashed the furniture and light fixtures in one of the private dining rooms and then, in a drunken rage, tried to rape his female companion. When the police finally arrived at Yar, Rasputin shocked everyone by undoing his trousers and exposing himself to the diners. He then began to yell that he acted this way in the presence of the tsar and that he often had his way with "the old girl"—a scandalous reference to the tsarina.[14] The police eventually managed to drag Rasputin away, the peasant unrepentant and "snarling and vowing vengeance."[15]

The deputy minister of the interior, Gen. Vladimir Dzhunkovsky, submitted a full report of the incident to the tsar. Nicholas II angrily summoned Rasputin and demanded an explanation. The peasant replied that he was a simple man and had become drunk due to bad judgment. But he denied that he had exposed himself or referred to the imperial family, despite the evidence to the contrary.[16] The tsar ordered Rasputin to leave the capital. Before he departed, however, Rasputin informed one of the police guards at his flat, "Your Dzhunkovsky's finished."[17]

The tsar gave his wife the report to read. Alexandra never claimed that it was untrue. But to admit Rasputin's faults raised the very real possibility that he would have to leave the capital forever. The loss of the drunken, corrupt peasant also meant the loss of the man whose prayers she believed preserved the life of her son. She wanted Dzhunkovsky dismissed. When she learned that the tsar's cousin Grand Duke Dimitri Pavlovich had read the report, she wrote angrily to her husband:

My enemy Dzhunkovsky . . . has shown that vile, filthy paper to Dimitri. . . . If we let Our Friend be persecuted we and our country shall suffer for it. . . . I am so weary, such heartache and pain from all of this—the idea of dirt being spread about one we venerate is more than horrible.

Ah, my love, when at *last* will you thump with your hand upon the table and scream at Dzhunkovsky and others when they act wrongly—one does not fear you—and one *must*—they must be frightened of you otherwise all sit upon us. . . .[18]

In September 1915, the tsar dismissed Dzhunkovsky.

Years later, Basil Shulgin, a monarchist member of the Duma, referred to Rasputin as "a Janus." He wrote:

To the Imperial Family he presented the face of a *starets*, in which the Tsarina felt she saw the spirit of God residing in a holy man. But to Russia, he presented his depraved mug, the drunken and lustful mug of a wood-goblin-satyr from the Tobolsk taiga. The cause of it all—All of Russia was indignant that Rasputin was in the Tsarina's chamber. While in the Tsar's chamber there was indignation and deep mortification. What were the people enraged about? That this holy man was praying for the unfortunate heir, a seriously ill child threatened with death by every careless movement. This annoyed them? Why? Thus this messenger of death stood between Russia and the Throne. He kills because he is two-faced. Because of his two-facedness the two sides cannot understand each other. With each hour increasing the mortification in their hearts, the Tsar and Russia lead each other, hand in hand, into an abyss.[19]

5

The Government Disintegrates

D URING THE YEARS of World War I, Rasputin stood at the pinnacle of his notoriety. He had survived scandals, rumor and intrigues. His position as a royal favorite was unassailable. Yet Rasputin's real power was minimal. His entire reputation rested on his influence over the empress and his ability to cure her son when he fell ill. His situation was dramatically altered in the fall of 1915, when Nicholas II assumed supreme command of the Russian army and took up residence at headquarters in Mogilev, hundreds of miles from the capital. The tsar left Alexandra in charge of the imperial government. Within eighteen months the Russian government had been brought to a state of virtual collapse. And the man most widely held responsible for this deplorable state of affairs was Gregory Rasputin.

The tsar hoped that his assumption of the supreme command would inspire the troops and consolidate his power to govern, eliminating the division between the civil and military branches. He also believed that, as tsar, his place was with his soldiers. In this, he was supported whole heartedly by the empress. Alexandra despised Grand Duke Nicholas Nicholaievich, who had held the post prior to her husband. Known in the imperial family as Nikolasha, the grand duke was married to Grand Duchess Anastasia, who, along with her sister Militza, had introduced Rasputin to the imperial couple and then become dedicated enemies of the peasant. When Rasputin had volunteered to come to headquarters to bless the troops, the grand duke replied swiftly, "Yes, do come. I'll hang you."[1]

With the tsar gone, the empress dealt with daily political business, but everyone in the capital assumed that Rasputin was the real power behind the throne. The peasant himself did nothing to correct this suspicion, and the unchecked rumor only added to his reputation. After the Revolution, no one had any doubt that he had been its chief architect. But the portrait of an all-powerful Rasputin, dictating governmental policy to an eager tsarina, who then demanded that her weak-willed husband carry it out, is one of Russian history's most pervasive falsehoods.

Certainly, a literal reading of the evidence seems to indicate Rasputin's dominant position. Along with pleas to be more autocratic, Alexandra repeatedly filled her letters with Rasputin's latest advice: "No, hearken to Our Friend, believe him," she wrote. "He has your interest and Russia's at heart— it is not for nothing that God sent him to us—only we must pay more attention to what he says. His words are not lightly spoken, and the gravity of having not only his prayers but his advice is great."[2] And, on the following day, she reported: "I am haunted by Our Friend's wish and *know* it will prove fatal for us and the country if it is not fulfilled. He means what he says when he speaks so seriously."[3]

This advice concerned not only government ministers but also extended to the military and actual draft pronouncements of imperial policy. Once, Alexandra sent a copy of such a draft to her husband with this message: "[Rasputin] begs you very much to send a telegram to the king of Serbia, as he is very anxious that the Bulgarians will finish them off. So I enclose the paper for you to use for your telegram—the sense in your words and shorter, of course."[4]

The empress also dispatched several parcels to her absent husband in Rasputin's name. One was a stuffed fish holding a bird impaled on a stick—a curious gift from the peasant to the tsar. "He used it first," she explained, "and now sends it to you as a blessing."[5] This was followed by a photograph of "Our Friend," which Alexandra implored her husband to keep near him at all times to give him courage.[6] Finally, she forwarded a small comb from Rasputin: "Remember to comb your hair before all difficult talks and decisions, the little comb will bring its help."[7]

But does a literal reading of this evidence reveal the truth? Given her faith in Rasputin as a "Man of God," it is perhaps natural that the empress turned to her friend for guidance on the matters of the day. His influence over the empress in political affairs, however, has been greatly exaggerated. Between 1915 and 1917, Russia had four prime ministers, five ministers of the interior, four ministers of religion, four ministers of justice, three ministers of agriculture, three foreign ministers, and four ministers of war. Twenty-six men held these seven positions over a twenty-month period. Of that number, only four ministerial positions can be said to have changed hands due to Rasputin. Eight of the men either resigned their positions or were relieved of their duties after disagreements with the tsar. Of the remainder, the empress actively campaigned for the removal of seven men.

Rasputin had no political sense; indeed, he cared little for the affairs of state and only concerned himself when the security of his position at court was threatened. He appears to have felt a certain patriotic duty toward advising the tsar and tsarina, but there is little evidence to suggest that either of them ever took his counsel seriously. What the evidence does suggest is that in almost every case where the empress mentioned Rasputin's name in connection with a particular official, the peasant had merely echoed her own beliefs. Rasputin had the ingratiating habit of repeating to the tsar and empress their own opinions of the men who held office. When, over and over again in her letters to the tsar, Alexandra writes that "Our Friend" does not like a certain individual, Rasputin seems simply to have told her what she wished to hear.

Regardless of the real dynamics between Rasputin and the empress, their relationship during World War I had a tragic effect on the internal stability of the empire. Even though the evidence indicates that Rasputin exercised little real power, no one knew the true circumstances. It was generally assumed that Rasputin was behind most of the internal chaos; this belief in his influence over the imperial couple further weakened the prestige of the monarchy. The hatred that most of the capital felt toward Rasputin soon attached itself to the tsar and empress as well, dragging the Romanov dynasty into scandal and disrepute.

Rasputin himself did nothing to correct this fatal misconception. Historian Martin Kilcoyne notes:

He used the remarks of the Tsarina as testimonials of his power. It was easy for him to create the impression that he was the dominant partner, that he originated ideas and saw to it that they were carried out by Alexandra, who automatically and obediently put her power at his disposal. . . . Despite his position as *starets* he was not free to dispute her. When she was certain of something she was certain beyond her ability to reflect and to question. Her intense assurance was something that even Rasputin dared not go against. In all their dealings she retained the upper hand. In fact, she was the dominant partner and could bend Rasputin to her will. He judiciously acceded to her frenzied importunings and agreed with her judgements of many situations. Without fully realizing what she was doing, Alexandra forced him to agree with her; then she was sure that her recommendations were the same as the will of God. Her faith in her own convictions could not be checked, even by Rasputin. She compelled him to assure her that God had approved her plans. She was not so smug as to think that she could discern His Will unaided. She needed Rasputin to interpret it for her, but conviction came first, then endorsement.[8]

Rasputin's supposed corrupting and incompetent influence over the Russian government became the talk of Petrograd during the war. Officials were scandalized at the thought that their careers were subject to the peasant's whims. But the biggest storm broke in September 1916, when Alexander Protopopov was appointed minister of the interior. Protopopov was an ultraconservative monarchist, a man whose political views appealed to both Nicholas and Alexandra. Although he had been a member of the Duma for some time, Protopopov had little political aptitude. But he had one important asset: Rasputin knew and liked him, although he had his doubts about the man's integrity—"his honour stretched like a piece of elastic," the peasant once observed.[9] Yet Alexandra put forth his name: "Gregory earnestly begs you to name Protopopov. You know him and had such a good impression of him—happens to be of the Duma and is not left and so will know how to be with them. ... I think you could not do better than name him. ... He likes Our Friend for at least four years and that says much for a man."[10]

Indeed it did. Gossips in Petrograd had a field day after Protopopov's appointment. On learning of his new position as minister of the interior, Protopopov ordered the uniform of an imperial gendarmerie, which he donned for an appearance at a Duma budget committee meeting; when he walked into the room, the other ministers burst into howls of laughter. More disturbingly, it was whispered that Protopopov was a necrophiliac.[11] He frequently spoke to an icon which he kept on his desk; when one man walked in and discovered it, the minister hastily explained, "He helps me do everything, everything I do is by his advice."[12] Such was the state of affairs in Russia at the time that much of the capital was prepared to believe that the most powerful official in the land was insane.

With the tsar away, Alexandra found it much easier to appoint and dismiss ministers on her own authority. She herself gave Protopopov the post of minister of agriculture to go along with that of minister of the interior. "Forgive me for what I have done—but I had to—Our Friend said it was absolutely necessary," she wrote to her husband.[13] Although the empress made the decisions herself, she invoked Rasputin's name, giving more credence to the belief that he possessed great power and influence.

This interference, this ministerial shuffle, and the seemingly unchecked influence of Rasputin at court was like a fatal disease, gnawing away at the stability and confidence of the imperial government. By the fall of 1916 the situation had reached a crisis stage. Members of the Duma openly began to campaign against the imperial couple. "If the young Tsarina is such a great Russian patriot," one politician asked Grand Duke Alexander Michailovich, "why does she tolerate the presence of that drunken beast who is openly seen around the capital in the company of German spies and sympathizers?" The grand duke, pledged to secrecy about Rasputin's role in the imperial household, said nothing.[14] One group actually had plans to "bomb the Tsar's motorcar from an aeroplane at a particular point along its route."[15] Other members of the Duma demanded that the empress be exiled to the Crimea for the remainder of the war.

Other members of the imperial family themselves felt that a catastrophe was unavoidable. The dowager empress gave her son an ultimatum: Either he send Rasputin away from the capital, or she would leave it. The tsar, of course, would do no such thing, and his mother defiantly took up residence in Kiev.[16] Grand Duke Alexander Michailovich made three different visits to headquarters, each time trying to persuade the tsar to send Alexandra and Rasputin away. "I believe no one but my wife" was the tsar's only comment.[17] Grand Duke Nicholas Nicholaievich came to headquarters to speak to his cousin about the political situation in Russia. For several hours the grand duke yelled at the tsar that he was allowing the ruin of the government. The tsar did nothing but continue to smoke. Finally, Nicholas Nicholaievich could stand it no longer. "I would be more pleased if you swore at me, struck me, kicked me out, rather than your silence!" he screamed. "Can't you see that you are losing your crown? Collect yourself while it's not too late. Give a responsible ministry. As long ago as June I spoke to you about this. You just procrastinate. For the moment there is still time but soon it will be too late." The tsar said nothing, but continued to smoke, observing the grand duke like an impudent schoolboy called to task by a stern headmaster.[18]

After these numerous appeals, Nicholas II received a long, prophetic letter from his cousin Grand Duke Nicholas Michailovich:

> Are you properly informed about the situation with the Empire, and particularly Siberia, Turkestan and the Caucasus? Do you know the whole truth or do they [presumably the Empress and Rasputin] hide most of it from you? Where does the root of the evil lie? Let me explain in a few words:
>
> So long as your method of choosing your ministers was only known to a small coterie, things could carry on for better or worse. But as soon as such matters were generally known and discussed in public, it became obvious that Russia could not go on being governed in that way.

You often told me that you trusted no one and were constantly being betrayed.

If this is true, the remark should apply above all to your wife, who, though she loves you, is constantly leading you in error—surrounded as she is by people in the grip of the spirit of evil. You believe in Alexandra Feodorovna. That is natural. But the words she utters are the outcome of clever intrigues, they are not the truth. If you are powerless to rid yourself of such influences, at least be always on your guard against the unceasing and systematic intriguers, who use your wife as a tool.

If you could prevent the persistent intervention of these evil influences, Russia's regeneration would take a great leap forward, and you would regain the confidence you have lost with the immense majority of your subjects.

You would find yourself faced with a people who, under a new regime, would be happy to work under your guidance.

I have hesitated for a long time before telling you the truth, but have now decided to do so on the persuasion of your mother and sisters. You are on the eve of new trials—new attempts against your person. Believe me, if I stress my desire that you should cast off the chains that imprison you, it is not for personal motives— as you know, I have none—but only with the hope of saving you and your throne and our dear country from the terrible and irreparable catastrophe that lies ahead.[19]

The tsar sent the letter, unread, to his wife. "I . . . am utterly disgusted," she wrote. "Had you stopped him in the middle of his talk and told him that, if he only once touched that subject [Rasputin] or me, you will send him to Siberia—as it becomes next to high treason. He has always hated and spoken badly of me since twenty-two years. . . ."[20]

By November 1916 the Russian Empire stood on the verge of collapse. Two devastating years of war, coupled with hyperinflation and constant ministerial shuffling, had left the country in chaos. The failure of the Brusilov military campaign against Austria that fall did more to dampen public morale. Confidence in the tsar, the army, and the ministers of the government struck bottom. And the man most widely held responsible for this sad state of affairs was Gregory Rasputin. He was undoubtedly the most hated man in all of Russia, believed to wield enormous influence and corrupting power over the imperial family. A few of his supporters continually defended the peasant against such accusations, but most citizens of Petrograd angrily denounced him as a scurrilous fraud, a manipulative, power-hungry Svengali who gloried in his malignant notoriety. He had carefully cultivated an aura of extraordinary influence. Now, with the country on the brink of ruin, Rasputin was about to fall victim to one of the most extraordinary and mythical murders of the twentieth century.

PART TWO

The Assassin

6

Enter the Assassin

UNLIKE HIS FUTURE VICTIM Rasputin, Prince Felix Youssoupov was the product of a privileged, lavish world. The Youssoupov family traced its descent back to the sixth century, to the prophet Ali, a nephew of Mohammed. A succession of ancestors fought, raped, and pillaged their way to power, including the famous general Ediguey-Manguite, Tamerlane's military chief. They remained narrow-minded, suspicious and isolated, striking terror into the Nogai hordes that they ruled. The Youssoupovs might very well have gone the way of other chieftains and fallen into obscurity but for one, Khan Youssouv, ruler of the Crimean peninsula, who had the dubious fortune of striking an alliance with Ivan the Terrible, grand prince of Moscow and first tsar of all Russia. As a consequence, Youssouv found himself drawn closer to the centers of power. His sons and daughter, true to their stubborn Tartar heritage, quarreled among themselves and plotted intrigues not only against their father's ally the tsar but also each other.

Youssouv's daughter, Queen Sumbeca of Kazan, quickly married a succession of husbands who had the nasty habit of murdering their predecessors to win her hand. A dispute between Khan Youssouv and the tsar resulted in a Russian siege of Kazan; soon the tsar's forces had captured the town and its queen. Although Youssouv threatened action against the powerful tsar, his own brother murdered him before he could spread the conflict, fearing the consequences if his family angered the unpredictable and violent Ivan the Terrible.

Such dissension between tsar and subject could very well have destroyed the family's fortunes. Recognizing the gravity of the situation, Khan Abdul-Murza Youssouv, one of Youssouv's great-grandchildren, made a bold and clever decision which probably saved the family from ruin: To please the tsar, he renounced both his Muslim religion and his claims to the Crimean khanite and converted to Russian Orthodoxy. The tsar, Feodor III, was so pleased that he immediately granted Abdul-Murza the title of Prince Dimitri Youssoupov; the once wild Tartar khanite family was thus raised to noble status in the kingdom of Russia.

Dimitri's son, Prince Gregory, set the pattern which members of the Youssoupov family were to follow for the next two hundred years: At the sides of tsars and empresses, the family served the state, basking in the imperial favor of the Romanov dynasty. In 1711, Peter the Great sent Youssoupov with an expeditionary force to fight in the Great Northern War against Sweden. Gregory did so well in battle that the tsar rewarded him by making Youssoupov his personal envoy and a fellow of the Military Institute. Through continued service and personal friendships with four sovereigns—Peter the Great, Catherine I, Peter II, and Empress Anna—Gregory consolidated his privileged position at the Russian court. His advantageous marriage to the daughter of wealthy Prince Lvov increased the family's fortune, power, and influence even further.

Gregory's son Prince Boris studied abroad at the Ecole d'Aspirants de la Marine Royale at Toulon and gained wide respect as a man of great intellect. He served as governor-general of Moscow, privy councillor and grand chamberlain of the imperial court. Boris was one of the founders of the famous Corps de Pages in St. Petersburg, and wrote much of the training manual for that military academy.

By the beginning of the nineteenth century, the Youssoupov family had risen to such heights that one of them, Prince Nicholas, acted as senior adviser to four Romanov sovereigns, Catherine the Great, Emperor Paul, Alexander I, and Nicholas I. He undertook the fashionable grand tour of Europe, visiting England, Germany, France, Italy, Spain, and Portugal. He purchased entire storehouses of furniture, paintings, porcelains, and sculptures, shipping them all back to St. Petersburg to adorn his glorious palaces. Everywhere he went, Nicholas was acknowledged as a man of great influence: He had audiences with King Louis XVI and Queen Marie Antoinette, Friedrich the Great, Voltaire, and Diderot. His interest in the arts led to his appointment as director of the Imperial Theatre in St. Petersburg; on his own, he patronized the poet Pushkin, who later dedicated several of his works to his benefactor. Nicholas married one of Prince Gregory Potemkin's nieces, Tatiana Engelhardt, an heiress, and increased his family's fortune once again. The marriage, however, suffered from the prince's marital infidelities; his reputation as a learned patron of the arts was surpassed only by tales of his insatiable appetite for feminine beauty. He kept an entire company of peasant ballerinas at his country estate outside Moscow; during a performance they had only to see a wave from the prince's cane to completely disrobe, much to the surprise of the audience. When he died at the age of eighty, Nicholas had just concluded an affair with a girl of eighteen.

Upon Nicholas's death the family fortune passed to his only son, Boris. Boris had been married twice, first to Princess Praskovie Scherbatov, daughter of one of Russia's most distinguished princely houses, and, after her premature death in 1820, to Princess Zenaide Naryshkin. Their union did not last for long; shortly after the birth of his son Nicholas, Boris fell ill and died unexpectedly. His beautiful wife, in sole charge of the rapidly growing Youssoupov fortune, spent little time mourning. Her lavish entertainments were famous for the wide-ranging circles they attracted. She carried on a long-standing affair with Tsar Nicholas I before finally leaving St. Petersburg to marry the Comte de Chauveau. She ended her days living in grand style in the Gothic Château Keriolet in France. Her great-grandson, Prince Felix Youssoupov, later recalled her as charming and gracious, though peculiarly miserly. She kept a box made of rock crystal and precious stones filled with moldy chocolates for her visiting relatives. Only her great-grandson would dare eat them, thus endearing himself to the elderly comtesse.[1]

Her son, Prince Nicholas Youssoupov, was a distinguished soldier and philanthropist. During the Crimean War he not only fought with great bravery but also spent thousands of rubles of his personal fortune on field hospitals, ambulance trains, and rehabilitative schools for the wounded. At the imperial court he acted as privy councillor, grand master of the court, and vice director of the imperial libraries. A talented amateur musician, he composed several symphonic works which received general public acclaim.

Nicholas married Countess Tatiana de Ribeauspierre, a member of an ancient and reknowned Alsatian family related through various unions to the Potemkins, Trubetskois, Sheremetievs, and Cantacuzènes, some of the most dignified and respected families in Russia. Tatiana was one of the famous beauties of her day, painted in romantic style by the great nineteenth-century artist Franz Xavier Winterhalter. They had two children, both daughters. Tatiana died when she was nineteen, leaving her younger sister Zenaide as sole heir to the immense family fortune.

Zenaide Youssoupov grew up to be an exquisite beauty, with deep blue eyes, a slender figure, and dark hair. With her charm and enormous wealth, she was courted by eligible scions from noble houses all across Europe. Grand Duke Constantine Constantinovich, a renowned poet and playwright, dedicated several of his works to her an in effort to win her hand in marriage, but to no avail.[2] Her portrait was painted by the best and most fashionable artists of the day, Serov and Flemeng, as well as by Grand Duchess Elizabeth Feodorovna. Among her hidden talents was said to be a gift of clairvoyance, or second sight, an extraordinary sense which her son Felix also later claimed to possess. Rather than making a grand match, she married for love, accepting the proposal of Count Felix Felixovich Sumarakov-Elston, a mere officer in the Chevalier Guards.

The Sumarakov-Elstons traced their descent from a Moldavian warrior clan. The family had migrated to Moscow and, through the centuries, frequently served in positions at the Romanov court. By marriage they were related to several other famous princely houses: the Obolenskys and Galitzines, as well as the Botkins, who served as court physicians under the last two tsars. Family legend declared that the name Elston derived from a clandestine affair between King Wilhelm IV of Prussia and one of his sister's maids of honor, Elizabeth Hitrovo. Unexpectedly, she found herself pregnant with the king's child; when he was born, the baby was called Felix Elston, a surname allegedly taken from the French *elle s'étonne*, which supposedly expressed her surprise. Like much of the Youssoupov story, however, this romanticized version falls short of the truth. An affair between Elizabeth Hitrovo and King Wilhelm IV undoubtedly took place, but it is doubtful that Felix was a royal bastard. More authoritative and less biased sources have named Baron Charles von Hugel as the father.[3]

Whatever the truth of his parentage, Felix Elston grew up a highly refined young man. He later married Countess Helen Sumarakov, the last of her line, and received permission to assume her surname and title for his children so that it would not pass into disuse. When they had a child, he received the name of Felix Felixovich, Count Sumarakov-Elston. Born in 1856, Count Felix became a career military officer. He joined the Corps des Pages and, on completing the course, was gazetted a second lieutenant in the Tenth Regiment of the Odessa Lancers in 1876. Six years later, he received his first commission in the Chevalier Guards Regiment. Tall and handsome, with a jaunty cavalry mustache and deep blue eyes, Felix possessed the upright bearing and reserved manner of a noble guards officer, making him infinitely attractive to the women at the imperial court.

Felix Sumarakov-Elston first met Zenaide Youssoupov at one of St. Petersburg's numerous social gatherings. Soon they were to be seen together at the most fashionable receptions and entertainments, attracting the curious attention of dowagers, who quickly spread word of the growing relationship. Zenaide's father, Prince Nicholas, liked Count Felix personally but expressed disappointment that his daughter had not selected a more illustrious fiancé. Nevertheless, he gave the union his blessing. Their courtship was a short one: On 4 April 1882, the pair married in the Chapel of the Chevalier Guards Regiment in the Russian capital.

The marriage between Zenaide and Felix was a study in contrasts. Husband and wife were complete opposites. Zenaide, cultured and cloistered, impressed everyone with her quiet grace and gentle beauty. She was without prejudice, bred with a sense of *noblesse oblige* which dictated her even and fair treatment of everyone she encountered, whether servant or grand duchess. Her passions were artistic: opera, ballet, music and painting.

Count Felix cared little for such things, although, as a concession to his wife's interests, he eventually assumed the presidency of the School of Imperial Arts and the Stroganov Institute, whose students Zenaide regularly patronized. However, at heart he remained a true soldier, never happier than when he could host regimental dinners and preside over reviews. Straightforward and somewhat tactless, Felix nevertheless won favor in St. Petersburg society with his easy charm and rather eccentric nature. For all of their differences, Zenaide and Felix were bound together by a dedication and love which made their marriage stable and lasting. Even after the Revolution, when they had fled their magnificent palaces and lived in exile, husband and wife remained touchingly devoted to each other.

As head of the house of Youssoupov, Prince Nicholas worried that his family's great name would fall into abeyance following his death. Upon the birth of his first grandson, Prince Nicholas Felixovich, Youssoupov applied to the Senate with the request that his son-in-law be allowed to take his surname and titles after his own death. When Zenaide's father died in 1891, the issue had still not been resolved. Two years later, Tsar Alexander III signed a special decree authorizing Felix Sumarakov-Elston to assume his wife's maiden name and honors. Thus, the proud and ancient House of Youssoupov, by imperial favor, was saved from oblivion for another generation.

After centuries of continued service and loyalty to the Romanov dynasty, the Youssoupov family had accumulated a mass of treasures, visible symbols of imperial favor. Their rewards were never as significant or extensive as those of other princes and dukes who composed the court and received numerous estates and thousands of serfs. But, unlike many of these recipients, the Youssoupovs carefully guarded and invested their riches with thoughts for the future. By the turn of the century they stood at the very pinnacle of Russian society both in status and in wealth.

Before the Revolution many Russian aristocrats lived lives of unimaginable luxury. They built summer and winter palaces, vacationed on the French Riviera, sent their laundry to Paris, and lavished huge fortunes on extravagant, hedonistic pleasures. There were 870 titled families in Russia at the turn of the century.[4] Only a small percentage had amassed the great wealth or risen to such heights as had the Youssoupovs. But riches were still to be had in Russia, if not from inherited fortunes, then through the newer but no less rewarding fields of industry and high finance. The Benckendorv family, for example, owned an industrial estate in the Siberian town of Lys'va which accounted for fully one half of the world's annual output of platinum.[5] The Youssoupovs themselves had invested wisely and made an immense industrial fortune. Even the Romanov dynasty, with their throne and all of its imperial trappings, were hard-pressed to match the wealth of this one princely family.[6]

At the time of Felix Youssoupov's birth in 1887, his family owned dozens of palaces and estates. They owned so many houses that they occasionally sold them off to the imperial government for use as official buildings. In St. Petersburg, a classical palace at no. 115 Fontanka Canal, designed by the Italian architect Giacommo Quarenghi, had been sold to the ministry of communications in 1815. This sale did not inconvenience the family in the slightest; they still maintained seven separate establishments in the Russian capital. Their principal St. Petersburg residence was the neoclassic palace at no. 94 Moika Canal; this was supplemented by large mansions on the Nevsky and Liteiny Prospects as well as four other residences scattered across the capital. They owned a Rococo villa at nearby Tsarskoe Selo and a dacha at Krasnoe Selo, the great military camp outside St. Petersburg. They kept five houses in Moscow, including one which had once been the hunting lodge of Tsar Ivan the Terrible; a few miles beyond the former capital, they owned an extensive country estate, Arkhangelskoe. To the south, they owned another large agricultural estate at Rakitnoe in central Russia as well as three separate estates on the Crimean peninsula. One of the family's estates in the Caucasus skirted the Caspian Sea for 125 miles. The area was rich in crude oil; it was so abundant that it simply soaked up through the soil, and local peasants had only to drive over this land to grease the wheels of their carts.[7] There were large mining tracts near the Don, Yaroslavl, and Astrakhan. In addition, the Youssoupovs owned industrial factories and brickworks in both Moscow and St. Petersburg. Such holdings made the family incalculably rich; one estimate of the real estate alone placed the value of their possessions at between $350 and $500 million in pre-Revolutionary figures. The same sum today would rank the family among the wealthiest in the world.[8]

It was impossible for the Youssoupov family to reside at all of these places. As a rule, they spent the winters in the Moika Palace in St. Petersburg, entertaining and enjoying the capital's social season. In late May they moved to nearby Tsarskoe Selo, following the imperial court as it retreated to Catherine the Great's summer palace. They would visit their dacha at Krasnoe Selo for the annual army manuevers in July before leaving St. Petersburg for Moscow.

At the end of the summer the family left Moscow for Rakitnoe, in central Russia. If possible, they always spent September there, timed to coincide with the rut which made the estate one of the best private hunts in Russia. In October they would journey to the Crimea to enjoy the warm, subtropical climate and healthy atmosphere before returning once again to the Moika Palace in St. Petersburg for the icy Russian winter. Because they owned so many establishments, the family could never visit more than a handful each year. Many of their houses, rarely occupied and in distant corners of European Russia, were simply forgotten. Incredible as it may seem, many of these forgotten estates, never visited, were allowed to fall into disrepair. They did not maintain on-site staffs except at their usual residences, so that careless curators in remote corners of the empire often did not fight the harsh elements. In 1912, Prince Felix Youssoupov set out to visit one of his family's old estates, Spaskoe Selo, buried deep in the Russian countryside and unoccupied for nearly a century. Beyond the still-barred gates he found the ruins of an elegant neoclassic mansion, its once elaborate stucco ceilings caved in, windows long gone, stumps of marble columns which had once supported colonnades and porticos dotting the overgrown garden. No one had come to stay there, and eventually the family forgot they even owned the house until Felix found the listing in the property ledgers.

The houses and estates the Youssoupovs occupied were rich museums unto themselves, filled with treasures accumulated through the centuries. The Youssoupovs had long been keen collectors and patrons, and the rooms of the palaces were hung with paintings by Rembrandt, Rubens, Tiepolo, Van Dyck, Gainsborough, Lorraine, David, Bouchier, and other European masters. The art collection was principally assembled by Prince Nicholas Youssoupov in the eighteenth century. At the turn of the century, it was the largest and most important private collection in all of Russia. The furnishings were a mixture of English and French antiques, many purchased by Prince Nicholas Youssoupov during his European grand tour. Their porcelain collections were especially rich, the Sèvres, Dresden, Wedgewood, and Meissen pieces supplemented by works from the Imperial Porcelain Factory and Gardner's Works in Moscow as well as examples from their own factories at Arkhangelskoe. The number of these works of art was staggering; today fully one-third of the present collection in St. Petersburg's reknowned Hermitage Museum was at one time owned by the Youssoupov family. The four hundred paintings, the furniture, sculptures, and china in the Moika Palace alone would have made it the fifth richest private museum in the world.

Along with the palaces, industrial estates, and works of art, the Youssoupovs accumulated a fortune in jewelry. In Victorian society, and particularly in the rarefied world of the St. Petersburg court, jewelry was as much an outward display of one's wealth, social standing, and imperial favor as palaces and yachts. No grand lady in society could possibly make do with less than a half-dozen parures of tiaras, necklaces, bracelets, earrings, brooches, and stomachers, and the higher one's position the more extensive the need for jewelry. Zenaide herself adored these fabulous pieces, and her collection of jewels was considered second only to those owned by members of the imperial family themselves.

She owned a number of historically significant and priceless jewels. These included the Polar Star diamond, just over forty-one carats; the Sultan of Morocco diamond, thirty-six carats; and the Ram's Head diamond, seventeen carats, which Catherine the Great had given to her favorite, Prince Gregory Potemkin. Particularly important were the tear-drop diamond earrings of the doomed Queen Marie Antoinette, weighing nearly thirty-five carats. Marie Antoinette had sewn them into her bodice when she and Louis XVI fled Paris in 1791. After her execution they were smuggled across Europe and eventually were purchased by the Youssoupov family in 1802.[9] Another rare piece was a long necklace of perfectly matched black pearls which had once belonged to Catherine the Great herself. But the most important and historic pieces in the entire Youssoupov jewel collection were two simple pearls, La Regente and La Pelegrina.

In 1887, when the French crown jewels were sold at auction, Zenaide acquired the famous La Regente, a tear-drop pearl pendant also formerly worn by Marie Antoinette. It was too large to use as a brooch, so Zenaide had it set so that she could wear it as a hair ornament.[10] The most extraordinary jewel in the Youssoupov collection was La Pelegrina, which had originally formed part of the Spanish crown jewels. The pearl had been given to Maria Therese by her father, Philip IV of Spain, upon her marriage to King Louis XIV of France. It disappeared in 1792 when the French crown jewels were stolen. In 1826, Princess Tatiana Youssoupov bought the pearl when it appeared in Moscow, and it passed into the Youssoupov collection.

Rich, cultured, and powerful, the Youssoupovs at the time of Prince Felix's birth in 1887 were recognized as the wealthiest and one of the most important aristocratic families in the empire. Their foresight and shrewd investments through the centuries had guaranteed an income beyond comprehension. One of their relatives, Prince Serge Obolensky, wrote that the Youssoupovs owned so much and possessed such vast amounts of money that even they themselves "didn't really know how much" they were worth.[11] It was into this enchanted world of luxurious palaces, fabled jewels, and priceless art treasures that Prince Felix Youssoupov was born.

7

A Privileged Childhood

His MOTHER EXPECTED A GIRL. She purchased a pink layette for the baby and made arrangements for a suitable wet nurse and nanny to be hired. Dresses covered with lace and ribbons, bows for the hair, and tiny patent leather shoes all awaited the arrival of the child. But on 23 March 1887, Zenaide Youssoupov gave birth to a second son, Felix. To compensate for this, the mother dressed her son as a girl until the age of five, making Felix even more feminine than was usual. This custom of dressing children of both sexes in expensive frocks and binding their long curls with matching ribbons was not unusual in Victorian society. Not surprisingly, most of the boys hated such treatment. Prince Felix's cousin Prince Serge Obolensky, who had himself suffered the same fate, later recalled: "For the first five years of my life my hair was kept long and I was dressed in skirts. This was humiliating to me. I even had curls. . . . My male cousins pulled my hair and made my life miserable, while my girl cousins liked to curl my ringlets, which was just as bad."[1] But, unlike his cousin, Prince Felix Youssoupov felt no shame at his feminine attire. He loved the frills and curls and petticoats; on walks with his nanny through the streets of St. Petersburg, he would frequently call out to strangers, "Look, isn't Baby pretty?"[2]

He grew up in his family's palace on the Moika Canal in St. Petersburg, the greatest of all the capital's private houses. One historian later wrote:

> This is not so much a unified town house, in the English sense, as an Oriental-type labyrinth in which generation after generation of Youssoupovs left their mark. There

67

was no fancy so extravagant, in this house, that it could not be indulged; nor any practice so bizarre that it could not be concealed from the rest of the family by a secret door hidden behind a bookshelf, or beneath an English billiards table, or in the intestinal area below where Rasputin was lured to his death.[3]

The Moika Palace did not originally belong to the Youssoupov family. It had been built in the eighteenth century by Field Marshal Count Peter Shuvalov, head of one of Russia's ancient, aristocratic families, but Shuvalov's house, a large, two-story structure in stone, was hardly a palace. In the 1760s, after the Youssoupovs acquired the property, they commissioned architect Jean Baptiste Vallin de la Mothe to enlarge the structure. He added a third story above the cornice, extended the house along the Moika, and encased the building in a stark yet elegant façade, dominated by a six-columned portico overlooking the canal.

No further major architectural work was carried out on the palace for more than fifty years. But over the course of the nineteenth century, no fewer than four different architects—the Russians Andrei Mikhailov and Alexander Stepanov, Italian Ipolit Monighetti, and the Swiss Bernhard Simone—worked on additions and renovations. Mikhailov extended the building farther along the canal, adding several ballrooms and private apartments on the lower floor. By the time of Prince Felix Youssoupov's birth, the Moika Palace stood as the grandest house in the Russian capital, on a scale with the residences of the tsar himself.

Visitors who crossed the threshold of the Moika Palace entered a world of sophisticated luxury. From the entrance hall, a wide, double flight of marble stairs ascended to the first floor; the walls and ceiling were richly decorated with stucco reliefs which shimmered in the soft light from the tall, curtained windows. Above hung an enormous crystal and ormolu chandelier, purchased by Felix's grandfather from a French château. At the head of the staircase, an anteroom opened to a ballroom overlooking the Moika Canal below. The cornice of the columned room was decorated with hundreds of gilded sconces to match the gilt-and-crystal chandeliers above; on evenings when the

Youssoupovs entertained, the room blazed with light, the sparkle reflected in a seemingly endless line of large pier glasses on the walls. To the right of this room Mikhailov created a second huge ballroom faced in artificial marble and decorated with screens of Corinthian columns and papier-mâché reliefs.

The formal state apartments, with views over the Moika, were arranged *en enfilade*, to provide a long vista. From the anteroom at the top of the staircase, double doors opened to the Green Drawing Room, named for its silk wall coverings and rich malachite chimneypiece. The furniture here was Karilian birch, decorated with ormolu lions' heads representing the family's coat of arms. The Imperial Drawing Room, the next room in the suite, was reserved exclusively for receiving members of the Romanov dynasty. The red silk wallhangings provided a brilliant backdrop for the Empire furniture, all heavily carved and gilded, and the allegorical ceiling painting, the work of the Italian Pietro Scotti. The floor of this room was an intricate mosiac, composed of eight different kinds of rare tropical woods, among them rosewood, sandalwood, ebony, and palmetto. In the adjoining Blue Drawing Room hung an eighteenth-century crystal and cobalt chandelier. The suite concluded with the Rotunda, a music room with eight scagliola columns supporting a dome painted by Scotti and another Italian, Marichi, to represent the sky.

At the eastern end of the first floor, the Exhibition Wing contained a series of formal reception rooms and galleries. These included the Picture Gallery, top-lit by two leaded-glass skylights and hung with a collection of Rembrandts, Reubens, Watteaus and Tiepolos; the Antique Hall, with an important collection of ancient Greek and Roman sculptures; and the Roman Hall, named for its painted ceiling depicting the death of a warrior after battle. The wing culminated in the Louis XVI–style theater, designed by Stepanov and decorated by Zenaide in cream, crimson, and gold. Artist Alexander Golovine, who had painted the magnificent curtain at the Mariinsky Theatre, also executed the curtain here. The private theatre could seat two hundred guests; above their heads swirled a sea of dancing cherubs, putti, and gilded garlands surrounding the ceiling painting, *Aurora Driving Away the Night*. Dominating the theater was the family box, at the rear of the first tier, entered through a Roman archway decorated with sixteen gilded "Y's" and other heraldic devices.

The Moika Palace was a labyrinth of galleries, halls, alcoves, secret staircases, and hidden rooms. On the lower floor was one such surprise: the Moorish Room, copied by Ipolit Monighetti from an apartment in the Alhambra. The Moorish Room was divided by painted arches, its windows screened with golden grilles. Divans and tables of sandalwood, along with plush pillows and water pipes, lay scattered across the inlaid marble and mosaic floor. An onyx fireplace stood against one of the marble walls, which were intricately decorated in a pattern of colored arabesques. In the center of the room stood an onyx fountain in which eight jets of water played at the touch of a switch. Around the cornice of the room, carved into marble and onyx panels, were inscriptions from the Koran, reminders of the Youssoupovs' Muslim heritage.[4]

The family's private apartments were no less luxurious. Zenaide's bedroom, hung with blue watered silk damask, contained long rows of glass cabinets filled with her priceless collection of jewelry. The furniture in the Private Drawing Room had belonged to Marie Antoinette; from the ceiling hung a rock-crystal chandelier from Madame de Pompadour's boudoir at Versailles. On the tables stood snuffboxes and ashtrays of jade, topaz, and amethyst, studded with diamonds and pearls, while crystal bowls, filled with uncut rubies, sapphires, and emeralds, served as mere decorations.[5]

In these rooms, the Youssoupovs held court, hiring opera and ballet companies to entertain their guests. Their elaborate balls and dinners were renowned throughout the capital, and invitations to the Moika Palace were among the most sought after of any society event. Their banquets were served on plates of solid gold and silver, enhanced with Sèvres porcelain and crystal from Bohemia. Special thousand-piece china services, made by the Youssoupov's own porcelain factory at Arkhangel-skoe, were commissioned to complement each dining room, with colors and patterns devised to match the interiors. This was only one of the many enchanting discoveries made by the hundreds of guests who luxuriated in the Youssoupovs' favor.

This degree of sophisticated style was made possible by Zenaide's huge fortune, but it was a veritable army of servants who carefully maintained the surroundings and standards. The extent of this style of life was exemplified by the fact that Zenaide employed one servant whose sole duty it was to care for her collection of fur muffs.[6] In the stables, grooms, drivers, and coachmen tended the horses and carriages, and later, with the introduction of motorcars came mechanics and chauffeurs. The family maintained a gilded gondola for use on the city's canals, complete with gondoliers in Venetian costume and tricorn hats. Chefs imported from Paris prepared the lavish dinners, served on gold plates polished by housemaids and handed to guests by footmen in the Youssoupov blue and gold livery. Scullery maids washed and cleaned, while flower girls cut and arranged roses, lilacs, and orchids throughout the rooms. Arabs and Tartars, attired in colorful native costumes, served as doormen.

Each year, with the approach of summer, the Youssoupovs, accompanied by a dozen steamer trunks and valises packed with clothing, jewels, and favorite objects, left St. Petersburg for Moscow. They traveled in their own railway carriage, a miniature palace of luxurious comforts that held a plush drawing room filled with overstuffed furniture, a dining room paneled in mahogany, bedrooms for the family and its servants, a kitchen, and an aviary. When the family traveled, the carriage was simply coupled to a regular passenger train bound for their intended destination. A similiar private carriage stood at the country's western borders for trips in Continental Europe.

The Youssoupovs' Moscow house, originally one of Ivan the Terrible's hunting lodges, had been designed by Barma and Postnik, the same two architects believed to be responsible for St. Basil's Cathedral in Red Square. When the Youssoupovs remodeled the house in the late nineteenth century, workers discovered an old basement passageway, bricked up hundreds of years before. Inside, chained to the walls, were the crumbling skeletons of dozens of men, victims of the depraved tsar.

After Ivan's death, the Russian court sold the mansion to the Volkovs, a wealthy boyar family. They lived within its walls for several decades before selling it to the Tolstoy family. In 1727, Empress Catherine I, wife of Peter the Great, presented it as a gift to the Youssoupovs; for the next century, the family rarely lived in the house, instead letting it out to other aristocratic Muscovites. There were several famous occupants, including the poet Alexander Pushkin, who spent his childhood there.[7]

The house looked rather forbidding, a sprawling red-brick mansion capped with steeply pitched copper roofs painted in a bright checkerboard pattern of medieval colors. Long rows of mica windows, encased in elaborate white stone frames carved with birds and foliage, dotted the façades, along with archways and arcades. Gables, dormers, and skylights pierced the roofs, decorated with wrought-iron railings and gilded finials. Its rambling form reflected the many centuries of construction and alteration, a pattern which continued until the end of the nineteenth century. In 1892 the Youssoupovs commissioned architect Nicholas Sultanov, who also did restoration work on the Kremlin palaces during the same period, to enlarge the mansion. On the eastern side of the house he created a series of reception and drawing rooms in a medieval-style addition, along with an entrance porch and a new grand staircase. He built a long wing to the north to contain the family's private apartments, connected to the old lodge by a glassed-in winter garden. He also enclosed the large courtyard to the east, creating tall arches and gates emblazoned with the Youssoupov coat of arms. Across the lane stood the family's private neoclassical theater.

Inside, the house was dark and somber, with low, vaulted ceilings painted with medieval frescoes; long, twisting passages; and narrow staircases which rose to shadowy alcoves. One chamber had been used as an audience room by Ivan the Terrible; the medieval paintings on the vaults depicted the tsar and his court on an imperial hunt. The *Krestovsky*, or Cross Hall, had been Ivan's ballroom; a large, square, vaulted chamber, it lay hidden behind massive golden grilles and was lit with nine solid-silver chandeliers and warmed by enormous multicolored porcelain stoves. The Chinese Salon was decorated with gilded dragons and lotus blossoms, while the ceiling of the Red Drawing Room featured painted roundels of former Youssoupov owners. These rooms were masterpieces of medieval decoration, the finest original interiors to survive in turn-of-the-century Moscow, with their painted, colorful birds, foliage, chevrons, and stamped and gilded leather wall hangings. In spite of its unquestionable beauty, the Youssoupovs disliked the house, finding the ominous atmosphere too powerful, and in the years before the Revolution, they used it principally for entertaining rather than living.

These receptions and banquets left a vivid impression on many of the guests. Infanta Eulalia, aunt of King Alfonso XIII of Spain, recalled the splendor of the Moscow house and the beauty of her hostess many years later:

> Of all the parties given in my honour, none impressed me more than that of Princess Youssoupov. The Princess was a most lovely woman, whose marvelous beauty stands out. . . . She lived in extraordinary luxury, in a setting of unsurpassed splendour, surrounded by works of art of the purest Byzantine style. . . . The magnificence and luxury of Russia, blended with the refinement and distinction of France, reached its culminating point in the Youssoupov Palace. . . . The Princess wore a court gown studded with the finest diamonds and pearls. Tall, exquisitely beautiful, she wore a *kokoshnik* set with enormous pearls and equally large diamonds, worth a fortune. A dazzling array of fantastic jewels from the East and the West completed her costume: ropes of pearls, massive gold bracelets of ancient design, pendants of turquoises and pearls, multi-coloured, glittering rings. . . . All these gave to Princess Youssoupov the majestic splendour of a Byzantine empress.[8]

The Youssoupovs much preferred Arkhangelskoe, their Moscow country estate. Surrounded by farmlands and forests, it fronted the Moscow River. It lay far beyond the suburban sprawl of the residential districts and industrial centers whose tall smokestacks belched their waste into the Moscow sky.

The Arkhangelskoe estate had originally belonged to the Galitzine family. Sometime in the late 1770s they drew up plans for a large house. The French architect Charles François de Gerne designed the residence, while the Italian Giacommo Trombaro laid out the park terraces. In 1810, Prince Nicholas Borisovich

Youssoupov bought the property from the Galitzines and commenced minor additions. The 1812 French invasion put a stop to this building activity, and when Napoleon's army left the city, Arkhangelskoe had been severely damaged not only by the ravages of war but also by a revolt among the local peasants. Subsequently, Youssoupov oversaw major renovations, including the redecoration of the interior by the architect Evgraf Tiurin and the painter Nicolas de Courteille after a disastrous fire.

The formal approach to the house cut through a forest of cedars, firs, and pines. Meadows grown over with colorful wildflowers stretched between groves of birch trees, with vistas to the winding breadth of the Moscow River beyond. At the end of the drive, a magnificent pair of gates, built in 1817 by Stephan Melnikov, stood between piers of Tuscan Doric columns crowned with an impressive pediment. These opened to the Court of Honor, surrounded by long colonnaded wings of double Tuscan columns on either side which stretched to join with the main house at the far end of the space. The two-story Ionic portico and pediment gave a hint of the glories which lay beyond the pale stone walls. Above, crowning the sloped green roof of the house, rose a small rotunda surrounded by Corinthian columns and pierced with French windows.[9]

Guests entered a marble hall decorated with statuary and bronze chandeliers. Twin Egyptian-style staircases led up to the second floor from either side, through trellised arches covered with trompe l'oeil ivy. The principal rooms of the house were arranged along both the northern side facing the courtyard and the southern, garden façade, all *en enfilade*. At the center of the southern enfilade was the Oval Salon, rising two stories to a domed ceiling. Bands of paired Corinthian columns circled the room, supporting the second-floor gallery, where musicians played during receptions. Above the heads of the guests hung an ormolu chandelier of 132 candles. The State Dining Room, in the northern enfilade, had walls decorated with grisaille panels. On the opposite side of the entrance hall was the Venetian Room, hung with the works of, among others, Tiepolo, including two enormous paintings, *The Feast of Cleopatra* and *The Meeting of Anthony and Cleopatra*.[10] The Antique Hall was filled with Prince Nicholas Youssoupov's collection of statuary, acquired during his tenure as ambassador in Turin. The library included over six thousand rare volumes. These rooms were filled with sculpture by Wolfee, Kozlovsky, and Canova; Sèvres, Wedgwood, and Meissen china and porcelain; and paintings by Van Loo, Hubert Robert, Tiepolo, Jacob Philippe Hackert, Doyen, Boucher, Watteau, Greuze, Claude, Fragonard, and Vigée-Lebrun. Today nearly all of this collection forms a major body of the collection of the Hermitage Museum in St. Petersburg. Everything was designed to bring the solitude of the gardens within. Walls were hung in soft linens or painted pastel colors to meld with the greens and blues beyond the windows. The gilding of the columns and cornices, along with the polished marble and shining, inlaid parquet floors, were meant to capture and suspend the golden rays of the summer sunshine.[11]

Three French doors opened from the Oval Hall to the southern stepped terraces, adorned with marble statuary and urns filled with fragrant roses. Twin flights of stone steps descended to the lawns, which stretched to the river in the distance. The grounds were a mixture of formal French-style parterres, with box hedge and pleached lime and beech trees, and the more expansive English-style park, with meandering paths, stretches of lawn dotted with classical statuary, and ornamental lakes and ponds. Four pavilions, which were connected to conservatories over six hundred feet in length, stood at the river's edge. The Youssoupovs filled these conservatories with palm and orange trees, banks of orchids, and free-flying hummingbirds. A classical rotunda with Corinthian columns and a low dome contained a portion of the immense estate library and was later used as a tea pavilion. The private chapel, the Church of the Archangel Michael—from which the estate derived its name—dated from 1667 and closely resembled the ancient medieval churches of the old capital, with its stepped rows of decorative arches and small onion domes. In addition to the church, the park also contained a whitewashed wooden theater, designed by Osip Bove and decorated in the Palladian style by Pietro Gonzaga, where the family frequently entertained their guests.

Like the Youssoupovs' other residences, that at Arkhangelskoe required hundreds of servants. Most were peasants, born on the estate and raised to serve the Youssoupovs. There were craftsmen: carpenters, architects, tailors, and shoemakers; artists: opera singers, ballet dancers, painters, and poets; those who worked on the estate farm: dairymaids, mowers, planters, agricultural supervisors, veterinarians; and those who worked in the house: the butler, footmen, maids, flower girls, scullery maids, kitchen boys, valets, and cooks. The Youssoupovs built model villages at Arkhangelskoe for these servants which were considered remarkable examples of enlightenment. The buildings included chapels, schools, libraries, shops, bath houses, and a hospital so that those born on the estate never had to leave its borders. With military efficiency, Felix's father regularly inspected the villages; the peasants who lived and worked on the estate faced immediate expulsion if they violated any of the rigid standards which he set. Every Sunday, when in residence, the Youssoupovs personally received the workers, listening to their suggestions, comments, or complaints. Once a year, Zenaide gave a dance to which all of those attached to the estate were invited and where the family mingled freely with their servants. Such benevolent treatment impressed many visitors; when the French painter Flameng left the estate after a visit, he said to Zenaide, "Promise me, Princess, that when my artistic career is over, you will allow me to become the honourary pig of Arkhangelskoe."[12]

Two private factories operated on the estate, one for porcelain, the other for glass. Items from the Arkhangelskoe craftsmen became highly prized. When Felix Youssoupov modernized the estate in 1912, he found crates of magnificent porcelain and crystal stored in one corner of the basement of the house. He took them back to the Moika Palace in St. Petersburg, where they can still be seen to this day.

Summer months at Arkhangelskoe were long and lazy. Felix and his elder brother Nicholas took turns rowing up and down the river or hunted for mushrooms in the forests. Zenaide hosted picnics in the woods, with servants carrying silver dishes of food to a portable table erected on an Oriental carpet. In the afternoons the boys rode or played lawn tennis with family and friends. Young Felix played badly; on one occasion, he returned a serve with such force and misdirection that it hit a visiting grand duke in the face. The unfortunate man had to seek immediate medical attention to save his eye.

At the end of the summer the peasants on the estate held an annual fair which the Youssoupovs attended. Children danced and played in the streets while Gypsies sang folk songs, accompanied by the balalaika and accordion. The last celebration came before harvest time. By August the heat of the summer days reached its peak. The family lounged on the terraces beneath the shade of canvas awnings, watching as long lines of peasants left daily for the fields to mow the wheat, an event of great importance.

The two most important and frequent visitors to Arkhangelskoe during Felix's childhood were the Youssoupovs' neighbors from the estate of Ilinskoe, Grand Duke Serge Alexandrovich and his wife, Grand Duchess Elizabeth. Serge had been appointed governor-general of Moscow in 1891; he quickly made himself the most despised member of the imperial family by his reactionary policies and ruthless domination of Moscow.

Felix later wrote that he "loved and revered" the grand duchess "as a second mother." At night, "nothing would have induced me to close my eyes until the Grand Duchess had come to say goodnight to me. She blessed me and kissed me and I was filled with a wonderful peace and went quickly to sleep."[13] But he disliked the grand duke, with his cold, arrogant manner. Serge Alexandrovich wore corsets, which, in the summer, could be seen through his white linen tunics. Felix liked to touch the stays, much to the grand duke's annoyance.[14] Felix's father had been appointed the grand duke's aide-de-camp when Serge took over the governor-generalship of Moscow, and so the two families had frequent contact. Although the grand duke and duchess were childless, Ella had a great love and understanding of children, and she and Felix got along very well. She remained a firm friend and later played an important role in the prince's life.

At the end of the summer, the Youssoupovs boarded their private railway carriage and set off for Rakitnoe, in the Kursk district. One of the larger of the family's holdings, Rakitnoe boasted a sugar plantation, several sawmills, a wool-spinning mill, a brick factory, and a racing stud. The Youssoupov horses often won the great races held in St. Petersburg and Moscow and were prized sires. The chief pursuits at Rakitnoe were riding and hunting. A pack of borzois led the chase across the forests and fields on these occasions, followed by riders in pursuit. On days when there were no hunts, shoots were held. Felix, expected to participate in these events, did so only reluctantly. He had no taste for blood sports. During one of these shoots, he wounded a small hare. "Its piteous scream made me feel so guilty," he later wrote, "that from that day I gave it up."[15] Later, he even gave away all of his expensive English guns, so intense was his dislike of violence, and refused to go to Rakitnoe with his parents. It is only one of the many ironies of his life that the young prince who was so affected by the sight of this wounded animal and gave away his collection of guns would later coldly plot the murder of another man.

8

Youth

PRINCE FELIX YOUSSOUPOV grew up a delicate and sickly child. He appears to have suffered from every known childhood disease and spent most of his early years in bed. Rarely did a night pass when the boy's screams and cries did not awaken the household. He sleepwalked, with nervous servants detailed to follow him round the palace at night to prevent an accident. This indulgent attention quickly spoiled him. He went through a long succession of nurses, governesses, and tutors, for none proved up to the challenge of raising him. His first nurse, a German woman, went mad, and the Youssoupovs sent her to an asylum. His second exhausted all her efforts on the child before she, too, left her post. Next came another German, who took to bed every night with a bottle of champagne. Felix's parents then hired a series of Russian, English, French, and Swiss tutors, all of whom left in exasperation. They finally engaged a Roman Catholic priest with the hope that he would be able to instill in Felix discipline and a love of learning. But he, too, failed in his task and went to work at the Romanian royal court. Many years later, Queen Marie of Romania told Felix that the poor man still suffered from nightmares as a result of his days in the Youssoupov household.

Despite his obstinacy, Felix went through the prescribed round of subjects—Russian grammar, arithmetic, history, French, German, English, and Latin. Every week, he attended dancing lessons with other children from noble families. Anna Taneyev, daughter of the minister of the interior and chancellor of the imperial court, was Felix's frequent partner at these classes. Felix disliked Anna, describing her as "tall and stout, with a puffy, shiny face and no charm whatever."[1] He wrote these lines many years later, however, after Anna had married Alexander Vyrubov and become notorious as the friend who passed communications between the empress and Rasputin.

Felix took pleasure in pushing his parents to their limits. He kept a small dog to which he fed chocolates and champagne; at parties he trotted out his drunken friend, who then relieved himself on the elegant guests, much to Felix's amusement. One day, however, he went too far: He dressed the dog as a prostitute, complete with dress and wig, face paint, and powder and sent him off into a drawing room where Zenaide sat chatting with the minister of religion. The dog promptly sprayed the illustrious visitor, driving the poor man out of the palace in a near fit.[2] On another occasion, Felix's father burst into the Moorish Room at the Moika Palace only to find his son standing before the fountain dressed in a makeshift sultan costume and wearing his mother's jewels, a half-naked Arab servant lying prone at his feet while the boy brandished a long ceremonial dagger. After this incident, Felix was forbidden to play in the Moorish Room for some time.[3]

In despair at their inability to control their son, Felix's parents sent him off on a tour of Italy with an elderly professor of art history. At night the old man disappeared from the hotel where they were staying, leaving Felix to explore on his own. One night the young prince ended up in a bordello, surrounded by naked women of all different ages. The madam of the establishment plied him with glass after glass of champagne, and Felix quickly became drunk, too drunk to take an interest in the proceedings, and the ladies left him alone. Suddenly, in his inebriated condition, Felix spotted his elderly tutor. He tried to hide beneath the table, but the professor caught sight of his charge and laughingly ordered a bottle of champagne for them. The tour of Italy continued in this fashion, the two visiting museums and cathedrals by day and bars and whore houses at night.

Not surprisingly, when Felix returned to Russia, his parents found him even more difficult than he had been before the trip. His father reacted swiftly. He fired his son's tutor and replaced him with, in prince Felix's own words, "a dirty, evil-smelling dwarf" who wore the same clothes six days a week, changing only for Sunday dinner with the family. Zenaide protested, but her husband was delighted and refused to relieve him of his duties. But soon Felix made even this man's life so miserable that he voluntarily quit as tutor. In response, Felix's father had all of the furniture removed from his son's bedroom and replaced it with a simple army cot, a stool, and a curious-looking cabinet. Felix tried to open the mysterious cabinet but found it locked. The following morning, his father's valet grabbed Felix out of the cot, stripped him of his clothes, and locked him in the cabinet. Immediately, a torrent of cold water poured from its top as Felix screamed and cried. When the servant finally opened the device, Felix fled, naked, down the hallways of the palace and out into the courtyard. His parents found him perched high in a tree, still naked, howling like a madman. He only agreed to come down on the condition that he not be subjected to such treatment again.[4]

His father decided to send him to military school, but Felix deliberately failed the entrance examination in an attempt to remain at home. This left only one alternative: the Goureievich Secondary School in St. Petersburg, which dealt only with the most difficult students. Felix again planned to fail his examination, but his parents, aware of the possibility, asked that he be admitted without the tests. The school, even with its reputation for harsh discipline, however, did little for Felix. When he left, he flung himself into his old habits, drinking and attending parties, "thinking only of satisfying my desires and impatient of any restrictions of my freedom."[5] His mother's friends found him impudent and rude; when they spoke to him in French, he answered only in Russian, which they considered ill mannered. He could be charming and sophisticated, though these qualities were tempered by arrogance and hedonism. But Felix, by this time nearly eighteen, seemed not to care what anyone thought of him. Instead, he threw himself headlong into the glamorous life of St. Petersburg society.

Felix could behave properly when it suited him, however. Carefully groomed and dressed, he often joined his parents and brother as they entered a family carriage and set off for the Mariinsky Theatre, several blocks down the Moika Canal from their own palace. The daughter of the British ambassador in St. Petersburg later recalled:

The ballet was given every Sunday and Wednesday at the Mariinsky Theatre, nearly all the stalls and boxes being taken by *abonnements*, which were themselves not always easy to obtain as they were very often hereditary and handed down from father to son. For the opera one could sit in any part of the house one liked but for the ballet no lady could sit anywhere but in a box and it was also considered highly unseemly to remain sitting in the box during the *entr'acte*, so, directly the curtain went down and everybody retreated to the little ante-room at the back of each box where one could smoke and talk and receive the visits of young men who had been sitting in the stalls. When I shut my eyes I can still feel the individual atmosphere of that huge theatre, the scent of ambre and chypre, of chocolates and cigarettes, the faint smell of heating, of leather and of the age and dust raised by hundreds of dancing feet. I can visualize the white and blue and gold of the decorations, the first four tiers of boxes, the dim, far-away gallery, the parterre of stalls crowded with artists, musicians, young diplomats, officers in brilliant uniforms, old, bald-headed generals. Now and then, defying convention, a young girl would lean from a box to smile a greeting at some young man below, a few old men grouped together in earnest discussion, would, for once not be talking politics but would be arguing about the technique of some dancer's step, shaking their heads mournfully as they agreed that the true art of choreography was deteriorating and that the last ballets lacked the beauty of the older performances. Fat ladies of the merchant classes munched chocolates brought to them in be-ribboned boxes by portly men with smooth faces, outside in the foyer young girls and boys from the gallery seats would walk solemnly round and round, watched by some anxious mother, sitting eating cakes and drinking weak, sugared tea.[6]

Felix enjoyed the capital's winter social season. St. Petersburg eagerly gave itself over to pleasure with the beginning of each new year, reveling in indulgent pastimes. Women spent their days at the hairdresser or in the great *couture* houses lining the Nevsky Prospect. In the afternoons they drove to the city's palaces, taking tea and exchanging the latest gossip. Gentlemen went to their private clubs: the English Club, the New Club, or, for the lucky few, the Imperial Yacht Club on the Morskaia. "His Majesty the Tsar," recalled Countess Kleinmichel, "had two kinds of subjects: those who were members of the Yacht Club, and those who were not. . . .

> How many people passing through the Morskaia used to raise their longing eyes to that Holy of Holies, the goal of their most ardent desires. I recollect the members of that select club gluing their noses against the window panes, pressing close against one another, persuaded of their superiority over all other beings, proud of their importance, and spending hours looking down the Morskaia. A young man who, the day before his admission to membership, was inoffensive, kindly and modest, eight days later would be self-important and abusive, and would disparage everything and everybody, except his club, of which he spoke as if it were the Senate or the Imperial Council.[7]

Although his father belonged to all of these exclusive clubs, Felix considered them boorish. He preferred the more bohemian attractions of the city's popular nightspots: the fashionable restaurants—Cubat's, the Bear and the Villa Rode, and the Aquarium Club, where fish swam behind the glass walls. He often drove to the islands to visit the Gypsies, drinking and joining in their dancing until dawn.

In summer, St. Petersburg took on an air of abandonment. A peculiar stillness settled over the city as members of the aristocracy fled to their country palaces. The Youssoupovs themselves followed the imperial court to Tsarskoe Selo, fifteen miles south of the capital. Their rococo villa stood near the imperial park, an eight-hundred-acre compound of lakes, gardens, and pavilions dominated by two palaces: the blue-and-gold Catherine Palace, built by Empress Elizabeth, and the smaller Alexander Palace, where the tsar and his family lived. After a few weeks the Youssoupovs traveled to Arkhangelskoe for the summer; then they moved on to the Crimea and Rakitnoe before returning to St. Petersburg to join in the pleasures of the season once again.

The Crimean peninsula was a semitropical paradise, a far cry from the long, harsh winters of St. Petersburg. After the imperial family purchased a villa there at the beginning of the nineteenth century, it became fashionable for members of the aristocracy to own houses along the seashore. From the outskirts of the town of Yalta, the Crimean coast along the Black Sea was home to dozens of members of the imperial family and the aristocracy. Behind high iron gates and carefully trimmed hedges stood summer retreats: the imperial family's Italian Renaissance palace at Livadia; Grand Duke Alexander Michailovich's Florentine-style Ai-Tudor; Grand Duke Peter Nicholaievich's Moorish-style Dulber; and the Youssoupov's Gothic-style Koreiz. The Youssoupovs, always at the forefront of the social spectrum, actually owned three Crimean villas as well as a number of vineyards and agricultural estates.

Koreiz, a rather ungainly stone mansion, sat in the middle of terraced gardens filled with rose beds, pavilions, fountains, and stands of palm and cypress trees. In one of his many bursts of enthusiasm for redecorating, Felix's father filled the park with bronze statuary representing sea nymphs, classical gods and goddesses, and family ancestors. During one of their absences from the Crimea, the estate curator took it upon himself to make further improvements; the family was shocked when they returned to discover all of the statuary in the park painted in brilliant flesh tones, an artistic statement which took several weeks to remove.

Kokoz, the other principle Youssoupov estate in the Crimea, was located in an inland valley surrounded by vineyards and agricultural lands. The name translated as "blue eye" in Tartar, and the theme was carried out in the decoration of the house, from the stained-glass windows to the wallpapers and carpets in the state rooms.

Life in the Crimea moved at a deliberately slow pace. Here more than anyplace else, Felix's father could give full reign to his renowned eccentricities, away from the wagging tongues of the capital. Once, on a whim, he purchased Ai-Petri, the highest mountain on the peninsula, as a gift for Zenaide. Every year while in residence in the Crimea, he presided over the Sheep Fair, which his son Felix recalled as a rather curious event. Members of the imperial family as well as the aristocracy were invited, and they strolled through the park at Koreiz while herds of sheep and goats grazed. Each sheep had a blue ribbon tied around its neck; each goat, a pink one. Footmen in livery, carrying trays of food and wine for the guests, moved among the freely roaming sheep, and while everyone enjoyed the afternoon, they all left, according to Felix, without the least idea of what had happened or why the animals had been present in the first place.

The Crimean holidays provided a welcome respite for Felix, who dreaded the rigors of his education in St. Petersburg. He barely managed to escape expulsion from the Goureievich Secondary School on several occasions. By the time of his twelfth birthday, he had fallen heavily under the dubious influence of his brother Nicholas, a student at the University of St. Petersburg. The two brothers shared a distaste for conventional St. Petersburg society and a love of more adventurous pursuits. By the time of his last year in secondary school, Felix regularly dressed as a woman and prowled the city's nightspots accompanied and encouraged by Nicholas. Even the jaded, decadent elements of St. Petersburg society were shocked once they learned of these transvestite activities.

Felix first began dressing himself in women's clothes at the age of twelve. One evening, while his parents were out, he and his cousin Vladimir Lazurov decided to leave the Moika Palace disguised as women. They raided Zenaide's wardrobe for suitable attire and her jewel cabinets for earrings and ropes of pearls. They woke her personal hairdresser, who supplied them with wigs. Wrapped in heavy fur cloaks, the two boys left the palace and strolled the Nevsky Prospect, where they were immediately mistaken for prostitutes and accosted by a group of drunken sailors. To escape their advances, Felix and Vladimir ducked into the Bear Restaurant, a fashionable St. Petersburg nightspot. They ordered champagne; after drinking several glasses, Felix became drunk and began to flirt with some men at a nearby table. The men invited the pair to dine with them in a private room. Before Felix could accept, he lost his head to alcohol. Taking his mother's string of pearls, he made a lasso and began aiming it at the heads of nearby diners. The string broke, the pearls scattered, and Felix had to admit the truth of the adventure when confronted by the manager. Not surprisingly, Felix's aunt forbade Vladimir to see him again, and Felix himself suffered the wrath of his furious and humiliated father, who confined him to his room for several weeks.[8]

Despite this incident and his father's disapproval, Felix, true to his love of pleasure, continued to indulge his taste for feminine disguise. He loved the adventure, and his brother Nicholas further encouraged him by taking Felix along when he and his mistress visited the city's clubs. "I then realized," Felix later wrote, "that my disguise allowed me to go wherever I chose, and from that moment I began to lead a double life: by day, I was a schoolboy and by night an elegant woman."[9] Nicholas arranged for his brother to be engaged as a singer at the Aquarium Club. Felix auditioned for the part in a gray tailored suit and hat, offering the latest Parisian tunes. On his opening night, he dressed in a gown of blue tulle embroidered with silver and a headdress of ostrich feathers. On the program for the evening, three stars were used in place of his name. At first the reception seemed cold, but by the third song, Felix held the audience captive, prancing about the stage in his gown and winking at men in the audience. After the performance, bouquets of flowers and invitations to dine with officers poured into his dressing room. He proved such a success that the manager booked him for six more engagements. On the final night, however, a member of the audience recognized a piece of Zenaide's jewelry which her son was wearing and informed Felix's parents of his curious nocturnal habits. To save his brother, Nicholas took the blame, though again Felix faced a lecture by his father on his peculiar lifestyle. The warning had no effect, for Felix refused to "give up the disguises which provided me with such delightful amusement."[10]

Events culminated in another visit to the Bear Restaurant. Felix attended a ball dressed as a woman and accepted the invitation of four officers to dine at the Bear. The officers engaged one of the private dining rooms, which were kept to satisfy the amorous appetites of the patrons. Once inside the room, the officers got drunk and tried to rip the clothes off Felix. To escape, he seized a bottle of champagne and hurled it at a mirror on the wall, then switched off the lights and fled. Felix's father soon learned of this latest adventure. He called Felix "a guttersnipe and a scoundrel, adding that people like me were not fit to breathe the same air as honest folk," the prince later wrote. All of St. Petersburg knew of his transvestite activities, his father continued, and by his repeated flaunting of his sexual peculiarities, the young prince had brought shame to his family. Saying that he no longer belonged in the Moika Palace but in a Siberian prison, the elder Youssoupov dismissed his son.[11]

Undoubtedly this denunciation had some effect on Felix, for he ceased to dress as a woman in St. Petersburg. But, on his frequent trips to Europe with his brother Nicholas—and away from the scornful gaze of his disapproving father—Felix continued his scandalous behavior. Once, in Paris, he and Nicholas attended a performance at the *Théâtre des Capucines*. Felix dressed as a woman. Throughout the first act, a fat, bewhiskered gentleman in one of the boxes stared long and hard at him. During the intermission, when the lights came up, Felix recognized the man as King Edward VII of England; one of the king's aides approached Nicholas, asking for the name of the lovely young woman with him.[12]

Felix's escapades were assisted by his "rather effeminate appearance," in the words of one lady who met him.[13] Another friend of the prince described him as "tall and slendour [sic], and almost too handsome. With his fine features, dark, melancholy eyes and ivory skin he might almost be called effeminate in appearance. One sees such men only in very old families where the vigour has begun to run low."[14] He had inherited his mother's chiseled nose and mouth and blue-gray eyes—"extraordinary . . . with long lashes," one of his friends recalled—with his father's fair hair and stature.[15] The epicene quality of his beauty lent Felix an ethereal, mystical quality, a vaguely feminine aura, which he carefully cultivated and enhanced.

The two brothers led a debauched life in Paris, visiting brothels and casinos, attending parties, and getting drunk every night. Once, Nicholas took Felix to an opium den. People in various states of undress lay on the floor, surrounded by a swirling haze of smoke. Felix had already smoked several pipes when suddenly the police burst into the establishment; he managed to escape through a rear door but quickly passed out in the street. The next day, he awoke with a terrible headache, vowing to never smoke opium again. "It goes without saying," he later wrote, "that I broke my word at the first opportunity."[16]

By the age of twenty, Felix Youssoupov had become accustomed to such pleasures. Along with drinking and drugs came sex. His first sexual experience occurred when he was twelve, on holiday in France. One evening, while out walking after dinner, Felix happened to pass by an open window and saw a young couple making love inside. On his return to the hotel he asked his mother what the strangers had been doing; Zenaide quickly changed the subject. But Felix, curious, went back to the house the following evening, only to find the couple gone. By chance, as he walked back to his hotel, he met the young man from the previous night, and Felix asked whether he was on his way to see his lady friend. For a moment the man stared at Felix, bewildered, then realizing that he must have been seen, he laughed and asked Felix why he wished to know. When Felix explained his interest, the young man invited him to join him and his friend later that same evening at a nearby hotel.

At the appointed time, Felix made his way to the hotel. The young man sat waiting on the porch. He had time only to tell Felix that he was from Argentina before the young lady arrived. They all went to a room in the hotel, and for the next several hours, Felix watched as the couple again made love. In his book *Lost Splendour*, Felix makes no claim to having been an active participant. Instead, in one of the most telling lines he ever wrote, he said, "I was so amazed by what I had learned that, in my youthful ignorance, I failed to discriminate between the sexes."[17]

Certainly, in light of his habit of dressing as a woman and the later rumors concerning Felix's sexual preference, his "failure to discriminate between the sexes" is highly revealing. The nature of Felix's sexuality remains something of an enigma. His frequent visits to brothels across Europe in the company of his brother were certainly not platonic, and it seems that his first sexual affairs were with women. But those who knew him throughout his life realized that he was an active homosexual, a judgment supported by contemporary rumor, the memories of his friends, and the stories told by Felix himself. Just when he may have crossed the line and begun to have homosexual affairs is not known. Felix himself later admitted to having many liaisons, none of which lasted very long because, as he frankly admitted, "I . . . cared for no one but myself." Addressing the rumors concerning his sexual preference, he later wrote, "I have often been accused of disliking women. Nothing is further from the truth. I like them when they are nice. . . . But I must admit that I have met very few who answered to my ideal of womanhood." Instead, he praised the "loyalty and disinterestedness" of the men he had known.[18]

In 1907, Zenaide and Felix Youssoupov celebrated their twenty-fifth wedding anniversary. They marked the occasion by hosting a number of sumptuous receptions, at which they were showered with expensive gifts. From her husband, Zenaide received a specially comissioned Fabergé egg in pink-and-opaque-white enamel studded with diamonds and pearls. A golden serpent circled the egg, its tongue pointing to the Roman numerals which marked the correct hour. Three miniature paintings of her husband and her two sons hung suspended from the shell. And Nicholas and Felix presented their parents with a Fabergé music box in pink enamel with rose diamonds. Six monochrome views on the top, bottom, and sides depicted the Moika Palace, Arkhangelskoe, Rakitnoe, the Youssoupov villa in Tsarskoe Selo, the Moscow house, and Koreiz in the Crimea; when opened, the box played a regimental tune called "The White Lady."[19] The presentation of these luxurious *objets d'art* marked the last occasion that the Youssoupov family were all together; within a few months, tragedy struck their house and plunged the family into grief.

9

Tragedy and Transformation

In THE EARLY-MORNING HOURS of 5 July 1908, two men stood facing each other across a field blanketed with dew just outside St. Petersburg; they were Prince Nicholas Youssoupov and Baron Arwid Manteufel. At the arranged time a carriage drew up, and several other men stepped out. One held a wooden box; when he opened it, the sunlight shone brilliantly on two silver revolvers. Youssoupov chose one first, then Manteufel, the other. One of the gentlemen from the carriage asked both men to step back thirty paces. At a given signal, both men fired. Nicholas Youssoupov fired his gun into the air. Manteufel fired directly at the prince, but he was so nervous that he missed his target. The gentleman giving the signal asked that both men approach fifteen paces closer. At the second signal, Nicholas again fired into the air. Manteufel, however, took careful aim. His shot rang out through the forest, shattering the early-morning silence. Prince Nicholas Youssoupov, heir to his family's great fortune, fell into the long, wet grass, dead of a single bullet wound to the heart.

In 1908, Prince Nicholas Youssoupov was twenty-five years old. Tall and handsome, with his father's dark hair and a pencil mustache, he was widely touted in St. Petersburg society as the prime bachelor of his day. At one of the many parties in St. Petersburg, Nicholas met Countess Marina Heyden. Prince Serge Obolensky described her as "much courted, extremely popular and a great flirt."[1] Nicholas quickly fell in love with her. At the time, she was already engaged to Baron Arwid Manteufel, a lieutenant in the Horse Guards Regiment. Manteufel could not compete with the enormous wealth and charm offered by Nicholas, nor could Marina resist. She and Nicholas quickly became lovers, but Marina kept her affair a secret from her fiancé. Nicholas approached his parents and informed them that he wished to marry the countess. Both Zenaide and her husband refused to consider the match; they thought that Marina Heyden was too "fast," not suitable, the subject of many rumors. Unperturbed, Nicholas confessed his desire to his brother, then twenty-one, but he, too, shared his parents' dislike of the girl and tried to dissuade Nicholas from continuing the affair.

In a bid for time, Marina informed Manteufel that the date for their wedding would have to be postponed. But Manteufel, suspicious, insisted on a definite date. Marina reluctantly agreed and went to Paris to purchase her trousseau. Nicholas followed her. Leaving Manteufel in the dark, they continued the affair. The countess declared to Nicholas that she would rather die than marry a man she did not love. But Manteufel eventually managed to persuade Marina that he would be forever dishonored in the eyes of his regiment if she refused to marry him. She returned to St. Petersburg, but as the wedding day approached, she became desperate. On the evening before the wedding, she summoned Nicholas to have dinner with her; Felix went along as well. As the night wore on, Marina repeatedly begged Nicholas to elope with her. In a panic, Felix rushed off to the Heyden mansion and returned with Marina's mother. He managed to pull Nicholas away from his mistress and back to the Moika Palace.

The following day, the wedding between Baron Manteufel and Marina Heyden took place as scheduled, and the couple left for Paris on their honeymoon. Everyone had feared that Nicholas would attempt to stop the marriage; to his mother, who had been particularly anxious, Nicholas declared that he no longer cared about Marina. A few days later, Nicholas informed his parents that he had decided to go to Paris to hear Feodor Chaliapin sing with the Russian National Opera; they could not stop him, but realizing that the decision to go to Paris had nothing to do with the opera and everything to do with Marina Manteufel, they sent Felix with him. In Paris, however, Nicholas disappeared. Felix discovered that the former lovers were again seeing each other and summoned his parents. By this time, Manteufel had learned of his wife's infidelities with Youssoupov. Although Nicholas refused to discuss it, his parents learned that Manteufel had challenged him to a duel. One day, however, Manteufel came around to the hotel where the Youssoupovs were staying and declared that he and Nicholas had settled the issue and that he intended to divorce his wife. With the crisis seemingly at an end, the Youssoupovs returned to St. Petersburg.

The peace did not last; goaded by his fellow officers, who convinced him that his honor and that of their regiment had been defamed, Manteufel again challenged Nicholas to a duel. The prince refused to discuss the matter with his parents, but he confessed to Felix that the duel would soon take place. Felix told his parents, but when they confronted Nicholas, he denied all. On the evening of 4 July 1908, Zenaide summoned Felix to her rooms. He found her sitting before a mirror, having her hair brushed by her personal maid. "I had a talk with your brother this evening," she said. "All the rumours of a duel are pure inventions; everything has been arranged. You can't imagine how happy I am."[2] Felix left unconvinced and went to bed, fearing the worst.

The following morning, Felix's valet rushed into his room, screaming, "Come quickly, something terrible has happened!" Felix ran through the hallways of the palace to his parents' rooms, passing silent but tearful servants along the way. He found his father standing over a stretcher on which lay Nicholas's bloodstained body. Zenaide lay on the floor beside her dead son, sobbing hysterically. Father and son managed to carry her to bed, and Felix sat with her while his father, pale and silent, went off to make the funeral arrangements. When Zenaide spotted Felix, she took him for his dead brother and began calling out, "Nicholas! Nicholas!" Felix could do nothing but call for a physician, who sedated her.[3]

For the next week, Nicholas's body lay in the chapel of the Moika Palace while services for the dead were conducted. At the end of the week, the family took his body to Arkhangelskoe, where he was interred in a temporary mausoleum in the park. A few years later, Felix's father commissioned the architect Roman Klein to build a magnificent Palladian-style mausoleum for the entire family. Long, curved colonnades in granite and marble stretched out in a half hemisphere; at their center lay a small temple ornamented with a pediment supported with Corinthian columns and a low dome over the interior chapel. The finest artists and craftsmen were hired to finish the elaborate chapel with varicolored marble and light gray granite. It took seven years to complete this neoclassic memorial; by the time Klein was done, the Revolution had broken out, and none of the Youssoupovs were ever buried in its splendid crypt.

The dramatic duel, with its tragic results, was the talk of St. Petersburg. Great sorrow was expressed over Nicholas's death, while Baron Manteufel was virtually ostracized even by members of his own regiment. His marriage to Marina did not last long; the pair soon divorced, and Marina lived the rest of her life as a lonely exile in Paris.

After Nicholas's death, the widowed grand duchess Elizabeth Feodorovna, whose husband Serge had been assassinated by a terrorist bomb in 1905, came from Ilinskoe to stay with the family. Felix's father concealed his grief and kept to himself, spending long days with his regiment. But Zenaide suffered a nervous breakdown. She underwent a complete transformation. She abandoned society, refusing to give parties or balls, and never again went to the theater or ballet. She forbade any member of the Horse Guards Regiment, to which Manteufel had belonged, from entering her house. Ella remained with her for weeks. She made Felix promise that he would stay at his mother's side until she recovered; but Felix, obsessed with thoughts of revenge, told the grand duchess that he planned to kill Manteufel.[4] Eventually, the grand duchess calmed Felix and asked that he come to see her in Moscow as soon as his mother's condition had improved.

One day, while still at Arkhangelskoe, Felix went for a walk in the park. He had never expected to be sole heir to the great Youssoupov fortune. Now, in time, all of the palaces, estates, and jewels would pass to him. "The idea that I would one day be one of the richest men in Russia went like wine to my head," he wrote. "Wealth, splendour, power: I could not imagine life without them."[5] But the thought of having to assume the responsibility of managing the family fortune preyed on Felix; he decided to go to Moscow to see Grand Duchess Elizabeth and confess his doubts.

After her husband's assassination in 1905, Elizabeth Feodorovna had sold all of her personal possessions, including her jewelry and wedding rings, and devoted herself to helping the poor. She founded a convent and became the abbess of the Order of St. Mary and St. Martha. Felix found her seated in her study; immediately, the pressures of his new responsibility and the effects of the tragedy surfaced, and he fell at her feet, sobbing hysterically. He confessed his anguish to her. "Happiness does not consist in living in a palace or enjoying a large fortune," the grand duchess told him. "These can be lost. True happiness is something that neither men nor events can take from you."[6] To show Felix the necessity of using his new fortune to benefit others, Grand Duchess Elizabeth asked him to join her in working for a number of charitable institutions in Moscow. Felix agreed and made plans to submerge himself in the shadowy world of the Russian working poor.

But his conscience still troubled him; he had told the grand duchess much about his life but found himself "tormented by the idea" of what he had concealed "and that she might still be cherishing some illusions about me." Once again, he went to speak with the grand duchess. He later wrote, "I confessed to her all the facts of my private life of which I supposed her to know nothing." Felix does not relate what these "facts" of his "private life" were, but, presumably, he confessed his homosexuality to Ella. When he had finished, the grand duchess kissed him and said:

> Don't worry, I know more about you than you think. That is why I am so much interested in you. Anyone who is capable of doing much evil is also capable of doing much good, if he sets about it the right way. No matter how serious the offence, it is redeemed by sincere repentance. Remember, the only thing that defiles the soul is spiritual sin; it can remain pure in spite of carnal weaknesses. It is your soul that I am thinking of and I want to lay it open to you.[7]

This conversation had a profound effect on Felix. He later wrote: "Her words filled me with a new hope and gave me strength to face the future."[8] Although Felix always had a tendency to exaggerate, especially where his place in posterity was concerned, the change seemed to have been genuine enough. Even his cousin, Prince Serge Obolensky, felt that following Nicholas's death and his confession to Grand Duchess Elizabeth, Felix "went through a profound religious conversion."[9]

Before Felix embarked on his charitable works with Grand Duchess Elizabeth he decided to visit the Larva District of St. Petersburg, where many of the factory workers and the poor lived. Never before had he ventured into such a squalid realm; along with two friends, Felix dressed as a beggar and stood on a street corner, asking for money. "Although I was only a fake beggar," he later wrote, "I was indignant when grand ladies covered with jewels and costly furs, and fine gentlemen smoking big cigars, passed me without so much as a glance." Having failed as beggars, Felix and his friends went to one of the houses kept for the poor; here they were given three soiled blankets on which to sleep. "All around us the dregs of humanity, both men and women, lay half-naked, drunk and filthy. The popping of corks could be heard as they drained bottles of vodka at a gulp and threw the empty bottles at their neighbors. The unfortunate wretches quarreled, copulated, used the filthiest language and vomited all over each other. The stench of the place was beyond description." Unable to stomach this scene, Felix fled. "It was difficult to believe that what I had just seen was real. How, in our times, could a government allow human beings to be reduced to such abject misery? I was haunted for a long time by memories of the horrible sights I had seen."[10]

The Larva District, however, could not compare with the horrors Felix witnessed when he began working with Grand Duchess Elizabeth in Moscow. She took Felix to the Khitrovka District, perhaps the most nightmarish place in all of Russia. Khitrovka sprawled on the banks of the filthy Yauza River, just across town from the Kremlin. A thick haze hung over the district. The stench of urine, feces, and vomit filled the streets. Only the most desperate, downtrodden people lived there. Every other building was a whore house, a tavern, or a doss-house, where the poor wretches fortunate enough to have the money to rent a bed for the night fled when the sun went down. Those who ventured out after dark risked their lives: Groups of pick-pockets and thieves gathered on the corners, waiting to attack anyone who crossed their path. Murders were commonplace; here screams and cries for help went unnoticed. In the mornings, the police made the rounds of the district, collecting the numerous bodies which lay in the streets; no policeman would venture into Khitrovka after dark. Men lay in the gutters, stabbed or strangled for a bottle of vodka; during the night thieves stole their vermin-ridden clothing, leaving the corpses naked. Whores plying their trade were often beaten, robbed, and left for dead. The bodies filled several carts each morning and were transported to the University of Moscow for use in anatomic studies.[11]

In this atmosphere children suffered horrible fates. Infants were rented to female beggars for twenty-five kopecks a day; three-year-olds went for 10 kopecks. The more wretched the infant, the greater the demand: Sickly, scab-covered children commanded greater sums. They were wrapped in rags and carried through the streets to arouse sympathy and generate income. If the child died from such treatment—as often happened—the beggar continued to use the corpse to raise alms. Babies were deliberately starved so that their cries would carry more anguish. The children who survived this existence often turned to the trade themselves; they knew of no alternative. Whores sold their infants to professional beggars at a public auction in the Khitrovka Market; ten-year-old girls went for fifty rubles each or were rented for half a ruble a night. Drunken young prostitutes sat in the streets, unable to stand from the effects of vodka. Child beggars quickly learned the tricks of the trade: They tore their clothing and hid their shoes, then marched off to Moscow's fashionable nightspots to stand in the snow for hours, pleading for money. This unbelievable quarter inspired Gorky to write his work *The Lower Depths*, in which he described the tragedies he had witnessed.[12]

Accustomed to luxury and privilege, Felix found Khitrovka "indescribable." The work with Grand Duchess Elizabeth opened his eyes to the other world of Russia, "a world of suffering more horrible than anything I had seen. ... I longed to snatch these poor creatures from their pitiful conditions and I was staggered by the immensity of the task."[13] He later wrote: "Until then I had lived only for pleasure, avoiding the sight of suffering in any form; I had not grasped the fact that there were any more essential values than money and the power that goes with it. I now felt the vanity of all of this. In discarding my thirst for power and my love for wordly possessions I had at last found freedom."[14]

Felix's change of heart was profound, and there is no reason to doubt his sincerity. In his newfound enthusiasm Felix decided to sell off his family's possessions and give the money to the poor, following the example of Grand Duchess Elizabeth. He planned to turn Arkhangelskoe into a center for the arts and provide free housing there for musicians, painters, and writers. The houses in Moscow and St. Petersburg would become hospitals and homes for the elderly; with proceeds from the sale of jewelry and paintings, he intended to build hospitals in the Crimea and the Caucasus. All of the vast estates would be given to the peasants who lived there, while the factories and workshops would become worker-owned.

Felix confessed his plans to Grand Duchess Elizabeth, who completely approved of them. But Zenaide would not hear of it; she lectured Felix on his duty as the last of the Youssoupovs. He must, she said, marry and produce an heir. Felix informed his mother that he did not feel fit for marriage and that the very idea held no attraction for him. But Zenaide insisted and somehow managed to win Grand Duchess Elizabeth to her side. Faced with this opposition from the two most important women in his life, Felix reluctantly gave up his ideas to dispose of the Youssoupov fortune.[15] He always suffered from momentary *idées fixes* whose initial appeal soon waned; it is impossible to say whether he would actually have followed through on his revolutionary plans to dispose of his immense fortune.

Shortly after Nicholas's death, Zenaide made arrangements for Felix to visit the empress at the Alexander Palace at Tsarskoe Selo. She hoped that Alexandra might convince her son of his duty. "Any self-respecting man," the empress began, "should serve in the army or take up a position at court. I am surprised that you do neither." Felix replied that as he had a horror of war, he could not consider a career in the military. As for the position at court, he claimed to be too outspoken and independent. One day, he told the empress, he would inherit an enormous fortune and his life would be dedicated to the management of his estates. By doing this, Felix said, he would serve not only Russia but the tsar. The empress bristled at this idea, saying, "But the Tsar is Russia." When Nicholas II entered the room, his wife turned to him and declared, "Felix's ideas are absolutely revolutionary."[16]

Unwilling and unable to please his mother about marrying, Felix made a dramatic decision: He would leave Russia and go to the university at Oxford. Both of his parents opposed the idea, but Felix was twenty-one and eager to break free of the stifling world of his parents. Zenaide still suffered from the effects of Nicholas's death and feared that if Felix went abroad, he would not return. She again asked the empress to intercede with her son. The talk took place on the eve of his departure. Alexandra expressed surprise at Felix's decision to leave his mother and tried to dissuade him from going. Like Zenaide, she, too, warned that if Felix left, he might find no place for himself when he returned to Russia.[17] But Felix had made up his mind; telling the empress that he would return to Russia at the end of his university career, he left the palace for England.

10

Oxford

FELIX WENT UP TO OXFORD at the beginning of Michaelmas term, 1909. The city continued to bask in the warm summer sunshine; from the neighboring villages of Hinksey and Elsfield, Oxford appeared like a vision, with a skyline pierced with golden towers, spires, and pinnacles. Along the High, which cleaved through the clusters of Gothic, medieval, and Victorian colleges, students in black gowns raced from one appointment to the next, making way only for the never-ending lines of bicycles circling the city. Across the High from Magdalen College, the more leisurely strolled through the Botanical Gardens, enjoying the last flowers of the summer. Behind the ornamented college façades, cloisters twisted around grassed-over quadrangles, narrow staircases wound into shadowy reaches, and a hushed silence reigned in the small, bare rooms occupied by the students. Couples lay in the grass of Christ Church Meadow, drinking champagne and watching the endless line of punts gliding by on the Cherwell. Farther up the river, male students frolicked naked at Parson's Pleasure, separated from their female counterparts at Dame's Delight by a bend in the Cherwell. Small groups of aesthetes and intellectuals gathered at the George Cafe to argue religion and drink themselves into blissful oblivion. As night fell, some students returned from days spent at the nearby estates of the great Oxfordshire families—the Marlboroughs, the Berties, the Stonors, and the Harcourts. At five minutes past nine, the great bell of Tom Tower began its nightly tolling, summoning the last of the students back to their colleges before the porters locked the gates and night settled over the cupolas and domes of the city's museums and churches.[1]

Acting on the advice of friends, Felix had applied for, and was granted admission to, University College on the High. For many years, legend had it that Alfred the Great had founded the institution—an erroneous assumption, as it turned out. Perhaps the most famous University College student had been the poet Shelley, who, in 1811, was "sent down" when he published a pamphlet called "The Necessity of Atheism." A marble monument showing the dying poet stood in the college, a measure of the rehabilitation of his reputation in the Victorian era. Logic Lane cut the college into halfs, each with its own quadrangle. Upon entering the college, Felix was received by the master, who explained how the university system worked. He then led the prince to a set of ground-floor rooms facing onto the High. These rooms were referred to as the Club, because, regardless of occupancy, students had the habit of gathering there. Felix moved in; today they are known as the Youssoupov Rooms, in honor of their most famous lodger.[2]

Life at Oxford proved very different from the luxurious surroundings at the Moika Palace and Arkhangelskoe. Felix had one scout to look after his clothing, prepare his food, and clean up his college rooms as opposed to the army of servants at his disposal back in Russia. The rooms were terribly cold, and water froze in the washbasin. The first term proved a tough adjustment for Felix; he knew only a few people, including his closest friend while at Oxford, Eric Hamilton, who later became dean of Windsor. Although he spoke Russian and French equally well, his English was poor. Once, his father asked him to order some cows for Arkhangelskoe; Felix sent the following cable to a farm: PLEASE SEND ME ONE MAN COW AND THREE JERSEY WOMEN.

After some deciphering, the farm filled his order. But a journalist managed to get ahold of the telegram and published it in a London newspaper, much to the amusement of Felix's Oxford comrades.[3]

His time at Oxford had a profound effect on Felix. Previously, he had immersed himself in a world of pleasure; now he dutifully attended his lectures and met weekly with his don. In between he went rowing on the Thames, learned cricket, played polo, and rode in the Oxfordshire countryside. At night, he often hosted parties in his rooms. Because they were on the ground floor of University College and faced the High, they provided a convenient means of entrance for students once the porter had locked the front gates. To assist them, Felix made a rope from knotted sheets; whenever he heard a knock at his window late at night, he simply lowered the line and helped the student into the college. This smuggling of students into college after hours continued until one night when Felix heard a knock, lowered the rope, and pulled up a policeman at the other end. Such an offense would normally have resulted in the student being sent down from college. But the bishop of London, who knew Felix, intervened on his behalf with the master, and the prince was only gated for the remainder of the term, an inconvenience Felix overcame by simply sneaking out at night.[4]

At the end of his first year, Felix took advantage of his right to live outside the college. He rented a small house on the outskirts of Oxford with two friends. Here he could freely indulge his expensive tastes; he hired a Russian chef, a French chauffeur, and an English valet. An elderly woman cleaned the house for him, while her husband took care of Felix's hunter and two polo ponies which were stabled nearby. Here Felix lived for the next two years while he worked toward his degree. His time at university passed too quickly for Felix, and at the end of three years, he received his Bachelor of Arts. When his cousin Prince Serge Obolensky asked Felix what he could expect at Oxford, the latter explained, "It will be difficult at the beginning. No one pays attention to you. But after the first term they get accustomed to seeing you around and then you will get to know them. But you just have to wait until they come to you."[5] He left Oxford in 1912 and always referred to the time spent at the university as "the happiest of my youth."[6]

Felix did not immediately return to Russia after he went down from the University. He decided to remain in London for another year. With a friend from Oxford, Jack Gordon, he rented two connecting flats in Curzon Street and hired two elderly sisters to look after them. Felix bought a new shiny maroon Delanay-Belleville, which he drove recklessly across London. On weekends he cruised along the Thames aboard his steam launch, carrying his friends from one party to another.

He threw himself into London society. His regular circle of friends included the duke and duchess of Rutland, Lord and Lady Ripon, King Manuel of Portugal, Prince Christopher of Greece, the Curzons, the duke and duchess of Marlborough, Lady Londonderry, Princess Daisy of Pless, the Astors, and Serge Obolensky. Felix made a deep, exotic impression on these new friends. "Seldom have I seen such a wonderful figure," recalled Mrs. Hwfa Williams, "such extraordinary eyes and a mouth that turned up at the corners. . . . Certainly he was the best looking man I have ever seen."[7] His good looks, wealth, and love of parties made Felix one of the brightest stars in London society. Occasionally the Russian Imperial Ballet came to London, and Felix knew most of the dancers personally—Vaslav Nijinsky, Tamara Karsavina, and Anna Pavlova. The latter was a close friend, and she and Felix spent many evenings at fashionable clubs and restaurants. After one round of partygoing, she declared to Felix, "You have God in one eye and the Devil in the other."[8] He was able to talk Pavlova into a special appearance at Oxford for his friends still at the university, and this added greatly to his reputation.

Felix eventually decided that he needed a larger flat. He signed a long-term lease on one at 15 Parkside Street, overlooking Hyde Park. This he decorated in his own bizarre fashion: black carpets, orange curtains, green walls, and blue furniture. He paid the rent for a decade in advance. A few years later, when the Revolution broke out and Felix lost most of the family fortune, he thus had a residence in London, which left him in a better position than many Russian exiles and also guaranteed that he could claim legal-alien resident status.

When Felix attended a charity ball at Albert Hall in London, his costume was so extraordinary that it made the front pages of the newspapers. He wore a gold brocade, short, *boyar* caftan trimmed with sable and embroidered with pearls and diamonds. His leather boots, into the tops of which were tucked baggy velvet peasant trousers, were sewn with medieval designs in jewels. On his head he wore a sable hat studded with a diamond-and-emerald aigrette. This image of the youthful prince dressed in sixteenth-century *boyar* costume has become the most enduring one of Felix through the years.

At this ball he met two of the daughters of the duke and duchess of Rutland, Marjorie and Diana Manners. In the weeks that followed, Felix spent a great deal of time with them, visiting their father's seat, Belvoir Castle in Leicestershire. He later wrote that he found both Marjorie and Diana attractive, but as time passed, Felix and Marjorie began to see each other exclusively. After a while there was talk of marriage. Felix does not mention these events in any of his books; but those closest to him knew the truth. Diana later wrote that Felix was "deeply in love" with her sister, and Serge Obolensky confirmed this.[9]

Marjorie Manners had been fond of Charles Paget, son of the marquess of Angelsey; however, he refused to commit himself to marriage, and in the spring of 1911 he left on a long cruise to consider the romance. At the same time that Paget left, Marjorie began to see Felix. This might have been the act of a desperate woman hoping to lure her former love back through jealousy, but Diana thought her sister's attachment to Felix was genuine. She later wrote, "I prayed for Marjorie to marry Felix. I bought her a *Hugo's Russian Grammer.*"[10] But Marjorie's first love got wind of the situation in London and hastily returned to propose to her. She accepted, and they married in 1912. After the death of Rasputin, Marjorie puzzled over her once-possible husband: "So, Felix is a murderer. Well, well, there it is. I have a feeling for the criminal classes and there it is and is and is. Dirty work, all round, it sounds. Does one write and congratulate, or condole?"[11]

While Diana had prayed for Marjorie to marry Felix, she herself was more than a little in love with him. Prince Serge Obolensky later wrote that he thought Diana hoped to marry Felix after Marjorie had returned to Charles Paget. But Felix, even if he had been in love with Marjorie, apparently had no interest in Diana. She later married Duff Cooper.

In London, Felix began having a peculiar problem with his eyes. At parties he saw certain people enveloped in a hazy cloud, or so he later claimed. After several weeks of this, he went to see a doctor, who, after examining him, declared that his eyesight was fine. A few weeks later, while riding to hounds, Felix again saw one of his friends in such a cloud; several hours later, this same friend, while jumping a gate, fell and suffered serious injuries. Felix said nothing. Then, when a friend of his parents' visited him, he saw the same vision. This time, Felix described it in a letter to his mother, saying that he felt certain that some danger awaited the man. Within a matter of days the man had mysteriously died. When Felix returned to the doctor and informed him of these events, the man said that he probably had some form of second sight. Just as suddenly as these visions began, according to Felix, they ended. Whatever the truth of the story, it is just one of the many enigmas still surrounding his life.

At the time Felix published his memoirs in the early 1950s homosexuality was still a criminal offense in most European countries, punishable by a long prison sentence and hard labor. Complete candor, even if desired, would have proved impossible. In *Lost Splendor*, the most revealing of his books, Felix carefully skirts the issue of his sexual inclination while at the same time dropping broad hints as to his tastes. His earliest liaisons were almost certainly with women, but as he grew older, Felix apparently began to indulge his taste for young men. Contemporary rumor in St. Petersburg tied him to affairs with members of both sexes before his tenure at Oxford. Even while he was in England, Felix allowed himself to develop a romantic liaison with Marjorie Manners. But at some point during his time abroad, Felix seems to have accepted once and for all his homosexuality. Within a year of his return from England, he married, but in spite of his wedded state, Felix seems not to have abandoned his romantic affairs with young officers.

Felix's amorous homosexual adventures were known among pre-Revolutionary St. Petersburg society. Rumors of his liaisons with handsome young officers were so widespread that they apparently even reached the isolated Empress Alexandra. Unfortunately, little evidence of this side of Felix's life remains; many of his intimates remained silent, and his descendants diligently guard his remaining private papers. Nevertheless, at least one alleged homosexual affair is well known.

In *Lost Splendor*, Felix describes Grand Duke Dimitri Pavlovich as "extremely attractive: tall, elegant, well-bred, with deep, thoughtful eyes. . . . He was all impulses and contradictions; he was both romantic and mystical. . . . At the same time he was very gay and always ready for the wildest escapades. His charm won the hearts of all but the weakness of his character made him dangerously easy to influence."[12]

Dimitri Pavlovich was born in 1891, the son of Grand Duke Paul Alexandrovich. His mother, Grand Duchess Alexandra, died giving birth to him. Dimitri and his sister, Marie, were raised by their father until 1902, when Grand Duke Paul contracted a morganatic marriage with Olga Pistolkors. The tsar forced the couple into a Parisian exile, and the two children from his first marriage were raised by their uncle and aunt, Grand Duke Serge Alexandrovich and his wife, Elizabeth. The children feared the grand duke and the grand duchess, who treated them as nonentities, and they were deprived of ordinary playmates.

In 1905, Serge Alexandrovich was assassinated when a terrorist threw a bomb as the grand duke left the Kremlin. Both Marie and Dimitri heard the explosion and rushed to join their aunt, who was already running across the cobbled square to the pile of smoking, twisted wreckage. They found what remained of their uncle: head smashed, arms and legs blown off, torso twisted into a mass of bone and blood. The grand duchess gathered up the largest pieces of her husband's body in the folds of her dress and rushed back to the Kremlin. Neither child would ever forget this terrible scene, and Dimitri suffered horrifying nightmares for many years. Following the grand duke's assassination, Elizabeth continued to act as guardian, sending Dimitri to military school and, a few years later, arranging a loveless marriage for his sister, Marie, to Prince William of Sweden.

Dimitri has often been portrayed as a golden youth. Writers speak of his sterling character, handsome bearing, and success as a lieutenant in the Third Cavalry Regiment of the Imperial Life Guards. A more balanced analysis, however, reveals a different picture. In reality, he was pale, thin, and nervous; his unpredictable moods and fits of depression were notorious. The grand duke was also an alcoholic, dedicated to the pursuit of pleasure in an attempt to combat his melancholy. Meriel Buchanan, daughter of the British ambassador, remembered him as "recklessly dissipated." She wrote that he suffered from a "lack of purpose, indecision and an inherent weakness."[13] And another of Dimitri's acquaintances, the Honorable Bertie Stopford, an aide at the British embassy in the capital, referred to the grand duke as "always helpless and desolate."[14] With such a character, Dimitri easily fell under the powerful influence of Felix Youssoupov.

The passage of time and destruction of relevant papers make it impossible to say precisely what the nature of the relationship between Felix and Dimitri may have been. But gossip at the time linked the two men romantically. Members of the Romanov family, the imperial court, and the aristocracy were all privy to information which confirmed the existence of such a relationship, if not the intimate details. Even today there are those who knew the principals in exile and recall frank, honest confessions of a romantic liaison. Many well acquainted with Felix and Dimitri seem to have accepted the fact that the relationship did indeed occur.

It has been argued that any homosexual relationship between the two would have been prevented by the imperial family. After his aunt Elizabeth became a nun, Dimitri spent most of the next few years living with the tsar and empress at the Alexander Palace. Alexandra, with her prim Victorian morality, would never have tolerated such a romance. This, however, does not mean that such a relationship could not have taken place or that it might have been short-lived. The nature of the relationship might merely have been romantic rather than sexual. If there was an affair, this fact in itself would have been reason enough for the two principals to have guarded the details, especially in light of Dimitri's close relationship with the tsar and tsarina. Felix, in his book, certainly leaves one with the impression that he was in love with Dimitri. During World War I, the empress's letters to her absent husband at headquarters frequently included warnings about Dimitri and his weak character:

> The Countess Benckendorff is shocked with Dimitri's goings on in town during the war and finds one ought to insist upon him returning to the regiment—I fully agree—town and women are poison for him.[15]

> We spoke long about Dimitri—he [Sablin, an official] says
> that he is a boy without any character and can be led by
> anybody. Three months he was under the influence of . . .
> [Sablin] and held himself well at Headquarters and when
> in town with him, kept himself like the others did and did
> not go out in the ladies' companies—but, out of sight,
> gets into other hands. He finds the regiment perverts the
> boy, in their coarse conversations, jokes are horrid and be-
> fore ladies too and they draw him down.[16]

In these letters the empress seems to hint at the rumors surrounding Dimitri's sexuality and the company he preferred to
keep. Although her first letter to her husband includes the phrase
"women are poison for him," it is her second note, in which she
confides that he "did not go out in the ladies' companies—but,
out of sight, gets into other hands," which is far more revealing.
For all of her Victorian censure, Alexandra heard the most reliable gossip and no doubt knew the tales prevalent in St. Petersburg. Again, to her husband, she implored that he order the
grand duke back to his regiment and away from St. Petersburg,
saying that Dimitri ". . . ought not to remain there, it's bad for
him, of your own accord, let him go, it's unhealthy doing nothing, when all are at war and now he lives in gossip and plays a
part in it."[17]

At the height of the friendship between the two men, the
empress wrote to her husband that Dimitri mixed with what she
termed "a bad set."[18] She had no illusions as to the effect of
Felix's influence over the grand duke, and condemned the Youssoupovs as "that wicked family!"[19] And Felix himself wrote,
"The Tsar and Tsarina, who were aware of the scandalous rumours concerning my mode of living, disapproved of our friendship. They ended by forbidding the Grand Duke to see me, and
I myself became the object of the most unpleasant supervision."[20] But neither Felix nor Dimitri would be put off so easily;
they simply carried on their relationship as before, but now conducted it in private, away from the prying eyes and wagging
tongues of court gossips.

11

Marriage

By 1913, BOTH ZENAIDE AND THE EMPRESS were insisting that Felix marry. The prince had always known that one day the conventions of the day must be satisfied. Felix was expected to provide an heir to the family fortune. Despite his homosexuality, Felix accepted this verdict. Knowing that he had to marry, he naturally wished to select the most beautiful and eligible young woman in imperial Russia. Even with his distinguished background, however, Felix would never have done as a husband to one of the young daughters of Tsar Nicholas II; he was well aware of the empress's hostility toward him, and, in any case, their rank as grand duchesses precluded what for them would have been morganatic marriages. He therefore set his sights on the next highest ranking member of the imperial family, Princess Irina Alexandrovna.

Felix first met the princess in the Crimea when he was eighteen. She was the only daughter of Grand Duke Alexander Michailovich and Grand Duchess Xenia, one of the tsar's sisters. Irina was beautiful, with deep blue eyes and luxurious golden hair. Quiet and shy, she had grown up the only girl in a household of six brothers. Her father devoted most of his time to things military—the navy and, on the eve of World War I, airplanes. Grand Duchess Xenia doted on her only daughter, and Irina enjoyed a happy childhood. Her parents, however, were far from happy, although they took great pains to conceal this from their children. The grand duke had carried on a long-running affair with a woman in the south of France with his wife's complete knowledge. Xenia played the part of the tolerant wife but refused to grant her husband the divorce which he constantly asked for.

As soon as Felix returned from Oxford, he began to pursue Irina. By the winter of 1913 he had made his decision. He approached Irina's father, Grand Duke Alexander Michailovich, and informed him that he intended to ask for his daughter's hand in marriage. The grand duke then called on Princess Zenaide to discuss the possible match between their two children. Having declared his love for Irina, Felix received the grand duke's permission and asked Irina to marry him. Although they had been seen together in public on numerous occasions, Felix and Irina did not know each other particularly well. Even so, she accepted his proposal. There is no evidence that Irina was in love with him, but, more importantly, the two quickly became good friends and confidants, and such things as romance normally played little part in dynastic marriages. In addition, both stood to gain by marrying the other: Irina was the tsar's only niece, beautiful and intelligent, while Felix was not only the wealthiest but the most handsome man in Russia. Whatever the reasons that drew them together, it must be said that their marriage was a happy and successful one which lasted over fifty years.

The engagement was officially announced at the end of September, with the wedding planned for the following spring. Felix immediately set about planning their new home. Rather than moving his wife into one of the empty Youssoupov palaces on the Nevsky or Liteiny or Litovsky, Felix decided to take up residence with his new wife in a wing of the Moika Palace. It had always been his home, and he felt more comfortable there than anywhere else. His parents, who still lived there, were frequently away, and their rooms were far removed from the section of the palace which Felix selected for himself and Irina. To the east side of the main palace block, Mikhailov had added a long, low wing across the front of the exhibition halls and theater wing, facing out on to the canal. Felix took a dozen rooms on the first floor and created a miniature private house.

However, once the initial excitement and enthusiasm over the forthcoming wedding began to wear thin, the inevitable problem arose: Felix's homosexual tastes were too well known to remain concealed from his future bride's parents for long. It is apparent that Felix told Irina of his past. "Far from being perturbed by what I had told her," he wrote, "she showed great tolerance and comprehension."[1] Her parents proved another matter.

Just after the engagement was announced, Irina went with her parents to Copenhagen to stay with her grandmother the dowager empress. Felix arrived a few days later, only to be met by Count Mordvinov, one of Grand Duke Alexander's aides-de-camp. Tersely, Mordvinov informed Felix that Grand Duke Alexander had recently learned of his future son-in-law's sexual proclivities and as a result the engagement had been terminated. Felix was told that he was not to try to see Irina or her parents. Stunned, he tried to question the aide, but Mordvinov refused to say anything further. Stubbornly, Felix went straight to see the grand duke and duchess; he burst into their rooms unannounced. Immediately, he confronted the issue head-on. According to one account, he declared that while he had been a homosexual in his youth, he no longer had such desires. Felix gives no details of the conversation in his book, but it must have proved persuasive. In the end, Irina's parents relented, accepted Felix's explanation, and declared that the engagement could resume.[2]

Felix had another obstacle, however, before all was well: The same rumors had reached the dowager empress, and she, too, had declared that her granddaughter could not be allowed to marry a man with such a scandalous past. At a luncheon with the dowager empress, Felix again confronted the rumors concerning his private life. She questioned him at some length before finally satisfying her doubts. At the end of the conversation, the dowager empress rose, telling Felix, "Do not worry, I will do what I can for your happiness."[3]

It seems that the source for most of this gossip about Felix's homosexual activities was Grand Duke Dimitri Pavlovich. When Felix first told Dimitri that he intended to marry Irina, the grand duke declared that he, too, wished to have her as his wife and that she would have to choose between the two of them. When Felix related this to Irina, she reassured him that she had already made her decision and that nothing could change her mind. Felix wrote, "Dimitri bowed before a decision which he realized was final but our friendship was to suffer and our relations were never the same afterward."[4] Presumably, Felix's wedding meant an end to whatever liaison he had enjoyed with Dimitri.

Although Felix does not name Dimitri as the source of these troubles, it is almost certain that the grand duke was responsible. In *Lost Splendor*, Felix writes that "the people who had tried so hard to damage me in the eyes of her parents were the very ones I had thought to be my real friends. I know that my coming marriage had upset some of them, but I now saw to what lengths they were prepared to go to prevent it."[5] Certainly, after the engagement was announced, Dimitri, in the words of one of his friends, became "more recklessly dissipated, his face whiter than ever, and there were deep shadows of exhaustion under his eyes."[6] It is impossible, however, to conclude if this was the reaction of a rejected suitor or a jealous former lover.

Felix and Irina's wedding took place on 9 February 1914 in the private chapel of the Anichkov Palace in St. Petersburg, the residence of the dowager empress. It was the last great royal wedding before the outbreak of World War I. Because Felix was not of royal blood, Irina had to sign an official document renouncing for herself and her descendants any claim to the throne; she was so far down the line of succession that this was a mere formality, but the wedding was one of the few officially sanctioned morganatic unions of Nicholas II's reign.

Before the wedding, the tsar approached Felix and asked what he would like as a wedding gift; Nicholas II himself considered offering Felix an official position at court. But Felix informed the tsar that the gift he would most appreciate would be unlimited use of the imperial box at the Mariinsky Theatre. With a laugh, the tsar granted this request. But he and his wife also presented the couple with a bag of twenty-nine uncut diamonds, ranging from three to seven carats each.

Typical of the luxury and splendor of the Youssoupovs' lives was the immense cache of jewelry which Irina received upon her wedding. Many of these jewels Felix later hid in both the Moika Palace and the Moscow house, where they were discovered by the Bolsheviks after the Revolution. An impressive number, however, were actually taken out of the country by Felix and Irina and later sold to various jewelers, Cartier among them.

The list of wedding jewels included over 150 separate pieces: some fifty uncut diamonds, twelve tiaras and bandeaus, two dozen necklaces, and a similiar number of earrings, a number of bracelets, several brooches, and a stomacher of diamonds and pearls. There were separate parures of emeralds, diamonds, pearls, diamonds and rubies, and demiparures of blue-and-white diamonds, diamonds and sapphires, and diamonds and rubies. The estimated value of these wedding gifts alone was several million dollars in pre-Revolutionary figures.[7]

On the day of the wedding, Irina arrived at the Anichkov Palace in a state coach drawn by four white horses. Her wedding dress was surprisingly modern, reflecting the influence of the current shapeless fashions. Irina had eschewed imperial tradition in favor of style and became the first Romanov bride to adopt twentieth-century dress rather than the more traditional Russian court gown dictated by years of precedent. Made of white satin, the skirt of her wedding gown fell in soft folds from the dropped waist to form a short train. The flat bodice was lightly ornamented with tiny pearls, as were the long, flowing sleeves. On her head Felix's wedding gift, a rock-crystal-and-diamond tiara commissioned from Cartier in Paris, anchored a lace veil which had once belonged to Marie Antoinette, and in her hands she carried a small bouquet of lilacs and orchids. One guest at the wedding later recalled her "severe, almost icon-like beauty."[8] She walked into the chapel on the arm of her uncle the tsar; Felix waited at the altar. Since he did not belong to any military regiment, he wore the uniform only of the nobility—a long black frock coat with gold lapels, white broadcloth trousers, and a ceremonial sword at his left side.

Following the ceremony, the newly married couple and their parents greeted the guests in the palace ballroom. Meriel Buchanan recalled the groom's mother as particularly beautiful. As the guests made their way through the receiving line, Zenaide occasionally smiled, but there was "a look of ineffable sadness in her still lovely cornflower blue eyes."[9] Another guest declared of Felix and Irina, "What an amazing couple—they were so attractive. What bearing! What breeding!"[10] The wedding luncheon of blinis, consommé, roe cutlets, and baked apples was served to the guests on solid-gold plates by an army of liveried footmen.

A carriage took Felix and Irina to the railway station. Family and friends had gathered at the siding to see them off on their honeymoon. As the train pulled out of the station, Felix noted that Dimitri Pavlovich stood apart from the rest of the group, watching their departure.

Felix and Irina spent their honeymoon in Europe and the Middle East. In Egypt they cruised down the Nile, climbed the pyramids, and explored the cool shadows of ancient temple ruins in the Valley of the Kings. In Jerusalem, where they attended Easter services, a crowd of more than five thousand Russian tourists gathered to cheer Irina as the tsar's niece. But the incessant heat proved too much for the pair, and they quickly returned to the less demanding pleasures of the Continent.

During the trip to Jerusalem, Felix picked up a new servant. While riding through the streets of the city in their carriage, Felix and Irina were accosted by a Negro who ran up to them and threw an envelope inside. It turned out to be a petition asking to be taken into service. Felix arranged for a meeting and hired him on the spot. His name was Thesphe; he came from Abyssinia and wore flowing white robes and colorful turbans, which appealed to Felix's sense of the exotic. Irina was less than pleased with her husband's latest acquisition, but Felix had made up his mind, and Thesphe remained, following them on the rest of their honeymoon and sleeping on the floor of his hotel room because he could not be induced to climb into a bed. He spent the greater part of his days endlessly flushing the toilet, fascinated by the indoor plumbing.

After a stay in London, Felix and Irina traveled to Kissingen, the German spa resort, to stay with his parents, who were on holiday. On 28 June 1914, came the news of two assassination attempts: in Sarajevo a young student had shot the heir to the Austrian throne, Archduke Franz Ferdinand, and his wife, and in Pokrovskoe an insane woman had stabbed Rasputin. The archduke and his wife died that afternoon, while Rasputin, after emergency surgery, survived. Events moved swiftly; the Austri-

ans began shelling Belgrade in a move designed to crush the
Serbian nationalist movement that had spawned the archduke's
assassination; in response, Russia mobilized her army against
Emperor Franz Joseph's forces. This brought the Kaiser into the
struggle; Wilhelm II, by the terms of a mutual defense treaty,
had to come to the aid of Austria. He ordered a mobilization of
German troops against Russia. France, Russia's only European
ally, quickly responded by putting her army on alert against
Germany and Austria. The stage was set for World War I.

At Kissingen the Youssoupovs were virtually cut off from
the latest news. No one believed in the possibility of a European
war. But the events under way could not be stopped. Germany
presented Russia with an ultimatum: She would have to cancel
her mobilization against Austria or face the consequences. Kissingen was a popular resort, and many Russians were on holiday
there that summer. As the deadline for Russian demobilization
approached, the Germans in the town began to demonstrate, and
the Youssoupovs quickly found themselves the objects of insults
and hatred. A telegram arrived from Grand Duchess Anastasia,
wife of Grand Duke Nicholas Nicholaievich, in which she advised the Youssoupovs to return to Russia before hostilities
broke out. Packing their things quickly, the family and their servants boarded the next train for Berlin.

On their arrival in the German capital the Youssoupovs and
their servants booked into the Continental Hotel. They then
learned that Russia had refused the ultimatum and Germany had
declared war. Within a few hours of their arrival, a squadron of
police came to their hotel suite and threatened to arrest the entire
family and all of their servants. The Youssoupovs locked themselves and their servants in one of the bedrooms and refused to
come out; eventually the police broke the door in and carted
everyone inside off to jail. At the station the inspector questioned
all of them at length, subjecting them to insults and warning that
those who had not left Berlin by nightfall would be incarcerated.
With that, the prisoners were released and returned to the hotel.

Irina telephoned her cousin Crown Princess Cecilie and
asked her to intercede on their behalf with her father-in-law the
Kaiser. A few hours later the crown princess informed Irina that
she had done all that she could to influence her father-in-law.

The Kaiser had promised that the Youssoupovs and their servants would be treated well but also that they were all to consider themselves prisoners of war. He offered them a choice of three country estates in which to reside for the duration of the war. Only after Felix's father appealed to the Spanish ambassador did the family finally receive permission to leave Berlin for Russia.

The following morning the Youssoupovs and their servants all drove to the Russian embassy, where they joined the ambassador and his staff as they boarded a caravan of automobiles and set off for Anhalter Station. No police or military escort accompanied them, and an angry mob hurled stones at the vehicles, shattering windows and striking some of the embassy staff. At the station the Russians quickly boarded the train set aside for their journey, and amid the jeering crowd, it slowly steamed out of Berlin toward the Russian frontier.

At the beginning of the war, in a surge of patriotism, the imperial family and members of the aristocracy threw themselves wholeheartedly into the effort. Upon returning from their honeymoon, Felix and Irina moved in to the east wing of the Moika Palace. The elder Youssoupovs were in residence in Moscow, where Count Felix held the post of governor-general, and so Felix and Irina were the only inhabitants of the massive building. With all of this room at his disposal, Felix decided to convert a wing of the Moika Palace into a hospital ward for wounded soldiers. The ballroom housed seventy soldiers, the portrait gallery became a workroom, and the main part of the entire first floor was given over to rooms for wounded soldiers and an operating room. In addition, the house on the Liteiny was also converted into a wartime hospital. Felix hired the best doctors and nurses to staff his new hospitals, and soon the ornate rooms of both palaces were filled with the wounded and dying.

Felix himself had no taste for war. He had not, as one might have expected, entered the Chevalier Guards Regiment which his father commanded, nor did he express any interest in the conduct of the war. He took advantage of a law which declared that only sons were exempt from military service. Although the law was designed to protect peasants and their meager rural holdings, Felix seized upon it as an excuse to avoid military service.

Public sentiment, however, rallied against the characteristic antipathy Felix displayed, and, as a concession, he decided to enter the Cadet Corps and take an officers' training course. He had no practical reasons for doing so and certainly gave no thought to actually joining a regiment when his term was completed. It was simply a charade, this time acted to appease the angry voices protesting his passivity. Still, Felix managed to continually fail his exams as a cadet and thus save himself from a commission at the front. One certainly gets the feeling that this failure was not an accident. No one was fooled by this behavior; in 1915, the tsar's eldest daughter, Olga, wrote to Nicholas II:

> We are in Petrograd today. I had the pleasure of two
> hours presiding in a big committee. . . . Then I went to see
> Irina. . . . Felix is a "downright civilian," dressed all in
> brown, walked to and fro about the room, searching in
> some bookcases with magazines and virtually doing nothing; an utterly unpleasant impression he makes—a man
> idling in such times.[11]

The day after the war began, a mob stormed the German embassy in St. Petersburg, smashing china, slashing pictures, and throwing furniture from the windows into the streets below. Mobs smashed the windows of German bakeries, German schools were threatened, and the music of Bach, Brahms, and Beethoven was banned from orchestral programs. The Holy Synod banned Christmas trees as a German custom.[12] In a bow to anti-German sentiment, the tsar changed the name of the capital from St. Petersburg to the more Slavic Petrograd.

The only bright spot in the first months of the war came on 8 March 1915, when Irina gave birth to a girl. They called the baby Irina after her mother, although she was always known in the family as Bebé. The entire imperial family attended the christening at the Moika Palace, and the dowager empress and the tsar stood as godparents. It proved to be one of the few happy moments in an increasingly troubled year for Felix and Irina. Soon the dark shadow of Rasputin would envelop Felix and change his life forever.

12

The Decision

PRINCE FELIX YOUSSOUPOV was not the first person to engage in an assassination plot against Rasputin. Many people wanted the peasant dead. His former supporter Serge Iliodor had arranged for the attempt on his life in Pokrovskoe in the summer of 1914. This appears to have been the first serious assassination plot. However, between 1914 and 1916, four further efforts were undertaken before the one successfully carried out by Felix. Maria rasputin remembered one unidentified woman who came to visit their flat in Petrograd. When the woman appeared, Rasputin grabbed the fur muff she carried and out fell a revolver. In January 1915, another attempt was made. While Rasputin took his afternoon stroll along the Kameni-Ostrovsky Prospect, a sledge tried to run him over, but Rasputin managed to jump out of the way just in time. The police arrested the driver; once in custody, he admitted that Iliodor had sent him to try to kill the peasant.

The third and fourth attempts came from members of the Russian government. In September 1915, Alexei Khvostov had been appointed minister of the interior. Both the tsar and the emptress like him, and he also proved to be a favorite of Rasputin's. Fat, ambitious, and of somewhat questionable honor, Khvostov moved quickly to consolidate his new power. Along with his deputy minister of the interior, Stephan Beletsky, Khvostov approached Prince Michael Andronnikov, a notorious homosexual whose apartment was strictly off-limits to all military cadets. Andronnikov acted as an intermediary for channeling bribes and appointments to various favorites. Khvostov and Beletsky arranged to funnel money to Rasputin through Andronnikov, for which the peasant would then convey their ideas to Tsarskoe Selo or, in some cases, refrain from giving his own advice to the empress. This arrangement worked for a time; then Rasputin, who never took much interest in money, simply began to ignore his benefactors' wishes. Khvostov could not very well cut out the payments to the peasant for fear that Rasputin would then turn around and expose the government's bribery. He eventually decided that the only way out of the situation was to have the peasant killed.

With this thought in mind, he asked Beletsky to consult with Michael Komissarov, a member of the police, to see if he might be willing to carry out the deed. Komissarov agreed, and Khvostov proceeded to make the arrangements. The first attempt called for Rasputin to be attacked by a gang of disguised policemen on his way out to dinner at a local restaurant. But at the last minute Rasputin refused to dine out—alerted, perhaps, by Beletsky, who was plagued with doubt about the morality of the proposed crime. Khvostov next suggested poison; Komissarov actually did get ahold of some poison and fed it to Rasputin's cats, which suffered agonizing deaths as a result. Rasputin thought that Andronnikov had been responsible and arranged with the tsar for his exile. Beletsky positively refused to consider another attempt, and Khostov, in an effort to silence him, had him appointed military governor of Irkutsk in Siberia. But Beletsky had his revenge: From Siberia, he wrote to both the empress and to Anna Vyrubova, informing them of the plot to kill Rasputin and of Khvostov's duplicity. Khvostov was fired shortly thereafter.[1]

We do not know when the idea of killing Rasputin first entered Felix's head. In his book on the murder, published in 1927, he wrote that it first occurred to him in 1915, during a conversation in which Irina complained that the peasant's influence would eventually destroy Russia. But certainly, if the idea struck a chord at that time, Felix must at least have considered the possibility at a much earlier date. His mother had frequently clashed with the empress over the issue of Rasputin, and the peasant's influence became a topic of conversation at the Youssoupov dinner table. Felix was himself clearly a member of the warring camp: Visits with Irina's grandmother the dowager empress and Grand Duchess Elizabeth often centered on discussions of the peasant and his malignant influence over the tsarina. Even so, a year passed before Felix finally made the decision to act.

The eighteen months between June 1915 and November 1916 are crucial to understanding Prince Felix Youssoupov's expressed motive for killing Rasputin. It was during this period that he apparently formulated his plans. In this he was influenced by both personal and military events. There is little evidence to indicate that Felix took much interest in the political situation of the Russian Empire before this time; it was only when the government and the army visibly crumbled that he concerned himself with the underlying causes of the rapid disintegration.

During the early days of World War I, Tsar Nicholas II appointed Felix's father as governor-general of Moscow, one of the most important civil posts in the empire. In times of war the office of governor-general carried military authority as well, and the elder prince Youssoupov was charged with maintaining order in the former capital through the use of a permanent garrison of soldiers attached to Moscow. In June 1915, Moscow suffered a violent wave of anti-German riots. One day a mob gathered in Red Square, demanding the empress's arrest, Rasputin's execution, and the tsar's abdication in favor of Grand Duke Nicholas Nicholaievich, the commander in chief of the Russian army. The crowd soon moved on to the Convent of Mary and Martha, where Grand Duchess Elizabeth ruled as abbess. She met them at the gate. They accused her and her sister the empress of being German spies and hurled rocks, screaming, "Away with the German woman!" A company of soldiers arrived and ordered the crowd to disperse; but as they walked away, they continued to hurl insults, calling the empress *Niemetzkaia bliad*—the German whore.[2]

When the empress learned of this, she demanded that the elder Youssoupov be fired from his post as governor-general for his inability to control the crowds. The tsar, also angry, confronted Felix's father over the crisis, and he, in turn, told the tsar precisely what he thought of the way Rasputin was being allowed to influence government affairs. Nicholas II fired Youssoupov on the spot.

Humiliated, the elder Youssoupovs retired to one of their estates in the Crimea. Both Zenaide and her husband blamed the empress for this public rebuke, and Felix received several letters from his mother in which she railed against what she believed to be Alexandra's unchecked power and Rasputin's corrupting influence. Zenaide's letters to her son suggested that for the welfare of the empire it was necessary that Rasputin be removed and the empress be exiled to a place from which she could no longer exert her control over government questions. Nowhere did the princess mention any assassination attempts; but Felix seems to have at least considered the possibility of murder at this early date.

In the fall of 1916, Zenaide asked the empress for an audience at the urging of Grand Duchess Elizabeth. When she appeared at the Alexander Palace, Zenaide could not fail to notice how coolly Alexandra treated her. And when Zenaide mentioned the name of Rasputin, Alexandra ordered her to leave. Zenaide, however, insisted on having her say. She spoke of the peasant's corrupting influence, denouncing his coterie of advisers and suggesting that the empress did not realize the true extent of the damage being done to the prestige of the monarchy. Alexandra listened in silence. When Zenaide finished, Alexandra rose, rang for a servant, and dismissed the princess. As Zenaide left, the empress angrily said, "I hope never to see you again!."[3]

Zenaide returned to the Moika Palace greatly upset and told her son of the scene which had just occurred. She wrote a full account of her audience to Grand Duchess Elizabeth. In despair, the grand duchess herself came to Petrograd to confront her sister. She arrived at the Alexander Palace in the gray nun's habit of her religious order. The conversation went badly. Alexandra refused to discuss Rasputin. "Remember the fate of Louis XVI and Marie Antoinette!" the grand duchess exclaimed.[4] At this, the empress rose, walked to her desk, picked up the telephone, and ordered a carriage to take her sister back to the railway station immediately. "Perhaps it would have been better if I had not come," Elizabeth said sadly. "Yes," the empress agreed, and the two sisters parted.[5] They would never meet again.

The grand duchess went straight to the Moika Palace. Felix, who was sitting with his mother, remembered that she entered the room "trembling and in tears." When Zenaide asked what had happened, the grand duchess cried, "She drove me away like a dog! Poor Nicky, poor Russia!"[6] The grand duchess, whom Felix adored, was devastated by her sister's refusal to even discuss Rasputin. She returned to her Moscow convent convinced that a revolution was inevitable, a view she had shared with Felix.

These were personal incidents, and Felix's reaction to them, while indignant, remained a matter of private concern. Far more disturbing, however, was what he believed to be Rasputin's military influence, and he later asserted that Rasputin was privy to all important decisions undertaken regarding the deployment and campaigns of the Russian army. While there is no evidence to support such a view, contemporary belief that this was the case pervaded society. This belief was especially damaging where the Brusilov offensive was concerned. This Russian thrust into the Austro-Hungarian Empire was one of the most tragic and devastating losses involving the tsar's troops in the war. Over a million casualties made it one of the heaviest setbacks suffered by the Allies.

Felix Youssoupov had little doubt that blame for the failure of the Brusilov offensive rested at Rasputin's doorstep. He would later describe how the peasant surrounded himself with men of dubious character and raised the possibility that these figures were in fact German spies. While he did not openly accuse the peasant of direct treason, Felix certainly believed that Russian military secrets passed through Rasputin's flat and that unscrupulous foreign agents made use of this information in their fight against the tsarist army.

All of these incidents, occurring over this crucial eighteen-month period, convinced Felix that Rasputin had become a liability to the monarchy. "No matter what I was doing, no matter to whom I was talking," he later wrote, "I was haunted by one persistent idea, the idea of delivering Russia from her most dangerous internal enemy."[7] At first, Felix seems to have been uncertain as to how best to achieve his aim. There was apparently some thought that Rasputin might simply be bribed to leave the capital, although the peasant's utter carelessness where money was concerned soon deflated this idea.

For all of the thousands of words spilled over the conspiracy to murder Rasputin, Prince Felix Youssoupov's precise motives in undertaking the plot remain unknown. There is some reason to doubt what he later related. In his books and interviews on the subject, he claimed that he acted out of patriotic duty. Certainly this is the reason that most of the other conspirators, including Vladimir Purishkevich and Dr. Stanislaus Lazovert, agreed to participate.

There is no shortage of evidence to suggest Rasputin's malignant influence over the imperial couple. Felix himself laid out a careful case for such a belief, and in this he echoed the general feelings of most of the tsar's subjects. The degree of Rasputin's actual sway over both Nicholas and Alexandra has already been discussed, but the public perception of this influence, whether real or imagined, caused just as much harm to the prestige of the monarchy.

Rasputin himself made no secret of the fact that he was against Russian participation in World War I. He felt—rightly, as circumstances would prove—that the country could not afford such total and destructive warfare and that the drawn-out conflict would eventually lead to internal strife. "It's time to end this slaughter," he once declared to Felix. "Isn't Germany our brother, too? The Lord said: 'Thou shalt love thine enemy as thine own brother.' That's why the war must cease."[8]

In his books, Felix implied that Rasputin was surrounded by German spies. On his visits to the peasant, he wrote, he often found "strange" men sitting around the dining table, "asking questions" of Rasputin and taking "notes of his replies." Rasputin referred to these men as "*zeleni*," the Russian word for "green." According to the peasant, these mysterious men lived in Sweden and came to the capital simply to meet with him on a frequent basis.[9] Rasputin knew a certain banker named Manus and dined with him every Wednesday evening. During these dinner parties Rasputin usually got drunk and spoke freely of all that the empress had told him. Maurice Paléologue had it on good authority that Manus was a German spy. Since the empress had access to secret government papers, it was therefore assumed that Rasputin had similiar knowledge. In this manner, or so Rasputin's enemies assumed, the Germans knew of all the Russian war plans in advance. General Alexeiev, the tsar's military chief of staff, recalled that after the Revolution, "when the Empress's papers were examined, she was found to be in possession of a map indicating in detail the disposition of the troops along the entire Front. Only two copies were prepared of this map, one for the Emperor and one for myself. I was very painfully impressed. God knows who may have made use of this map."[10] Because she shared all with Rasputin, it is reasonable to assume that he, too, knew of the map. This, however, is the entire case for Rasputin having been a German spy, and no further evidence has since come to light which would support Felix's accusations.

Felix also suggests that he feared for the continued wellbeing of the tsar. In the fall of 1916 many of those around Nicholas II noted his growing sense of lethargy, his inability to maintain coherent speech, and the dazed look in his eyes. According to Felix, Rasputin told him that the tsar was "given a tea which causes divine grace to descend on him. His heart is filled with peace, everything looks good and cheerful to him."[11] After hearing this confession, the prince believed that the tsar was being drugged through herbal teas concocted by the Tibetan Dr. Badmayev and then administered to the emperor by his wife. There is indeed some evidence that the tsar suffered from the effects of drug use in the fall of 1916. But there is nothing to suggest that these drugs were ever administered by his wife. On the contrary, the letters exchanged between Nicholas and Alexandra contain repeated references to the imperial couple's frequent use of opium, cocaine, and similiar narcotics for the treatment of various ailments. Use of such substances might have resulted in the symptoms attributed to the tsar, but they were certainly not prescribed by the mysterious Dr. Badmayev.

Taking these circumstances into account, it can reasonably be argued that Felix acted out of a misguided sense of patriotism. He worked himself into such a state of hysteria that he unquestionably believed that this was his divine mission in life. To Felix, such a role clearly followed family tradition: the Youssoupovs had always been strong, vibrant, and bold, serving the Romanovs and preserving the integrity of the Russian Empire. The army suffered defeat after defeat, the government disintegrated, the imperial family receded further and further into the background—all due to the ominous, pervasive influence of Rasputin. Reasonable men recognized the problem, but only Felix Youssoupov was resolute enough to respond. This belief drove the prince to act. If he carried out his plan, he had every expectation that his action would later be recognized as a great patriotic sacrifice, a bold strike against the decay and internal turmoil threatening to overwhelm the country. Felix would kill Rasputin and be hailed as a hero for his action.

Rasputin's murder took on a more historic tone as Felix continued his plot. He began to envision himself as a figure of great importance, a second Alexander Nevsky, sent to deliver his country from a dangerous threat. He had no doubt that by killing Rasputin he would assure his place in history. Once Felix perceived the murder in this light, he easily overcame whatever remaining moral doubts he might have had by justifying his action as being necessary for the good of the country.

Rene Fulop-Miller suggests that Felix partially undertook the murder out of boredom. Plotting and carrying out the death of Rasputin—"a worthy victim"—in Fulop-Miller's words, would provide Felix with excitement and "stir both his own jaded blood and the whole country at the same time."[12] The idea that Felix carried out Rasputin's murder simply for excitement is an interesting one. Certainly, as the plot progressed, Felix himself fell victim to the sweeping drama he had instigated. But such a belief assumes that Felix already possessed a murderous character. There is no evidence of any kind to support this conclusion.

There can be little doubt that Felix Youssoupov himself was convinced that the murder of Rasputin was a patriotic act and that this belief motivated his decision. There are numerous incidents and discussions which may have influenced Felix in this, all of which seem compelling. But do they form the sole basis for his action? In her final book, Maria Rasputin suggests that Felix was in love with her father and that Rasputin's rejection of Felix's homosexual advances led to his murder. She records that her father once entered his study to find Felix lying naked on the couch. "There was no doubt what he had in mind, and Papa was dismayed to see that all his efforts had been in vain."[13]

It has been suggested that there was an active homosexual relationship between the prince and the peasant and that this led in turn to Rasputin's murder. Speaking of such allegations in 1971, Cedric Salter, one of Felix's friends after the Revolution, wrote:

> This was Youssoupov's own unvarying version of the events leading up to, and taking place on, the fatal night, given to me and many others in long pavement café talks in Paris in 1932, nearly half a century ago . . . in 1932, no one would have dared to put it in print that they or anyone else living, were homosexual, so that many renderings of Rasputin's death glossed over this vital fact. However there is certainly no doubt that Rasputin and Youssoupov had a close homosexual relationship, that this influenced the course of events and that anyone who knew Rasputin and Youssoupov, even slightly, was aware of the fact.[14]

This certainly contradicts every accepted theory about the relationship between the prince and the peasant. Rasputin's sexuality has never been questioned before, and nearly all of the evidence suggests that he was strictly heterosexual. Surprisingly, there is further evidence to support the homosexual idea. After the Revolution, Aaron Simanovich, who acted as Rasputin's secretary during World War I, strongly hinted that the peasant had been sexually attracted to Youssoupov.[15] Simanovich, who saw Rasputin every day, was certainly in a position to know whereof he spoke. And Felix, as Salter stated, himself advanced this theory to his close friends, knowing full well that it would never become known beyond his inner circle of friends until after his death. He apparently was privy to intimate details of Rasputin's sexual prowess, for he later described the peasant's penis, which seems to indicate firsthand knowledge.[16] Once, at a dinner party, Felix must have confided something of the sort to Noël Coward, for that night, in his diary, the playwright recorded, "The truth, I think, is that Rasputin had a tiny little letch on Youssoupov himself."[17]

It is tempting to conclude that any homosexual relationship between Felix and Rasputin existed only in Youssoupov's mind. The peasant seems to have held a strong attraction for the prince, and it is likely that much of this was, by the very nature of Rasputin himself, colored by a degree of sexuality. Felix himself always maintained that he found Rasputin repulsive; yet he appeared to be fascinated with the peasant's crude sexuality and powerful manner. The rumors surrounding Rasputin's amorous escapades would undoubtedly have enthralled Felix.

A great degree of mystery also surrounds Rasputin's midnight visit to the Youssoupov palace on the night of his murder. If a relationship between the prince and the peasant did, in fact, exist, it would help to explain away some of the inconsistencies attached to that night. Felix always claimed that the peasant had come to the Moika Palace to meet his wife, Irina. Irina was actually in the Crimea at the time of the murder, staying with the elder Youssoupovs. We do not know if Rasputin was aware of this. But on the night of the murder itself Felix entertained the peasant until nearly three in the morning; it is unlikely that Rasputin sat up until such a late hour and still expected to meet the princess. And, near the end of his life, Felix claimed that Rasputin had come to the Moika Palace on that fateful night for reasons other than those he gave in his written accounts and that the visit had nothing to do with Irina herself. So the question remains: Why did Rasputin accept this midnight invitation? It is just possible that the answer may lie in the nature of the relationship between Felix and Rasputin.

It is impossible to say whether Maria Rasputin's claims of a spurned homosexual relationship had any bearing on Felix's decision to murder the peasant. Circumstantial evidence does suggest that the friendship between Felix and Rasputin may have encompassed some sexual element; but whether this feeling was mutual, real, or imagined will never be known. In addition, Felix had a confusing habit of changing his story as the years went by. He certainly confided potentially scandalous details of

Rasputin's murder, and the nature of their relationship, to many of his friends, further obscuring the truth.

It is likely that Felix arrived at his decision to murder Rasputin independent of any intimate relationship between the two of them. By his own admission he did not cultivate a friendship with Rasputin until the fall of 1916, and it seems certain that by this time Felix had already reached his fateful decision. There is little doubt that Felix truly believed that by killing the peasant he could save the Romanov dynasty from ruin. Convinced that this role had been predetermined by divine providence, Felix proceeded under an aura of near-religious exaltation, a hysterical obsession to deliver his country from Rasputin's evil clutches.

13

The Deception

BEFORE FELIX DECIDED on which course of action to take, he had to renew his acquaintance with Rasputin. He wished to determine for himself just how influential the peasant had become and also win his confidence in the event that any action should become necessary. This did not prove difficult, as Munya Golovine was continually asking Felix to come to her house for another meeting with Rasputin. But he was careful to remain skeptical in appearance.

"How do you explain this good man's habit of defiling his saintliness with drunken revels?" he asked Munya one day.

"You surely realize," she replied, "that all those tales are nothing but black and slanderous lies? He is surrounded by envy and malice. Evil minded people invent charges and purposely distort facts, in order to blacken him. . . ."

Felix then tried another approach, arguing that Rasputin's presence at court did great harm to the prestige of the imperial family. He pointed out that whatever the truth of the accusations against Rasputin might be, the public, both in Russia and in Europe, believed the rumors. But Munya would not listen, declaring, "Nobody has the right to criticize the actions of the Emperor and Empress. What they do concerns no one. They stand by themselves, above all public opinion."

Felix realized that these were the views of the imperial couple themselves. He left convinced "that it was impossible to fight against Rasputin's influence with mere words. Logic was of no avail. The clearest arguments would not convince those whose judgement was clouded."[1] He later wrote that he spent many sleepless nights pacing up and down his bedroom, trying to reach a decision. He had no doubt that Rasputin's continued presence was damaging the prestige of the monarchy and the welfare of the empire.

It is indicative of just how strongly Felix felt that he had reached this point. No one who knew Felix well ever thought him particularly strong-willed or resolute, yet his decision—certainly the most important he would ever undertake— was made only when he became convinced that there was no other course of action. This decision may well have rested on two different motivations: Felix's desire to end Rasputin's influence and some obsessive sexual tension which Felix felt he needed to exorcise. It was no longer a question of bribing Rasputin to leave the capital; only the peasant's death would accomplish his goals. Yet Felix apparently had to spend some time convincing himself not only that murder was the only choice open to him but that he was capable of carrying out such a plan. For a man like Prince Felix Youssoupov, continually coddled and indulged, to suddenly and with determination concoct a murder plot required intense conviction. Eventually, Felix worked himself into a state of near-religious exaltation, apparently believing that he had a divinely inspired mission to rid Russia of Rasputin. The idea of cold-bloodedly plotting his murder, therefore, became not a question of an ordinary assassination but rather one of patriotic duty. "All my doubts and hesitations vanished," he later wrote. "I felt a calm resolution, and gave myself over to the set purpose of destroying Rasputin."[2]

Felix drew two others into his confidence. The first was his friend Dimitri Pavlovich. After the temporary break following Felix and Irina's wedding, the prince and grand duke had renewed their friendship and were once again close confidants. "For many reasons," Felix later wrote, "I attributed great importance to his participation in the plot."[3] The second conspirator was Lt. Ivan Sukhotin, an officer in the Preobrajensky Guards Regiment, who was being treated for wounds received in action. Felix met the handsome young man and formed a great attachment, visiting him on a daily basis. Both men agreed with Felix that Rasputin's murder was necessary for the salvation of the empire. Few details were discussed, however, and the plan did not extend beyond a decision that one of the three should gain entrance to the peasant's flat and shoot him on the spot.[4]

In order to advance his plot, Felix had to cultivate a relationship with the peasant. They had met only once, at Munya Golovine's mansion in 1909; now Felix arranged to visit Munya the next time Rasputin came to her house. He found the man much changed. "His face was puffy, his form seemed to have become lax and flabby. He was no longer clad in an ordinary peasant's coat, but in a blouse of pale blue silk over wide velvet trousers. There was something extraordinarily repugnant about his whole appearance."[5]

Felix told Rasputin that he was suffering from a disease for which the doctors could find no cure. He asked if Rasputin could help him. De Jonge speculates that Felix may have raised the issue of his homosexual desires and sought Rasputin's help. Certainly, in her last book on the subject, Maria Rasputin indicates that this was the case. She writes that Felix told her father, "You must know, of course, that I have homosexual desires as well as heterosexual, and the former is interfering with my marriage."[6] Unfortunately, we have only Maria's word for this explanation of Felix's "illness." But the possibility cannot be ruled out. In any case, Rasputin agreed to begin regular sessions of healing, and thus, Felix achieved the objective of gaining his trust.

Accordingly, Felix made his way to Rasputin's flat on the appointed day to begin treatment. He later wrote:

> We left the kitchen and went into his bedroom. It was small and simply furnished. In one corner, along the wall, there was a narrow bed; on it lay a cover of fox fur—a present from Vyrubova. Nearby there was a huge chest. In the opposite corner hung icons, with lamps burning in front of them. Here and there on the walls were portraits of the Tsar and of the Tsarina, and gaudy coloured prints depicting scenes from the Holy Scriptures. From the bedroom Rasputin took us into the dining room where tea was laid. The samovar was already boiling. On the table were glass dishes of jam and fruits, and quantities of plates filled with cakes, biscuits, sweets and nuts. In the

Rasputin, about 1906

Unless otherwise credited, all photographs are from the author's collection.

The Winter Palace from Palace Square in St. Petersburg, photograph taken around 1900

Empress Alexandra with Tsarevich Alexei after his christening, August 1904

Tsar Nicholas II and Tsarevich Alexei, 1912

Rasputin, standing in the middle of the group, surrounded by his family at Pokrovskoe, about 1900

Rasputin with his children in Pokrovskoe, about 1910

Rasputin with Bishop Hermogen and the Monk Iliodor, about 1906

Tsarevich Alexei in the uniform of a
Russian Army private, 1915

Anna Vyrubova, 1917

Rasputin, 1913

Rasputin, 1914

Rasputin surrounded by his admirers at tea in his flat, 1915

"Russia's Ruling House," a cartoon by Ivanov, 1915

The entrance to Rasputin's apartment block in St. Petersburg, contemporary photograph

(Below) Portrait of Prince Boris Nicholaievich Youssoupov, Felix's great-grandfather, painted in 1809 by A. Gros Collection of the Pushkin Museum of Fine Arts, Moscow

(Above) Portrait of Princess Tatiana Youssoupov, Felix's great-grandmother, painted by Franz Xavier Winterhalter, 1858 *(The Hermitage Collection, St. Petersburg)*

Portrait of Princess Zenaide Youssoupov and her son Prince Felix at Arkhangelskoe, 1894, painted by François Flameng *(The Hermitage Collection, St. Petersburg)*

Count Felix with his two sons Prince Nicholas and Prince Felix, 1892 *(Private collection)*

The Youssoupov family, 1895 *(Left to right)* Nicholas, Felix, Count Felix, and Princess Zenaide *(Private collection)*

Prince Felix Youssoupov, painted by Valentin Serov, 1904 *(The Hermitage Collection, St. Petersburg)*

The Youssoupov Family on the terrace steps at Arkhangelskoe, 1905 *(Private collection)*

The front doorway of the Moika Palace, contemporary photograph

The grand staircase at the Moika Palace, contemporary photograph
(Collection of Nils Hanson)

The ornate interior of the Moika Palace, contemporary photograph

middle stood a basket of flowers. The furniture was of
massive oak—high-backed chairs and a cumbersome sideboard loaded with crockery. Paintings, badly executed in
oils, adorned the walls; over the table hung a bronze
chandelier with a large glass shade. There was a telephone near the door leading to the hall. The whole contents of the flat, from the cumbersome sideboard to the
crowded and abundantly stocked kitchen, bore the stamp
of *bourgeois* well-being and prosperity. The lithographs
and badly painted pictures on the walls were fully in
keeping with the owner's taste.[7]

Following tea, Rasputin led Felix to his study. Felix recalled:

The *starets* told me to lie down on the couch. He stood in
front of me, looked me intently in the eyes and began to
stroke my chest, neck and head. He then suddenly knelt
down and—so it seemed to me—began to pray, placing
his hands on my forehead. He bent his head so low that I
could not see his face. He remained in this position for a
considerable time. Then he suddenly jumped to his feet
and began to make passes. He was evidently familiar with
certain of the processes employed by hypnotists. His hypnotic power was immense. I felt it subduing me and diffus-
ing warmth throughout the whole of my body. I grew
numb; my body seemed paralysed. I tried to speak but my
tongue would not obey me, and I seemed to be falling to
sleep, as if under the influence of some strong narcotic. Yet
Rasputin's eyes shone before me with a kind of phospho-
rescent light. From them came two rays which flowed into
each other and merged into one glowing circle. This circle
now moved away from me, now came nearer and nearer.
When it approached me it seemed as if I began to distinguish his eyes; but at that very moment, they would again
vanish into the circle, which then moved further and further away. I was conscious that the *starets* was speaking
but I could not make out the words; I could only hear the
sound of a vague murmur. Such was my condition as I lay
motionless, unable to call out or stir. Yet my mind was still

free, and I realized that I was gradually falling into the power of this mysterious and sinister man. But soon I found that my own inner force was awakening and was of its own accord resisting the hypnosis. This force grew stronger within me, enveloping my whole being in an invisible armor. Into my consciousness floated a vague idea that an intense struggle was taking place between Rasputin and myself, and that my own personality in battling with his made it impossible for him to dominate me completely. I tried to move my hand and it obeyed me. But I did not alter my position; I waited until Rasputin himself should tell me to do so. By now I could clearly distinguish his figure, face and eyes. That terrible circle had completely disappeared. . . . "Well, my dear, that'll be enough for the first time," he said. He kept watching me closely, but evidently he was able to note only one aspect of my sensations; my resistance to the hypnosis had escaped him. There was a self-satisfied smile on his face; and he spoke to me in the assured manner of a person conscious of his entire mastery over another. He was obviously convinced that I had been completely subjugated by him, and that henceforth he could count me among his submissive followers. With a brusque movement he pulled my arm. I sat up, feeling dizzy and weak. With an effort, I rose from the couch and took a few steps about the room; but my legs seemed half paralyzed and would not fully obey me. Rasputin continued to observe every movement I made. "This is God's grace," he said. "Now you'll see how soon it will heal you, and drive all your illness away." We parted, and he made me promise to visit him again very soon.[8]

"This description of him lying helpless and immobile in the thrall of a powerful and evil man," writes De Jonge, "sounds more like the erotic fantasy of a passive homosexual than an accurate account of what really happened."[9] But certainly, whatever may have happened during this visit, Rasputin made a powerful impact on his "patient."

Further visits to Rasputin proved very disturbing. Rasputin began to speak freely of the power he claimed to hold, and of his plans for the future. "Don't be afraid of me," he once said to Felix. "When you come to know me better, you'll see what sort of a man I am. . . . I can do anything. . . . If the Tsar and Tsarina obey me, surely you can. . . . I shall be seeing them soon, and I'll tell them that you've been to tea with me here."

This is exactly what Felix did not wish; in order for his plan to work, he had to maintain secrecy, and had Alexandra known about the visits, she surely would have questioned Felix as to his reasons. "No, Gregory Efimovich," Felix replied, "don't say anything about me at Tsarskoe Selo. The less people know about my being here the better."[10]

In his book on Rasputin, Felix detailed their many conversations; again, these must be treated with some caution, for Felix relied on his memory to record these long passages and was not above distorting the truth when it served his own ends. Even so, the conversations are worth examining at some length, because they form the basis of Felix's expressed motivation for killing the peasant.

Of the Duma, Rasputin said, "They're always speaking ill of me there and getting the Emperor upset. . . . Their babblings won't last much longer. I'll dissolve the Duma soon and send all the deputies to the Front." He also spoke of his relations with the imperial family: "The Empress is a very wise ruler. . . . With her I can do anything, I can get anything I want. But as for him— well, he's a child of God. There's an Emperor for you. Why, he ought just to play with children and flowers, and get busy in a vegetable garden—not rule the country; that's a bit difficult for him, so, with God's blessing, we help him."[11] And again, at some length on the same subject:

When it's all settled, we'll hail Alexandra as Regent for her young son and we'll send him to Livadia for a rest. . . . There! Won't that be a treat for him? To be a market gardener! He's worn out—he must have a rest. . . . Yes, and mark you, down there in Livadia, among the flowers, he'll be nearer to God; and he's got plenty to pray about—the war for one thing, and all it has cost. A whole life of prayer won't be enough to wipe that out. . . . Now the Empress herself—she's a wise ruler, a second

Catherine. Why, she's been governing alone for some time past.[12]

Once, according to Felix, Rasputin offered to make him a minister in the government. "I realized how easy it was for him to obtain anything," Felix wrote, "and I also knew what a scandal might ensue."[13] With this offer, Felix knew that he had successfully achieved the peasant's trust. "My meetings," he said, "left me with an overpowering feeling of contamination."[14] Nevertheless, Felix continued to receive "treatments" from Rasputin throughout the fall of 1916. There is some disagreement as to the number of visits that took place between them. After the Revolution, Munya Golovine testified that Felix met the peasant only twice in the fall of 1916, once at the end of November and again in early December, and that each visit took less than an hour.[15] To the contrary, Felix states in his book that numerous visits took place in the fall of 1916; because the prince asked Rasputin to keep these visits a secret, it is possible that Munya Golovine did not know of their existence.

With each visit, Felix later wrote, he felt a growing confirmation of his decision to destroy Rasputin. His belief that he alone had been selected by fate to deliver the Russian Empire from what he saw as impending disaster had developed into an obsession. There was no retreat. "I was forced to the conclusion that it would be necessary to resort to extreme measures in order to deliver Russia from this evil genius."[16]

On 20 November 1916, Vladimir Purishkevich rose to speak in the great columned chamber of the Duma, once Potemkin's Tauride Palace. A short, fat, balding man in his mid-forties, Purishkevich came from a wealthy Bessarabian family and had entered politics at the turn of the century. Although he had been a member for nearly a decade, Purishkevich had only disdain for the Duma. He frequently interrupted the legislative proceedings, hurling abuse at speakers and even at the president. Once he went as far as to throw water at another member who had the floor; on another occasion, he appeared wearing a red carnation in the fly of his trousers. As a result, he was often expelled from the chamber. In spite of all this, Purishkevich remained an immensely popular figure not only with his fellow legislators but with the public as well. His picture was sold on street corners, and toys were even named after him. Now, as he walked to the podium, the entire Duma held its breath in anticipation of what he might say.

Purishkevich spoke for two hours, bellowing against the "dark forces" which threatened Russia. "It requires only the recommendation of Rasputin to raise the most abject citizen to high office," he exclaimed. At the close of the speech, he challenged the ministers to go at once to the tsar at headquarters and protest against the peasant and his influence. "Have the courage to tell him," Purishkevich cried, "that the multitude is threatening in its wrath! Revolution threatens, and an obscure *moujik* shall govern Russia no longer!"[17]

The entire Duma rose to its feet and gave Purishkevich a thunderous round of applause. But Maurice Paléologue noticed that Prince Felix Youssoupov, sitting in the visitors' gallery, remained seated, pale and trembling.[18]

When the legislature adjourned, Felix made his way back to the Moika Palace. On arriving, he immediately telephoned the Duma and asked to be connected to Purishkevich. Felix explained who he was to the deputy and asked that he be allowed to meet with him in private as soon as possible to discuss "Rasputin's role at Court" and other matters which he termed "awkward." Purishkevich agreed and set the appointment for the following day.[19]

At nine o'clock the next morning Felix appeared at Vladimir Purishkevich's flat. "I was very much taken with both his external appearance, which radiated inexpressible elegance and breeding, and particularly with his inner self-possession," Purishkevich later wrote.[20] According to Purishkevich, Felix spoke for two hours. "Your speech," he told the Duma member, "will not bring the results you anticipate. The sovereign does not like having pressure brought to bear on him, and Rasputin's importance, you must realize, will not only not lessen but, on the contrary, will increase—thanks to his complete influence over Alexandra Feodorovna who, since the sovereign is at Headquarters engaged in military affairs, is really governing the country."

"But what can be done?" Purishkevich asked.

"Get rid of Rasputin," the prince announced with a chilling smile.

"That's easy to say," Purishkevich replied, "but who will do it? There are no decisive people in Russia now, only a government which, while it could do it and skillfully, only clings to Rasputin and guards him as if he were the apple of its eye."

"Yes," Felix agreed, "you can't depend on the government, but, all the same, people will be found in Russia."

"You think so?"

"I am sure of it. And one of them stands before you." As Purishkevich listened in silence, Felix poured out his plans to assassinate Rasputin.[21] Purishkevich himself had thought long and hard about killing the peasant and was clearly enthusiastic about Felix's proposal. The deputy expressed some concern over the fact that the peasant was so well guarded; but Felix dismissed this objection, saying that he himself had befriended Rasputin and now enjoyed easy access. After Felix informed Purishkevich of the joint cooperation of Dimitri Pavlovich and Lieutenant Sukhotin, the Duma deputy agreed to meet with the group and discuss further plans.

Felix was quite taken with Purishkevich—"an amazingly kind and decent fellow"—he wrote in one letter.[22] He was convinced that Purishkevich would prove a valuable addition to the group of conspirators. Stirred by the speech in the Duma and fresh from his meeting with the deputy, Felix wrote to his mother ominously: "I don't know how it will all end. We seem to be living on the slopes of a volcano and the same thoughts lurk in all our heads."[23]

PART THREE

The Crime

14

The Conspiracy

IT TOOK SURPRISINGLY LITTLE TIME for the conspirators to act. Purishkevich had made his speech in the Duma on 19 November; within three weeks, Rasputin would be dead. Together these men formed a powerful alliance against the peasant. Prince Felix Youssoupov represented the aristocracy; Grand Duke Dimitri, the imperial family; Ivan Sukhotin, the Preobrajensky Guards Regiment; and now, with Purishkevich, they could lay claim to a representative of the imperial government itself. As a group, these men acted out of misguided patriotism in the belief that only Rasputin's death could alter the disastrous course which threatened to overwhelm the Russian Empire. By striking out against Rasputin, the conspirators hoped to diminish the empress's influence over her husband; the tsar would then be free to listen to the warning voices of his ministers and grant the reforms necessary if Russia were to survive the turmoil of the war. If they were ever charged in Rasputin's disappearance, the participation of Grand Duke Dimitri ensured that the conspirators would be immune from regular prosecution, since members of the Romanov dynasty were exempt from ordinary judicial and civil regulations and were subject only to the authority of the tsar himself. This immunity also extended to any coconspirators.

At first, Felix wished to shoot Rasputin in his own flat. With some difficulty, the others pointed out that doing so involved too great a risk: Rasputin's apartment was nearly always filled with petitioners and devotees. Even if Felix succeeded in shooting his victim, there was no guarantee that he himself would escape unharmed. After much discussion, the conspirators agreed that Rasputin should simply disappear and that his murder should remain a secret. There was some worry that a direct assassination attempt would be viewed as a protest against Nicholas II himself. Because the conspirators were acting in an effort to save the monarchy, this they wished to avoid at all costs. Finally, they decided to kidnap Rasputin, kill him, smuggle his body onto Purishkevich's hospital train, and dump it on a field near the front, where it would later be discovered by the military authorities.

Purishkevich suggested that a friend of his, Dr. Stanislaus Lazovert, should join the conspiracy. He thought that Rasputin might perhaps be fed poison after he was abducted and that his friend could assist in obtaining the necessary substances. Because Felix was the only one of the conspirators who had actually met Rasputin, it seemed natural that he should be the one to bait the peasant. Their chief difficulty lay in evading the police who kept an around-the-clock watch at Rasputin's flat and followed him everywhere he went. Felix said this should not present a problem given the right circumstances.

Felix approached Vassili Maklakov, a brilliant and respected lawyer and member of the Duma, and asked for his participation. He had heard Maklakov deliver an inflammatory speech in the Duma against Rasputin and thought he might prove to be a useful connection. Maklakov, however, was less than enthusiastic, commenting sourly, "Do you think I keep an office for assassins?" The lawyer declined to take part. On the other hand, he told Felix, he did not wish to stand in the way of the conspiracy. He advised Felix against hiring an assassin: "It will pay him better to betray you; but if decide to do it yourself, see me and I might warn you against inadvertent mistakes." He advised Felix that in order for Rasputin's death to have any effect on the internal situation in Russia, his body would have to be found and the crime known. Maklakov did agree with Felix that the identities of the conspirators should remain a secret.[1]

Felix had a second conversation with Maklakov in early December. Maklakov was adamant in his refusal to join the conspirators. This time, however, he took Felix a little more seriously. Maklakov told Felix that he and his fellow plotters should be careful to divert any suspicion which might settle upon them following Rasputin's disappearance. It was he who suggested that after carrying out the deed, they place a telephone call to one of Rasputin's favourite restaurants, the Villa Rode, asking if he had arrived. The lawyer also told Felix that should events warrant his intervention, he himself would volunteer to act as legal counsel.[2]

During his talk with Maklakov, Felix noticed a heavy steel-and-leather club in the deputy's office. When Felix asked about it, or so he later wrote, Maklakov handed it to him, saying, "Take this, in case you might ever want it."[3] Following publication of this version, however, Maklakov himself disputed that he had offered the club, declaring instead that it had been Felix who had asked for its loan.[4] Purishkevich later claimed that Felix also obtained from Maklakov a quantity of cyanide in both liquid and crystal form.[5]

The conspirators met in late November to discuss the plot. Felix explained Maklakov's view that Rasputin's body must be found and argued that they should abandon the idea of simply dumping him on a battlefield. Instead, he suggested that they should kill Rasputin in Petrograd and dispose of his body in the capital. Felix proposed that he invite Rasputin to the Moika Palace and poison him there. The other conspirators agreed. The only question left was the date. Purishkevich and Grand Duke Dimitri were scheduled to be away from Petrograd for the first week of December, but both planned to return by the middle of the month. In addition, Dimitri had several social engagements, none of which could be canceled for fear that this would later arouse attention. The first evening Dimitri had free was 16 December, a Friday. After some discussion, the conspirators agreed to this day. This would also allow Felix to entertain Rasputin in a more isolated part of the palace. Some minor renovations were just being completed to the eastern wing of no. 94 Moika, including work on a few rooms in the cellar. With this finished, Felix could choose a room far removed from the rest of the house, and, more importantly, from the presence of the numerous servants.

"The prospect of inviting a man to my house with the intention of killing him horrified me," Felix later wrote. "Whoever the man might be—even Rasputin, the incarnation of crime and

vice—I could not contemplate without a shudder the part which
I should be called upon to play—that of a host encompassing the
death of his guest. My friends fully understood my feelings." After discussing his reluctance with these friends, however, Felix decided that "where the destiny of all Russia was concerned, all considerations or feelings of a personal nature should be set aside."[6]

On 29 November, Purishkevich visited Felix at the Moika
Palace. Together they spent the afternoon walking through the
basement labyrinth, looking at various storerooms and trying to
select a location for the intended crime. Because a police station
was located just across the Moika, they wanted to be certain that
nothing would be heard in case any difficulties arose with the
plan. Eventually, they settled on a vaulted chamber, directly beneath the prince's study, whose two small windows overlooked
the canal. The room was isolated, located at the eastern end of
the palace, far away from the quarters occupied by the servants.

Although the conspirators had agreed that the plot to kill
Rasputin should remain a secret, Purishkevich formed the rather
indiscreet habit of bringing it up whenever he found himself in
the presence of important persons. He also openly bragged in
the Duma press room that the peasant was about to be killed,
completely oblivious of the presence of dozens of his fellow legislators. He cornered Vassili Shulgin, a monarchist deputy in the
Duma, in a secluded area of the Tauride Palace's Catherine Hall
and whispered dramatically: "Remember the sixteenth of December."

Shulgin was completely puzzled. "What for?"

"You'll see," Purishkevich replied airily. "Farewell." Then,
apparently changing his mind, he turned and said, "You can be
trusted. We're going to murder him on the sixteenth."

"Who?"

"Grishka," Purishkevich declared. He explained the details
of the conspiracy as deputies pushed and shoved their ways
past. But Shulgin was unimpressed.

"Don't do it," he urged.

"What! Why not?"

"I don't know," Shulgin replied. "It's repulsive. . . ."

"You're a weakling, Shulgin," Purishkevich countered.

"Perhaps," the deputy answered. "But maybe it's something else. I don't believe Rasputin has any influence."

"No?"

"It's all nonsense. He simply prays for the heir. He has no influence on the ministers. He's a clever peasant. . . ."

"So," Purishkevich asked, "in your opinion, Rasputin is not bringing evil upon the monarchy?"

"Not only does he not bring evil, he kills it."

"Then I don't understand you."

"Why, it's perfectly clear," Shulgin replied. "Killing him won't help. There are two aspects. The first is what you yourself have called the 'leapfrog' of ministers. The leapfrog occurs either because there is no one to appoint or because, no matter whom you appoint, you do not please anyone, because the country is wild about the idea of people who have the public trust, and they are precisely the people the Sovereign does not trust. Rasputin has nothing to do with all this. Killing him will not change anything."

"What do you mean, will not change anything?"

"Why, things will go on as before. The same 'leapfrog' of ministers. And the other aspect is that what Rasputin does will not be destroyed by killing him. It's too late. . . ."

"What do you mean?" Purishkevich demanded. "Excuse me, but what are we supposed to do, sit idly by? Endure this disgrace? Do you understand what that means? It is not for me to say or for you to listen. The monarchy is perishing. . . . I tell you, the monarchy is perishing, and we along with it, and Russia along with us. . . . We cannot sit by, no matter what. We'll follow through to the end. It can't get worse. I'm going to kill him like a dog."[7]

On 1 December the conspirators all met on Purishkevich's hospital train to discuss the final arrangements. Dimitri Pavlovich asked whether Rasputin was likely to accept an invitation to the Moika Palace: "What is his attitude toward you, Felix? Does he trust you?" "Oh, completely," Felix said laughing. "I am above suspicion. He likes me very much. He even regrets that I don't hold an administrative post and promises to make me into a great statesman."[8]

The conspirators sat up late that night in Purishkevich's train, working out the intricacies of the plot. Felix agreed to issue an invitation to Rasputin to come to the Moika Palace, ostensibly to meet Irina. According to the contemporary accounts given by Felix, Rasputin had often expressed an interest in the princess, and her presumed presence was used to bait the trap. Felix himself would call at Rasputin's flat to collect the peasant late on the night of 16 December. Because Felix was adamant that none of his servants should be involved in the crime, it was arranged for Dr. Lazovert to don a heavy fur cloak and hat and act as the Youssoupov chauffeur.

Once at the Moika Palace, Felix would lead Rasputin to the room in the basement which he and Purishkevich had previously selected. Here the peasant would be fed poisoned cakes and wine. Once Rasputin was dead, his body would be wrapped in a curtain, loaded into Purishkevich's motorcar, and driven across the city to the Petrovsky Bridge, linking the Petrovsky and Krestovsky islands. Here it would be pushed beneath the ice of the frozen Neva River. Weighted down with chains, it would sink to the bottom. The site had been carefully selected; it was isolated, at the far end of the city, in the Islands, where many middle-class merchants kept summer dachas. The heavy current which swept the waters of the Neva out into the Gulf of Finland would also carry with it Rasputin's body. They expected that it would not be found until the spring thaw. At the same time, Dimitri Pavlovich and Lieutenant Sukhotin would take Rasputin's clothes back to Purishkevich's hospital train and burn them. Finally, a call would be placed to the Villa Rode restaurant asking if the peasant had arrived in order to divert suspicion away from events at the Moika Palace.

Felix visited Rasputin at his flat in the first few days of December. Casually, he asked the peasant if he would like to come to the Moika Palace to meet Irina and suggested the sixteenth. Rasputin agreed at once. He further eased the conspirators' plans by asking that Felix arrive at midnight and that he use the back entrance to avoid the watchful eye of the Okhrana agents who regularly stood guard at the peasant's front door. Rasputin hoped to visit the Moika Palace unobserved; Felix could not have wished for a more cooperative victim.[9]

A few days before the event, Felix wrote a curious and ambiguous letter to his absent wife: Irina knew that her husband had formerly talked about killing the peasant and immediately replied:

> Dear Felix,
>   Thank you for your insane letter. I could not understand the half of it. I realize that you are about to do something wild. Please take care and do not get mixed up in any shady business.[10]

The plot was too far gone, however, to change direction, and Felix himself showed no hesitation about carrying it through to the end.

Ten days before the murder, the Hon. Bertie Stopford wrote:

> Went to supper at Schubines, where I found—amongst many friends—Grand Duke Dimitri. I had not seen him for many months. He called me aside into another room, where he discussed with me at great length the whole internal policy situation. Having had knowledge both of my loyalty and discretion, he confided to me the steps he thought must be taken to arrest the continued reactionary policy of the Empress, into which she was dragging the Emperor, and how imperative was the removal of evil counsellors.[11]

By now much of Petrograd knew of the plot. Three days before the event, the conspirators met one last time. According to Felix, they decided to simulate a party in the palace by using a gramophone; the prince would explain to Rasputin that Irina was entertaining guests and would be down to visit them shortly. By this time, the poison would have acted, and Rasputin would be dead.

As the date of his visit to the Moika Palace grew nearer, Rasputin became apprehensive. He repeatedly told those around him that he felt his life was in danger. At his last meeting with the tsar he refused to give Nicholas his usual blessing, saying, "This time it is for you to bless me, not I you."[12] A few days before his death, he sat down and wrote a strangely prophetic letter. Headed "The Spirit of Gregory Efimovich Rasputin of the village of Pokrovskoe," it was directed to the tsar:

> I write and leave behind me this letter at St. Petersburg. I feel that I shall leave life before 1 January. I wish to make known to the Russian people, to Papa, to the Russian Mother, and to the Children, to the land of Russia, what they must understand. If I am killed by common assassins and especially by my brothers the Russian peasants, you, Tsar of Russia, have nothing to fear, remain on your throne and govern, and you, Russian Tsar, will have nothing to fear for your children, they will reign for hundreds of years in Russia. But if I am murdered by *boyars*, nobles, and if they have shed my blood, for twenty-five years they will not wash their hands from my blood. They will leave Russia. Brothers will kill brothers, and they will kill each other and hate each other, and for twenty-five years there will be no nobles in the country. Tsar of the land of Russia, if you hear the sound of the bell which will tell you that Gregory has been killed, you must know this: if it was your relations who have wrought my death, then no one of your family, that is to say, none of your children or relations will remain alive for more than two years. They will be killed by the Russian people. . . . I shall be killed. I am no longer among the living. Pray, pray, be strong, think of your blessed family.
>
> Gregory.[13]

The morning of Friday, 16 December 1916, dawned cold and clear in Petrograd. Looking out of her windows at the Alexander Palace, Empress Alexandra noted the "wee pink clouds" scattered across the blue sky.[14] As the afternoon wore on, workers quickly finished their jobs, stores closed for the weekend, and troikas raced couples down the Nevsky Prospect to late teas at the private clubs lining the Neva embankments. By midnight the city lay slumbering, dark and snowbound.

Rasputin rose late that Friday morning. After a late morning visit to church and a bathhouse, he returned to his flat to receive visitors. He immediately began drinking. His secretary Simanovich estimated that by the time he left for the Moika Palace, the peasant had consumed at least a dozen bottles of Madeira.[15] Rasputin had mentioned the midnight visit to several persons that day, including the minister of the interior, Alexander Protopopov. Although Protopopov argued against accepting the invitation, Rasputin clearly was looking forward to the evening and would not be put off.

That afternoon, Anna Vyrubova visited the peasant to give him an icon from the empress. Rasputin informed her of his proposed midnight visit to the Moika Palace to see Princess Irina. The lateness of the hour struck Vyrubova as odd, but she said nothing. Later that same evening, when Anna mentioned the visit to the empress, Alexandra replied, "But, there must be some mistake, Irina is in the Crimea." She fell silent; then, after a few minutes, repeated, "There must be some mistake." The pair did not speak of the visit again that evening. "Next morning," Anna Vyrubova recalled, "soon after breakfast, I was called on the telephone by one of the daughters of Rasputin. . . . In some anxiety, the young girl told me that her father had gone out the night before in Youssoupov's motorcar and had not returned."[16]

15

The Crime

FELIX SPENT THE GREATER PART of that Friday worry-
ing over the decoration of the basement room where the murder
would be carried out. The room was divided in half by low
arches. Two small windows high in the gray stone walls looked
out onto the canal. The larger section of the room was furnished
as a dining area, with curved couches set into an apse at the
eastern end. Felix selected the pieces of furniture from the numerous storerooms of the palace: carved oak chairs, a mahogany
sideboard, and small tables were placed about the room. An ebony cabinet stood in one corner, heavily decorated with little
mirrors and columns of bronze. On the cabinet was placed a
sixteenth-century Italian rock-crystal-and-silver crucifix. Pieces
of china and small *objets d'art* lined the red granite mantelpiece,
and Persian carpets covered the cold stone floor. Before the fireplace lay a white bearskin rug. From the other side of the room
a narrow wooden staircase wound up to the first floor of the
palace and opened into the octagonal anteroom decorated with
eight mirrored doors and lit by a skylight. Four of the doors were
false, the others opened to the staircase, Felix's study, Irina's
apartments, and a hallway leading to the rest of the palace. Halfway up the staircase from the basement to the first floor, a concealed doorway led into the small private garden which connected to both the rear courtyard and to the Moika Canal. Felix
called his servants and told them to prepare a late-night tea for
six persons; then he left the palace to study for his exams the
following morning at the Cadet Corps.

That evening, Felix went to the magnificent Cathedral of
Our Lady of Kazan. He walked past the great Corinthian col-

onnades, copied from Bernini's model at St. Peter's in Rome, and entered the granite-and-marble sanctuary. In the dark shadows of the church he prayed for two hours. As he prayed, he was surrounded by the noble banners of Napoleon's Grand Armée, captured during the retreat from Moscow in 1812. By the time he left, Felix had worked himself into a state of religious hysteria, convinced of his divine mission to kill Rasputin, or so he later claimed: "I had a strange feeling of lightness, of well being, almost of happiness."[1] He had dinner at his father-in-law's palace before returning to the Moika late that night.

By eleven o'clock at night all was ready. A fire burned in the granite fireplace, spilling its ashes onto the stone floor. Two stained-glass lanterns cast their glow over the room. Bottles of wine and glasses stood on the sideboard. In the middle of the room, at the table where "Gregory Efimovich was to drink his last," a samovar smoked.[2] Plates of cakes and biscuits were set out on a silver platter. Felix told his servants to wait in another wing of the palace until they were summoned. The room, in Felix's words, was "isolated from the rest of the world and it seemed as though no matter what happened the events of that night would remain forever buried in the silence of those thick walls."[3]

At midnight the other conspirators began arriving. Felix took a small box containing the cyanide from the ebony cabinet and handed it to Dr. Lazovert. The doctor put on a pair of rubber gloves and carefully ground the crystals into a fine powder. He sliced the pink and chocolate cakes in half and, in the center of each, sprinkled a quantity of the powder, saying that such a dose was sufficient to kill several men. A few of the bottles of wine were also poisoned. Lazovert then threw the gloves into the fire; within a few minutes, the entire room was filled with thick smoke, and the conspirators had to open the windows to clear the air. They decided that the room should appear as if a party had already taken place; they poured wine into several of the glasses, crumpled napkins, disarranged chairs, and left cake and biscuit crumbs on the table. At twelve-thirty, Lazovert dressed in his chauffeur's cloak and cap, while Youssoupov himself donned a fur coat and low hat. The other conspirators went upstairs to Felix's study to wait for the return of the prince with

Rasputin. Felix and Lazovert climbed into Purishkevich's black automobile and drove off into the night.

The motorcar bearing Felix pulled to a stop in the rear court-yard of Rasputin's apartment block. With his hat pulled low over his face, Felix slowly made his way up to the peasant's flat. The doorman immediately stepped into his path, demanding to know whom this late caller wished to see. Felix replied that he had a meeting with Rasputin, and the doorman reluctantly allowed him to pass. At the door, Felix rang the bell.

"Who's there?" Rasputin called out.

"It's I, Gregory Efimovich," Felix replied. "I've come for you."[4]

Rasputin unlocked the door, and Felix quickly entered the flat. The peasant immediately noticed his strange attire and asked, "Why are you trying to hide?"

"Didn't we agree that no one was to know you were going out with me tonight?"

"True, true," Rasputin agreed. "I haven't said a word to anyone in the house." Again, this is not the truth, for many people knew of the proposed visit to the Moika Palace. But Felix seemed to calm at this news and began to carefully examine his intended victim. Rasputin wore a white silk shirt embroidered with blue cornflowers, black velvet trousers and a thick raspberry-colored cord around his waist. He had neatly combed his hair and beard, and Felix noticed a strong smell of cheap soap. "I had never seen him look so clean and tidy."[5]

Felix urged Rasputin to finish dressing so that they might leave. The peasant looked all over his flat for his boots, saying, "It's those children again, they've hidden them. They don't want me to go out."[6] It is curious that Felix fails to mention this in his books. He wrote that the peasant put on his snow boots and heavy overcoat, then turned to him and suggested a visit to the Gypsies. If this is true, it lends further weight to the belief that Rasputin had not expected to meet Princess Irina but intended to spend the evening only with Felix.

As Felix watched Rasputin dress, he later wrote, "a great feeling of pity for the man swept over me. I was ashamed of the despicable deceit, the horrible trickery to which I was obliged to resort. At that moment I was filled with self-contempt, and won-dered how I could even have thought of such a cowardly crime. I could not understand how I had brought myself to decide on it." But just as quickly as the doubt crept over him, Felix recalled all of the stories he had heard about the peasant and his evil influence.[7] He told Rasputin that it was time to leave and helped him into his overcoat.

They left the flat by the back staircase and walked to the motorcar where Lazovert waited. After a circuitous route through the dark streets of Petrograd to throw off any police who might be following, Lazovert drove to the Moika Palace. In spite of these precautions, however, the Okhrana agent on duty at Rasputin's apartment block, Tikhomirov, had not only witnessed and made note of Felix's arrival and departure with the peasant but had actually followed them in another motorcar through the capital to the Moika Palace. Tikhomirov now watched as the automobile entered the inner courtyard and deposited Rasputin and his host at a side entrance. They disappeared inside. It was one o'clock in the morning.

Upstairs, in Felix's study, the other conspirators, hearing the arrival of Felix and his victim below, turned on the gramophone; oddly, Felix had only one record, the American marching tune "Yankee Doodle." For the next two hours, the song played over and over again, until it was burned into Purishkevich's mind.

The sounds from the first floor drifted down into the basement room. "What's all this?" Rasputin asked. "Is someone giving a party?"

"No," Felix answered, "just my wife entertaining a few friends; they'll be going soon."[8]

On entering the room, Rasputin threw off his heavy overcoat and began to inspect his surroundings. He seemed particularly taken with the little ebony cabinet by the fireplace and, according to Felix, "took a childlike pleasure in opening and shutting the drawers, exploring it inside and out."[9]

The pair sat down at the table in the middle of the room. In *Lost Splendour*, Felix wrote that he made one last attempt to persuade Rasputin to leave St. Petersburg and that his refusal "sealed his fate."[10] This detail is missing from his earlier book,

Rasputin, published in 1927, and it seems likely that he inserted it for his own benefit.

Felix knew that Protopopov had called on the peasant earlier that day; he asked Rasputin if the minister feared some kind of conspiracy. "Why, yes, my dear boy," Rasputin replied. "The aristocracy can't get used to the idea that a humble peasant should be welcome at the Imperial palace. . . . They are consumed with envy and fear . . . but I'm not afraid of them. They won't do anything to me. I'm protected against ill fortune. There have been several attempts on my life but the Lord has always frustrated these plots. Disaster will come to anyone who lifts a finger against me."[11] To Felix, sitting across the table from his intended victim, these must have been chilling words indeed.

Although Felix offered Rasputin something to drink and eat, the peasant refused. In exasperation, Felix excused himself and disappeared up the narrow staircase to consult with the other conspirators. "Just imagine, gentlemen," he announced, "nothing is going right. The beast will neither eat nor drink. No matter how much I urge him to warm up and accept my hospitality."[12] The others urged Felix to return to the basement to try again; with a shrug, he descended the staircase.

Again, he offered the peasant a plate of cakes; but according to his published accounts, he could not bring himself to offer any of the poisoned pastries. Rasputin again refused, saying, "I don't want any, they're too sweet."[13] But, soon enough, he gobbled down several of the cakes without cyanide. Felix thrust the plate of poisoned cakes at Rasputin, who, finally ate a few of these as well. The poison, according to Lazovert, should have taken effect immediately; however, it appeared to have absolutely no effect. Felix watched in astonishment as Rasputin went on talking calmly. He then suggested that Rasputin might enjoy a glass of Crimean wine from the Youssoupov vineyards; again, Rasputin refused. But Felix moved to the sideboard and poured two glasses of wine—one for himself and one for his guest. Cyanide powder had been sprinkled into several of the glasses but Felix again was reluctant to use a poisoned one. Taking the two glasses, he set down one before Rasputin and himself began to drink from the other. Eventually, Rasputin also drank his wine. He then called for some Madeira. This time Felix was determined to use a poisoned glass, but the peasant insisted that it be poured into the empty wineglass.

"You can't mix red wine with Madeira," Felix protested as he took the glass from the table.

"Never mind; pour it into this glass, I tell you," Rasputin answered.[14]

Felix agreed but managed to break the first glass. He picked up a second one from the sideboard, this one containing cyanide, and filled it with Madeira. Rasputin drank this down slowly, sipping "like a connoisseur."[15] Felix waited for the poison to take effect; but Rasputin continued to sit upright, only occasionally holding his throat as if he were having trouble in swallowing.

"The Madeira's good," Rasputin suddenly said. "Give me some more."[16] Felix filled another glass containing poison and handed it to the peasant, who quickly drained it. "My head reeled," Felix recalled.[17] Rasputin stared at him, smiling one minute and then looking at him deeply, with "fiendish hatred."[18] In an instant, Felix believed that Rasputin knew he had been poisoned. "We seemed to be engaged in a strange and terrible struggle," he wrote. "Another moment and I would have been beaten, annihilated. Under Rasputin's heavy gaze, I felt all my self-possession leaving me; an indescribable numbness came over me. . . ."[19] He later wrote that, at that moment, he nearly fell upon Rasputin and strangled him. Instead, he managed to pull himself together and, saying that he was going upstairs to see whether Irina could join them, excused himself and disappeared up the staircase. From the first floor, the sound of "Yankee Doodle" still filled the palace.

As the night wore on, the other conspirators anxiously awaited Rasputin's death. When Felix appeared for the second time, he looked, according to Purishkevich, "distraught and pale."

"No," Felix exclaimed, "it is impossible. Just imagine, he drank two glasses filled with poison, ate several pink cakes and, as you can see, nothing has happened, absolutely nothing, and that was at least fifteen minutes ago. I cannot think what we can do. . . ."[20] The prince reported that Rasputin lay on the couch below, saying nothing; the only effect he could observe was that he seemed sleepy and complained of a burning in his throat.

"Go back," the others urged him. "The poison is bound to take effect finally but if it nevertheless turns out to be useless, come back after five minutes and we will decide how to finish him off. Time is running out. It is already very late and the morning could find us here with Rasputin's corpse in your palace. . . ."[21] Felix returned to the basement room; it was two o'clock in the morning.

When Felix reentered the basement, he found Rasputin sitting at the table in the middle of the room. The prince offered him a cup of tea, which the peasant accepted. This seemed to revive him. He spotted a guitar and said to Felix, "Play something, something cheerful. I love the way you sing." Felix protested that he did not feel much like singing, but Rasputin begged him, and he reluctantly picked up the guitar and began a Gypsy song.[22] When he finished, the peasant called for another, then another. This went on for the next half hour; when Felix could bear it no longer, he again excused himself and climbed the staircase to the first floor.

By this time, Lazovert's nerves had completely given way; he had already fainted once. When Felix appeared again, the others looked at him in amazement. The prince was hysterical, screaming that he could take no more.

"Ah, well," Grand Duke Dimitri said, "let's forget it for today, let him go in peace. Perhaps we will be able to send him packing in some other way another time and in different circumstances."[23]

"Never!" Purishkevich exclaimed. "Your Highness, don't you understand that if he gets away today, he will have slipped away forever? Do you think that he will come to Youssoupov's tomorrow once he realizes he was tricked? Rasputin cannot, must not, and will not, leave here alive."

"What is to be done, then?" Dimitri Pavlovich asked.

"If the poison doesn't work," Purishkevich replied, "then we must show our hand. Either we must all go downstairs together or you can leave it to me alone."[24] After some hurried consultations, the conspirators decided to attack Rasputin en masse and strangle him. Together they began their descent down the staircase: Purishkevich, resolute in his determination to kill the peasant, leading the way; Felix, completely hysterical; Lazovert, so overcome with anxiety that he could barely walk; and Dimitri Pavlovich and Lieutenant Sukhotin, indifferent and plagued with doubts. Halfway down the staircase, Grand Duke Dimitri suddenly tapped Purishkevich on the shoulder and asked him to wait. He then whispered a few words to Felix, and the group returned to the octagonal hall.

"Will you object if, come what may, I shoot him?" Felix asked. "It will be quicker and simpler." Apparently, Dimitri had suggested this to Felix as a means of ending their nervous game.

"Not at all," Purishkevich replied. "It is not a question of who kills him, but that he be killed, and without fail, tonight."[25] This sudden, decisive action on Felix's part may very well have stemmed from his determination to be the sole assassin of Rasputin, either to lay claim to the glory which he believed would follow or to settle some personal vendetta with the peasant. He took Dimitri's Browning revolver and crept down the staircase once more.

He found Rasputin sitting at the table, his head hung low, his breathing labored. Possibly the poison was, at last, beginning to take effect.

"Are you feeling unwell?" Felix asked.

"Yes, my head is heavy and my stomach is burning. Give me another glass—that will ease me." Felix complied, pouring another glass of poisoned Madeira. In Rasputin's condition, Felix might have expected—even hoped—that this last drink would finally have killed the peasant and thus relieve him from having to shoot him in cold blood. But instead of having any adverse effect on Rasputin, the drink seemed to revive his spirits. Suddenly, according to Felix, and for the second time that evening, he suggested a visit to the Gypsies on the Islands, winking heavily at Felix and saying, "With God in thought but with mankind in the flesh."[26] This remark, if true, once again lends credence to the theory that Rasputin came to the Moika Palace that night only to visit Felix, for if he still expected to meet Irina, he would scarcely have suggested that the pair leave before this had taken place.

Felix finally decided to act. He walked to the ebony cabinet and stared long and hard at the crucifix atop it.

"What are you doing over there so long?" Rasputin finally asked.

"I love this cross," Felix answered. "It's a very beautiful thing."

"Yes, it's a nice thing," Rasputin agreed. "Cost a lot of money, I'm sure. How much did you pay for it?" Without waiting for the answer, he walked to the cabinet. "This is what takes my fancy most," he declared, and again began to examine it in detail.

"Gregory Efimovich," Felix said slowly, "you had better look at the crucifix and say a prayer before it."

Rasputin stared at Felix for a moment, a look of fear in his eyes. Then, wrote Felix, "I saw a new and unfamiliar expression in his eyes, a touch of gentleness and submission. He came right up to me, looking me full in the face, and seemed to read in my glance something which he was not expecting."[27] Later, Felix explained to Maklakov his reasons for leading Rasputin to the crucifix:

> He conveyed to me the sense of horror which overcame him when Rasputin swallowed all the poison they had for him without any effects. Youssoupov, who believed a supernatural force existed, thought that one of these was protecting Rasputin. It might also render a bullet harmless. He decided to exorcise it by a classic method—the Sign of the Cross. Leading Rasputin to the crucifix he reproached him for not crossing himself. And, when Rasputin started to make the Sign of the Cross, thus sending the evil forces away, Youssoupov shot him.[28]

With Rasputin's back turned to him, Felix pulled the revolver from his jacket and took aim at his heart. He eased the trigger back, and the shot rang out. With a "wild scream," Rasputin fell onto the white bearskin rug.[29]

On hearing the shot and the scream, the other conspirators rushed down the staircase to the basement room. On the way in, one of them accidentally brushed against the light switch on the wall, plunging the room into darkness. When they turned the lights on, they saw Felix standing over the body on the floor, a wisp of smoke rising from the revolver muzzle, his features wildly distorted.

No one said a word. Felix himself appeared as if he were in a trance. He continued to point the revolver at Rasputin. The peasant lay on the floor; his breath came in long, agonized gasps, and at times he twitched convulsively. He had covered his eyes with his right hand. A bloodstain slowly seeped across the white silk shirt which he wore. Then Grand Duke Dimitri broke the silence, saying, "We must get him off the rug quickly, just in case, and put him on the tiled part of the floor. His blood might ooze out and stain the bearskin."[30] Dimitri Pavlovich and Purishkevich pulled the body onto the stone floor, and Lazovert bent over to examine him. Soon the twitching stopped, and the doctor proclaimed him dead. Felix turned out the lights, and the conspirators went up to the first floor. It was just after three o'clock in the morning.

In Felix's study, Purishkevich turned off the gramophone, which had been playing "Yankee Doodle" incessantly for the past two and a half hours. The conspirators congratulated each other: All felt that by killing Rasputin they had saved Russia from ruin. Lieutenant Sukhotin dressed in Rasputin's heavy fur overcoat and beaver cap, while Lazovert again donned his chauffeur's uniform. Grand Duke Dimitri joined them this time, and the trio left the Moika Palace for Purishkevich's hospital train to burn the peasant's coat and boots. They would return later to collect the corpse.

Purishkevich settled himself into a comfortable armchair and began to smoke a cigar, while Felix disappeared into his parents' apartments. For unexplained reasons, Felix returned to the basement. He wrote that an "irresistible force impelled me to go down to the murder room."[31] He found the body in the same position as it had been a few minutes earlier. According to Felix, he felt for a pulse; there was none. Then, in a burst of rage, he seized the corpse by the shoulders and shook it violently. He threw the body back against the floor, then again knelt down beside it. Suddenly, the left eye twitched and then opened. In a few seconds, the right eye also opened. "I then saw them both—the green eyes of a viper—staring at me with an expression of diabolical hatred," Felix wrote. "The blood ran cold in my veins. My muscles turned to stone. I wanted to run away, to call for help, but my legs refused to obey me, and not a sound came from my throat."[32]

With a wild roar, Rasputin stumbled to his feet. Flailing his arms about in the air, he managed to grab Felix and rip one of the epaulets from his tunic. His eyes bulged in their sockets, and a thin stream of blood trickled from his lips. Calling, "Felix! Felix!" he again reached for his assassin. "I realized now who Rasputin really was," Felix later wrote. "It was the reincarnation of Satan himself who held me in his clutches and would never let me go until my dying day."[33] Filled with terror, Felix managed to knock the peasant backward and ran for the spiral staircase. Rasputin, crawling on his hands and knees and screaming "like a wounded animal," followed him.

Purishkevich, still smoking his cigar, heard "a wild, inhuman cry" from the basement. Felix burst through the anteroom door, screaming, "Purishkevich, shoot! Shoot! He's alive! He's escaping!" The prince rushed past the older man, his face "white as a sheet," his eyes "bulging out of their sockets," and ran screaming down a palace corridor.[34]

Purishkevich grabbed his revolver and waited at the top of the staircase for Rasputin. But he heard the concealed door on the landing opening into the courtyard and guessed that Rasputin must have found it. He ran down the staircase to find the door ajar.

A few feet ahead of him, Rasputin staggered across the snow-covered courtyard, crying, "Felix! Felix! I will tell the Tsarina everything!" The small courtyard at the side of the palace was enclosed by a low stone wall into which a decorative wrought-iron fence had been set. In the middle of the low wall a set of gates opened to the street. As Rasputin stumbled across the courtyard, the Moika Canal and the dark buildings lining its opposite bank were clearly visible through the railings. He trudged toward the iron gates leading to the Moika Canal. Purishkevich took aim and fired. The shot shattered the stillness of the night. But Rasputin continued to run for the gate: Purishkevich had missed. He took aim a second time and fired but again missed. By this time Rasputin had nearly reached the gate. In a few seconds he would be free. Purishkevich stopped and, with all of his concentration, fired at the distant figure. This shot struck Rasputin in the back. A fourth shot hit him in the head. He fell face first into a snowbank. Purishkevich ran up to him and violently kicked Rasputin in the head. The peasant could not move; his hands clutched convulsively at the snow in an effort to escape, but he could only snarl at Purishkevich. In a few seconds, the movements stopped.

Purishkevich could not drag the body back into the palace by himself; he hurried off to the main entrance, where two soldiers were on guard duty. "Boys," he announced, "I killed Grishka Rasputin, the enemy of Russia and the Tsar." The pair took the news as Purishkevich had hoped, saying, "Thank God, about time."

"Friends," Purishkevich declared, "Prince Felix Felixovich and I rely on your absolute silence. You must understand that if this business is discovered, the Tsarina will not commend us for it. Can you keep quiet?"

"Your Excellency," they answered, "we are Russians, you need not worry, we won't betray you."[35] Purishkevich then embraced and kissed both men, asking them to drag Rasputin's body from the courtyard gate to the small hall at the bottom of the cellar staircase.

Purishkevich went off to find Felix, who was nowhere to be seen. Felix wrote that he had gone round to the front of the Moika Palace to cut off Rasputin's exit should he make it to the courtyard gate. As he raced along the canal, Purishkevich's shots echoed through the night. Felix waited outside the gate, looking up and down the street, but Rasputin failed to appear. After a few minutes, he entered the courtyard and followed the crimson trail across the snow to the peasant's body, lying in a bloody snowbank near one of the gates. The two soldiers Purishkevich had spoken with also ran out, to carry the body inside. Just at that moment, however, a policeman named S. F. Vlasyuk walked through the far set of courtyard gates. Felix carefully placed himself between the body and the gate so that the official would not see the corpse.

"Your Highness," Vlasyuk said, "I heard shots. Has anything happened?"

"No, nothing serious," Felix answered, at the same time directing the policeman toward the gate. "A stupid business. I had some friends with me tonight and one of them drank rather too much, and began shooting and making all this disturbance.

If anybody asks you what's going on just say that everything is all right."[36]

When Felix returned to the body, it had changed positions. Overcome by the thought that Rasputin might still be alive, he fled into the palace, passing the two soldiers who picked up the corpse and carried it into the entrance hall. Purishkevich finally found Felix in his parents' bathroom, leaning over the basin, vomiting. He kept repeating to himself the last words the peasant had spoken to him: "Felix! Felix! Felix! Felix!"[37] Purishkevich put his arm around Felix and led him down the staircase to the entrance hall.

When they entered the hallway, Rasputin lay in a pool of blood on the stone floor. Seeing the corpse, Felix suddenly lost control. He grabbed the steel-and-leather club Maklakov had given him and, rushing at the body, began to beat it about the face and chest.[38] Purishkevich and the two soldiers stood stunned as the prince continued to batter the corpse, spraying blood on the walls of the hallway. Then, coming to his senses, Purishkevich ordered the two soldiers to restrain the prince, who was screaming at the top of his lungs, "Felix! Felix!" As the men pulled him from the corpse, Felix vomited again, then fainted. The men carried him up the staircase and put him on a couch in his nearby study. Felix was completely spattered with Rasputin's blood.

Purishkevich remained in the entrance hall, trying to clean up the bloodstains on the walls and floor. One of the soldiers hurriedly entered and informed him that a policeman had called to inquire about the shots. Purishkevich went to meet him and saw that it was Vlasyuk. He decided to be completely honest with the man.

"Officer," he began, "did you come here a little while ago to inquire about what had happened and why there had been a shooting?"

"That is right, Your Excellency," the policeman replied.

"Do you know me?" Purishkevich asked.

"That is right, I do."

"Who am I, then?"

"State Duma member Vladimir Mitrofanovich Purishkevich."

"Right. But do you know this gentleman?" Purishkevich asked, pointing to the crumpled figure of Felix lying on the couch.

"I do," Vlasyuk answered.

"Who is he?"

"His Highness Prince Youssoupov."

"Right. Listen, brother, answer me honestly: do you love our holy Tsar and Mother Russia? Do you want the victory of Russian arms over the Germans?"

"Of course, Your Excellency, I love the Tsar and the fatherland and I want victory for Russian arms."

"And do you know who is the most evil enemy of the Tsar and of Russia, who hinders our war effort . . . who controls the Tsarina and, through her, makes short work of Russia?"

"Yes!" the policeman exclaimed, "I know. Grishka Rasputin."

"Well," Purishkevich replied, "he's no more. We killed him—it was him we were shooting at just now. You heard, but if anyone asks you, you can say, 'I saw nothing and I know nothing.' Can you manage to be quiet and not betray us?"

"It's like this, Your Excellency," the officer replied slowly. "If they ask me, and I am not under oath, then I will say nothing, but if they put me under oath, then it can't be helped, I will have to tell the whole truth. It would be a sin to lie."[39] With this, Vlasyuk left the Moika Palace.

While this conversation was taking place, the two soldiers from the main door had wrapped the corpse in a heavy blue curtain and bound it with ropes. Purishkevich directed the servants to finish cleaning up the blood and sat down in an armchair to await the return of the other conspirators. Within a few minutes, Dimitri, Sukhotin, and Lazovert walked into Felix's study. Purishkevich quickly informed them of what had transpired during their absence, including the two police visits. All agreed that the body must be removed as quickly as possible. Purishkevich, Grand Duke Dimitri, Dr. Lazovert, and Lieutenant Sukhotin all carried the heavy blue bundle to the motorcar in the courtyard and placed it in the rear seat. This time, Dimitri drove the automobile, with Lieutenant Sukhotin sitting next to him. In the rear seat, on either side of the corpse, were Purishkevich and one of the soldiers from the palace. Lazovert, whose nerves could take no more, stayed behind.

On the floor of the motorcar, Purishkevich noticed Rasputin's heavy overcoat and boots, which were to have been burned by the others. With some irritation, Purishkevich asked why this had not been done and was informed that due to their bulk they had been too difficult to burn. "We'll throw them into the water with the body," he announced to the others. He later remembered that "a nervous tremour" ran through him "at each bump as my knees touched the repulsive, soft corpse" jostling next to him in the rear seat.[40]

The automobile hurried across the frozen, silent city toward Krestovsky Island. At the edge of Petrovsky Island, where a narrow, wooden bridge connected the two strips of land, the motorcar came to a halt. At the far end of the bridge, on the Krestovsky Island side, a tiny hut glowed with light, indicating that the night watchman was on duty. But when the conspirators cautiously checked, they discovered that the man was sleeping. They crept back to the automobile, removed the corpse from the rear seat, and with great effort flung it over the railing into the icy Neva River. The chains and weights which they had purchased to sink the body to the bottom had been forgotten on the floor of the car; these were wrapped around Rasputin's overcoat, which was also hurled into the murky blackness below. In their haste, the conspirators neglected one of Rasputin's boots at the edge of the bridge.

Just after five in the morning, the automobile returned to the Moika Palace. The remaining blood was scrubbed off, and those servants who had been witness to the terrible events that night were gathered and sworn to secrecy. Felix left the Moika Palace for his father-in-law's house, and the other conspirators dispersed to their own residences throughout the frozen capital. "No one noticed us," Purishkevich noted in his diary. "Everyone about us was sleeping in a dead sleep."[41]

(Previous page) Prince Felix Youssoupov, photographed while a student at Oxford University, 1909

(*Above left*) Prince Felix Youssoupov and Princess Irina Alexandrovna, engagement photograph, 1913
(*Above*) Felix in boyar dress for the costume ball at the Albert Hall, London
(*Left*) Felix and Irina with their daughter Irina, 1915 (*Private collection*)

Unless otherwise credited, all photographs are from the author's collection.

The Youssoupov Palace on the
Litieney Prospect in St. Petersburg,
contemporary photograph

The Youssoupov Palace on the Fontanka
Canal in St. Petersburg, designed by
Quarenghi, garden front, contemporary
photograph

Arkhangelskoe, the Tiepolo Room,
contemporary Photograph (*Private
collection*)

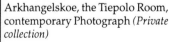

Vladimir Purishkovich
(*Private collection*)

Grand Duchess Elizabeth in the uniform of the Nursing Sisters Order of Mary and Martha, which she founded, 1910

Dowager Empress Marie Feodorovna

Irina modeling a gown from Irfe
(Private collection)

Grand Duke Dimitri Pavlovich and his sister Grand Duchess Marie Pavlovna, 1908

Tsar Nicholas II, 1914

(*Above*) The murder cellar in the Moika Palace as it appeared on the night of 16 December, 1916 (*Private collection*)
(*Right*) The Youssoupov's Moika Palace in St. Petersburg, seen from the canal bridge, contemporary photograph
(*Below*) Rasputin's corpse (*Private collection*)

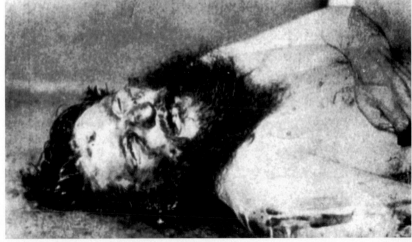

(*Above*) The Petrovsky
Bridge over the Neva
River, from which
Rasputin's body was
thrown by the
conspirators,
contemporary
photograph
(*Right*) Felix and Irina
presiding over a booth at
their Red Cross charity
bazaar, London, 1920
(*Private collection*)
(*Below*) The items
discovered by the Soviets
which Felix had hidden in
the secret room of the
Moscow House (*Private
collection*)

(Above) Felix and Irina on board the *Berengaria* during their visit to America, 1923 *(Private collection)*
(Right) The wedding of Irina Youssoupov to Nicholas Sheremetiev in Rome, 19 June, 1938 *(Private collection)*
(Below) Felix and Irina arriving at court during the CBS Television trial in New York *(Private collection)*

16

The Police Report

Felix awoke just after four in the morning; he had passed out on the sofa in his study. The others had already left to take Rasputin's corpse to the Neva. For some time, he wandered alone through the empty palace, from the murder room to the entrance hall, retracing the pattern of Rasputin's death. He found the soldier who had been left behind, and the two of them tried to clean up the blood. Because the police now knew that Rasputin had been killed in the Moika Palace, Felix quickly took precautions; he decided that a dog would be shot and dragged over the crimson trail in the snow-covered courtyard. When the police inquired, the prince would tell them that one of his guests, after drinking too much, had killed the animal, thus accounting for the bloodstains.

He called in all of the servants who had been present at the Moika Palace that night and informed them of what had happened. All seemed to understand the need for secrecy and pledged to say nothing. At five o'clock that morning, according to Felix, he left the Moika Palace and drove to his father-in-law's house nearby, where he would spend the rest of the night. Upon entering the palace, he found Irina's brother Prince Feodor awaiting his arrival. "Thank God you've come at last!" he said. "Well, what has happened?"

"Rasputin is killed, but I can't say anything more just now. I'm too tired." With this, Felix retired to bed.[1]

This, then, is how the night came to an end, according to Felix. Over the years he never wavered publicly from his version of the events that night—a version supported by Purishkevich's published diary. Of the other conspirators—Dimitri Pavlovich,

Lieutenant Sukhotin, and Dr. Lazovert—none ever spoke publicly of the murder, and so it is on the accounts of Felix and Purishkevich that we have come to rely for information about it. However, these two orthodox versions of the murder are not the only ones we have. There are several other contradictory explanations of the events of that night, all of which need to be examined.

On Saturday, 17 December 1916, an official police report on the disappearance of Rasputin was filed with the chief of the Petrograd military gendarmes. Because it forms an official contradiction in many instances, of the version which Felix later gave it is worth quoting in full:

> Today, at about 2:30 in the morning the policeman who stands on guard at the house of the Home Office situated on the Morskaia heard a detonation from the palace of Prince Youssoupov situated on the opposite side of the Moika. As this post is a special one and the policeman on duty is forbidden to leave it, he went into the Home Office premises and communicated by telephone with the police sergeant on duty at the adjoining station. Then the news of the shooting was passed on to the Kazan police district in which the palace is situated. The chief police officer, Colonel Rogov, with a detachment of men, proceeded to the spot. Examination of the doorman on duty at the adjoining house elicited the fact that the shot had been fired from the young Prince's side of the palace. In order to ascertain the cause of the shooting in the palace, the assistant police officer, Captain Krylov, was ordered to enter the building and he was informed by the butler that a reception was proceeding inside, and that one of the guests, while practicing at a target, had missed his aim and fired into the window, in proof of which Captain Krylov was shown the broken window on the ground floor overlooking the forecourt of the adjoining house. The data obtained through the investigations were communicated by Colonel Rogov the same night to the Police Master of the Second Division, Major-General Grigoniev,

and to M. Chaplygin, the official on duty at the Prefecture.

Scarcely had the police officers left the palace when a motorcar drove up along the Moika Canal quay and stopped near a small footbridge almost facing the palace; four men were seen to alight from the car. The moment they had left it the chauffeur extinguished the lights, and putting on full speed, made off along the canal. This scene was witnessed by a detective belonging to the Okhrana, named Tikhomirov, who had been detailed by the police department to look after Rasputin. Tikhomirov—presuming that the men who entered the palace, not by the main entrance but from a door situated on the side of the palace and opening into the forecourt of the adjoining house, were robbers—hurried across the canal to the police station, and thence telephoned a report of what he had observed to the Chief of the Secret Police.

Colonel Rogov had no sooner returned to his house than he was notified from the Okhrana that information had been received relative to an attack on the palace of Prince Youssoupov. A number of police officers were again dispatched there. The butler came out and explained to them that some very highly placed guests had just arrived from the environs of Petrograd. A report about this was made during the course of the night to the Prefect, General Balk.

Shortly after 6AM, at the police station beside the palace, while the police officers who had come off duty were being questioned in the ordinary course as to the events of the night, the sound of several police whistles was heard from the street. This drew the constables and police sergeants to the windows, whence they perceived that from the main entrance of the Prince's palace two women were being helped out, and that they were offering resistance to their ejection, and refusing to enter a motorcar, and doing their best to force a way back into the palace. In response to their protestations the detectives stationed along the canal had sounded the alarm. By the

time the police rushed out of the police station the motorcar was already whirling off along the quay. Hastening
out after his men, the police inspector, Colonel Borozdin,
hailed the motorcar belonging to the secret police, which
was permanently on duty at the Home Office, and started
off in pursuit. At the same time his men were hurried to
the palace. It was impossible to overtake the fugitive car
on account of its superior speed; moreover, it carried neither numbers nor lights. To the police who came to inquire at the palace the explanation was offered that two
ladies belonging to the *demi monde* had been misconduct-
ing themselves and had been invited to leave the palace.

On the nocturnal adventures on the Moika a joint
personal report was made to the Prefect in the morning
by Colonel Rogov and Captain Borozdin. The whole affair
seemed to be at an end when suddenly from the forecourt
alongside the palace four shots were heard in rapid succession. Once more the alarm was sounded in both police
stations and again detachments of police appeared at the
palace. This time an official wearing a colonel's uniform
came out to them and announced categorically that within
the palace there was present a Grand Duke and that
H.I.H. would make in person to the proper quarters any
explanations that might be necessary. After such a decla-
ration, the police inspector, unable to obtain any enlightenment whatsoever, returned to his office, leaving a patrol
on the opposite side of the Moika by way of precaution.
About an hour had passed when suddenly from the direction of the Blue Bridge a motorcar drove up to the palace.
The servants, assisted by the chauffeur, in the presence of
an officer wearing a long fur cloak, carried out what
looked like a human body and placed it in the car. The
chauffeur jumped in and, putting on full speed, made off
along the canal side and promptly disappeared. Almost at
the same time, General Grigoriev was informed from the
Prefecture that Rasputin had been killed in the Youssoupov Palace.

The police officials on arriving at the palace were
met this time by Prince Felix Youssoupov, who told them

that it would be necessary to draw up a report as to the killing of Rasputin. At first this announcement was not accepted seriously in view of all the strange occurrences of the night. But the police officials were invited to come to the dining room in the basement and there were shown the spot where the body had been lying. They saw on the floor a pool of congealed blood, and traces of blood were also visible on the snow in the forecourt of the adjoining house. In answer to the question where the body was, the Prince replied that the body was where it should be, declining to give any further explanation.

Soon afterwards the palace was visited by the Director of the Police Department, the Chief of the Secret Police, and the whole of the Generals of the Gendarmes. The police patrols were then relegated to their various stations, and at the subsequent investigation sent over to the officials of the police department. At five o'clock on the following afternoon a secret telegram was sent to every police station with a view to ascertaining the itinerary of the motorcars which had come up to the Prince's palace during the night, and of the one which had removed Rasputin's body in the morning. At the same time numerous police patrols were dispatched to the islands in the Neva and to the suburban districts.[2]

This report calls into question the versions of the murder as given by Felix and Purishkevich in many respects. First, there are obvious problems with the times given by the conspirators and those listed in the police report. The report records the first shot at two-thirty in the morning, which is close enough to the time Felix says he shot Rasputin in the basement. But from that point on the accounts diverge. Half an hour after the first shot, Captain Krylov was led to a room in the basement of the Moika Palace and shown a broken window; at this time, Rasputin allegedly still lay in the cellar. Either Krylov was shown a different room, or Rasputin's body had been moved. Neither Felix nor Purishkevich mentions this visit in their accounts, although both were certainly aware of it. There can be no question that it indeed took place, and its omission suggests that other details of events that evening were deliberately altered or ignored by both of the two participants who left accounts of the murder.

Just after this, an automobile drew up at the side entrance of the palace, and four men exited. The car then drove off. We know from both the accounts left by Felix and Purishkevich that Grand Duke Dimitri Pavlovich, Lieutenant Sukhotin, and Dr. Lazovert left the palace after the initial shooting to dispose of Rasputin's fur coat; they did not return, however—according to Purishkevich—until well after Rasputin had been killed in the courtyard. As the police report makes clear, the two other cars which arrived at the palace that night carried no passengers with them. Therefore, this car must have been the one bringing the men back to the Moika Palace or bringing four other participants in the murder. Because we know that Lazovert was allegedly driving Purishkevich's motorcar, he could not have been one of the four men who exited at the palace; although Grand Duke Dimitri and Lieutenant Sukhotin were with him, this still leaves two unnamed men who entered the palace. If we discount Purishkevich's account that Lazovert was driving the automobile and accept that he was one of the four passengers, this still leaves one man unaccounted for, according to the police report. Neither Felix nor Purishkevich mentions anyone else present other than themselves, Dimitri, Lazovert, and Sukhotin. But clearly, from the official report, at least one, and perhaps two, other men were at the palace that night. It is possible that one or both of these mysterious men could have been the young officers who assisted Purishkevich in the removal of the body, although the timing of the event conflicts with the versions as given by both Felix and the Duma member.

It is also clear from the police report that two women were present at the palace during the murder. They were seen being forcibly ejected just after six in the morning. Again, neither Felix nor Purishkevich mention this fact. Just after this, four shots were heard; these can only have been Purishkevich's shots as he chased Rasputin across the courtyard. But both Felix and Purishkevich put this event nearly three hours earlier, shortly after three o'clock. A few minutes later, the police officer dispatched to the palace met with an unknown man in a colonel's uniform who informed him that a grand duke was present in the house. This man's identity remains a mystery.

According to the police report, Rasputin's body was not removed from the palace until sometime between seven and seven-thirty in the morning—again, significantly later than both Felix and Purishkevich claim. Sometime between seven-thirty and eight o'clock, Felix himself showed a visiting official the bloodstained basement room and told him that Rasputin had been killed. Not only does Felix fail to mention this important fact in either of his two books dealing with the subject, he also says that at five o'clock in the morning he was at Irina's father's house going to bed.

These discrepancies call into question both Felix's and Purishkevich's accounts of the murder. There is no reason to disbelieve the police report; however, if Rasputin had been killed in a manner different from that given by the two principal assassins, they may have wished to keep this fact a secret. One might conclude that the police report was simply wrong in its details but for the fact that there is independent confirmation for much of what it contains.

On the question of the unknown men who were at the Moika Palace, a private police memorandum circulated in Petrograd the day after the murder disclosed their names: Feodor and Nikita Alexandrovich, Felix's brothers-in-law. Neither of these two men ever admitted to being in the palace on the night of the murder. This same report also confirms that two women were present at the palace. In addition, it gives an account of Rasputin's murder unlike those of either Felix or Purishkevich. According to the memorandum, Rasputin, once in the basement room, was handed a loaded revolver and told that he must either commit suicide or be killed. Rasputin refused to kill himself; instead, he took aim at Grand Duke Dimitri. The bullet missed, smashing into one of the windows. The others in the room then killed the peasant.[3]

This story matches nicely with the known facts. It accounts for the mysterious presence of the two unknown men at the palace as well as the women who were ejected in the morning and also explains the broken window shown to Captain Krylov on his visit. On the question of the women present, this fact seems to have been common knowledge at the time. Bertie Stopford, a friend of Felix's who heard the details of the murder from the prince himself, recorded, on the basis of this information, that two women had been present that night.[4] Anna Vyrubova wrote in her book that she knew one of these women personally.[5] There seems little doubt that two women were present at the palace and that both Felix and Purishkevich deliberately kept this fact a secret. Additionally, another of Felix's cousins on his father's side, Vladimir Lazurov—who, as a boy had joined the prince in his early transvestite escapades—apparently declared that he, too, had been present at the Moika Palace that night and had participated in the murder. All of this again raises questions as to both Felix's and Purishkevich's veracity concerning other events of that night.

Prince Serge Obolensky, another of Felix's cousins, also had his doubts as to the honesty of the prince's published version of the murder. "I could not imagine Felix cold-bloodedly carrying out a murder plot," he wrote. "He was not in any way a conspirator or killer. On the contrary, he was too generous and too kind, a man with a great heart, fundamentally religious and deeply mystical."[6] Obolensky, of course, was writing in defense of his cousin. But he heard the details of the event from Felix and in his book related that he believed Felix's Abyssinian servant Thesphe had participated in the murder, fixing the poisoned drinks and actually shooting the peasant.[7]

Aaron Simanovich, Rasputin's secretary and trusted adviser, left a very different account of his master's murder. He was sufficiently well informed that one would expect his sources to be reliable. Simanovich personally spoke with not only Rasputin's daughters and members of his small household but also with the tsarina, Minister of the Interior Alexander Protopopov, and Vera Korelli, a cousin of Felix's. Simanovich later wrote:

> What actually happened we were told later by a cousin of Youssoupov's, who herself had fired a shot at Rasputin. Those involved in the plot, among others, were Grand Duke Dimitri Pavlovich and two sons of Grand Duke Alexander Michailovich. As Rasputin entered all assembled

fired at him with the exception of Vera Korelli, a dancer and cousin of Youssoupov's. Rasputin fell to the floor and, thinking him dead, the plotters bundled him into his coat and took him down to the cellar. Astonishingly, Rasputin revived after a time, left the cellar and tried to climb out of the grounds over a high wall. This proved to be too much for him and he fell back unconscious. Dogs found him and their barking brought the Household to the scene.[8]

The most startling version of the events of that night comes from Rasputin's daughter Maria. In 1977, in the last of her three books on her father, she related:

Suddenly his tormentors came for him *en masse*, as he desperately tried to push them away. But it was useless. He caught sight of Felix, whose eyes were glassy and set, and said, "May God forgive you."

Having used him sexually, Felix finally pulled forth the gun and fired a single shot into Papa's head as he was struggling to his feet. Papa fell backward, onto the bearskin rug. Blood began to spread across the white fur from the wound in Papa's head.

"Is he dead?" asked Youssoupov.

"No, a little wine will fix him up," volunteered one of the men as he grabbed a half-filled glass and promptly threw it into Papa's face.

"What do they want of me?" Papa mumbled, half-conscious, "what do they want?"

Suddenly, things began to happen more swiftly. As if programmed for this very moment, the men moved in unison and with precision over my father's body. There was much kicking, punching and gouging at the inert body lying on the now bloodstained rug.

One of the men drew a dagger and, pushing aside the man who was still straddled across the lower extremities of my father, rapidly tore away at the remains of his trousers. Some say it was Felix who wielded the knife; others say differently.

In any event they all hovered close, watching as the deed was committed. With the skill of a surgeon these elegant young members of the nobility castrated Gregory Rasputin and flung the severed penis across the room.[9]

Patte Barham, who coauthored this last book with Maria Rasputin, related that she heard this story from the sister-in-law of one of the prince's servants, a butler called Paul. Coincidentally, the head butler in the Moika Palace was named Paul. Barham also writes that on a visit to Paris she was actually shown the severed penis, kept in a velvet case and jealously guarded by a group of fanatical émigrés.[10] It should be pointed out that after Rasputin's body was recovered from the Neva, an autopsy was begun, and the report contained no mention of castration.

Much of this secondary evidence is contradictory in itself. None of the versions agree with each other or with the accounts left by Felix and Purishkevich. Yet obviously, on the basis of the official police report, the tale told by both main participants is inaccurate in many instances. All of those involved in the events of 16 December 1916 are now dead. The best that we can do is fit the known facts into a sequence of events and speculate on what may have happened. Based on the available evidence, it is possible to reconstruct a plausible scenario for Rasputin's murder, contradictory in many respects to the accounts left by Felix and Purishkevich but in accord with the known facts.

Felix and Rasputin arrived at the Moika Palace shortly after one o'clock in the morning. It seems likely that poison was the intended method of death. As Alex De Jonge points out, "Poisoning is a splendid method for a would be-killer in cold blood who is also the victim's host. At no stage does he actually have to reveal that he is about to commit murder, he simply watches and waits. He thereby avoids the terrible moment of naked embarrassment when both parties know what is about to happen and look one another in the eye."[11] Although the poison failed to take immediate effect, as the conspirators had hoped, there is nothing supernatural in this. Considering Felix's stated reluctance to offer Rasputin any of the poisoned cakes and wine, we cannot accurately know how much poison the peasant ingested. Maria Rasputin later wrote:

I am convinced that certain details given by the assassins were added partly to make the story more picturesque and partly to excuse the slaughter. . . . I am positive that my father did not eat poisoned cakes, for he had a horror of sweet things. If he drank a glass of muscat mixed with cyanide, doubtless the poison had not dissolved but settled at the bottom of the flask, and it was for that reason that he did not feel its effects.[12]

There is another explanation for the poison's failure to act. In *Rasputin and the Fall of the Romanovs*, Colin Wilson relates that the peasant suffered from acute alcoholic gastritis, which would have lengthened the time needed for the poison to take effect.[13] There were also repeated rumors of a deathbed confession by Lazovert in which he alleged that he had deliberately substituted a harmless chemical at the last minute. In any case, when the poison failed to have the desired effect, the conspirators resorted to other means.

It is likely, based on the evidence, that when Felix reentered the basement room for the last time, he was not alone. According to his cousin Vera Korelli, Felix, Purishkevich, Dimitri Pavlovich, Lazovert, Sukhotin, Princes Feodor and Nikita Alexandrovich, one other woman, and herself all turned on the peasant. He may or may not have been given the choice of either killing himself or being killed. In any event, one shot was fired—the shot recorded in the police report at two-thirty in the morning. If this first shot struck the basement window shown to Captain Krylov, then obviously Rasputin was killed by other means—possibly by being beaten or strangled. The appearance of the corpse after its discovery in the Neva supports the conclusion that he was subjected to many severe blows—blows which, according to Felix, came only after the four shots fired by Purishkevich but which could in fact have been inflicted much earlier.

It is difficult to determine how many conspirators were present in the Moika Palace; because neither Felix nor Purishkevich mentions Princes Feodor and Nikita Alexandrovich or the two women, it is possible that there were others in attendance as well. Although the evidence suggests that the two sons of Grand Duke Alexander Michailovich were there, the time of their arrival at the palace remains a question. Vera Korelli places them in the murder room at the time of the first shot—that is, at two-thirty. But they may not actually have arrived at the Moika Palace until just after three, when the mysterious car drew up outside the entrance and deposited the four men. In this case, it is likely that they were collected by another of the conspirators, perhaps Dimitri Pavlovich, and brought to the palace to help in the disposal of the body, arriving after the actual murder.

At six in the morning the two women left the Moika Palace and were observed by the policeman on duty. Their departure may have been an attempt to distract or confuse the police. Between three and six, Rasputin's body must have lain in the cellar. At some point, Felix returned to the basement room, which corresponds with the account of Purishkevich and also with that of the prince himself. Purishkevich later hinted that something strange had happened between Felix and Rasputin while the prince was alone with the body, but gave no details.[14] Alex De Jonge thinks that Felix "abused the body sexually in some way."[15] By this time, Felix was indeed probably capable of such action, and certainly his dealings with the peasant were dominated by a sexual fascination.

As to the allegation that the prince castrated Rasputin, this would have been entirely in keeping with the character of the murder and added an ironic twist to the killing. The removal of Rasputin's penis would have been a symbolic act in light of the scandalous rumors surrounding his sexual adventures. In addition, if some form of homosexual relationship existed between Felix and Rasputin, castration might have been a further way for the prince to free himself from the sexual hold the peasant had on him. But there is no authoritative evidence that Rasputin was castrated.

Whatever happened in the basement room, Rasputin recovered sufficiently to make an escape attempt. Purishkevich chased him across the courtyard, firing the four shots noted in the police report. These proved fatal to the peasant. By seven in the morning, the body had been removed from the palace and thrown into the Neva.

The only remaining mystery is why Felix, after taking measures to ensure the secrecy of the act, led a visiting police official to the murder room, showed him the bloodstains, and announced that Rasputin had been killed. The answer to this most probably lies in Felix's motivation for killing the peasant; whatever circumstances or personal feelings may have caused him to act, he believed that by removing Rasputin, he would be hailed as Russia's savior. Affecting an air of self-importance, therefore, would have been entirely in keeping in a man convinced that he was fulfilling a role predetermined by destiny.

We will probably never know with any certainty the true nature of the events of that night at the Moika Palace. But it clearly would be a mistake to accept without question the accounts left by Felix and Purishkevich. Time and the stories of others have shown that Felix used his version of the murder to achieve his own ends and carefully presented the version which served him the best. In the end, truth, as well as Rasputin, fell victim to Prince Felix Youssoupov.

17

Discovery

Aт TEN O'CLOCK ON THE MORNING of 17 December, a servant woke Felix with the news that General Grigoriev, the Kazan District chief of police, wished to speak with him regarding the disturbance at the Moika Palace the previous night. According to Felix, Grigoriev declared that Rasputin was missing and that police reports filed early that morning seemed to indicate that this disappearance was somehow connected with what had happened at the Moika Palace. Specifically, according to Grigoriev, Purishkevich had bragged to one of the policemen that he had shot the peasant.

From the official report filed later that day, we know that Felix himself had also confessed to participation in Rasputin's murder. Now, confronted with the true implications of the act and more sober in thought, he apparently tried to conceal the assassination. To Grigoriev, he explained that Rasputin had telephoned just after midnight and asked the prince to join him on a visit to the Gypsies. Felix, who declared that he had been hosting a small party that night, told Grigoriev that he had declined Rasputin's invitation. The party at the Moika Palace had ended around three that morning, when Grand Duke Dimitri Pavlovich, in a drunken state, had shot one of Youssoupov's dogs in the mouth. As for Purishkevich's confession, Felix explained this away by stating that the Duma member had also been drunk and had merely been comparing Rasputin to the dog.

To bolster this story, Felix showed Grigoriev the body of a large dog, which lay in the palace courtyard against a bank of snow. The dead animal explained the presence of the bloodstains, which were clearly visible spread across the white courtyard. Felix had actually instructed one of his servants to shoot a dog in the mouth and drag the corpse around the courtyard in an attempt to disguise the trail left by Rasputin. He had also taken scent bottles and poured their contents across the bloody trail. In a final effort to avert suspicion, Felix declared, "The people who organized Rasputin's murder—if that has actually occurred—planned carefully and deliberately to connect the crime with me and my party." But Grigoriev was not fooled. He returned to police headquarters and informed the chief of the Petrograd police, V. V. Vassieliev, that the disappearance of Rasputin was almost certainly connected to the events of the previous evening at the Moika Palace.[1]

Later that same morning, Munya Golovine rang Felix up, demanding, "What have you done with Gregory Efimovich?"

"With Gregory Efimovich?" Felix asked. "What a strange question."

"What?" she exclaimed. "Wasn't he with you yesterday? Then where is he? Come and see me quickly, for God's sake! I am in a terrible state of mind." Felix reluctantly complied. When he arrived at the Golovine house, Munya greeted him hysterically, crying, "Tell me, for God's sake, where is Gregory Efimovich? What have you done with him? They say that he was killed in your house and that you are his murderer." Munya told Felix that she had already spoken with the empress at Tsarskoe Selo and that Alexandra felt certain that Rasputin had been killed at the Moika Palace.

"Ring up Tsarskoe at once," Felix asked Munya. "If the Empress will receive me, I will explain everything to her."[2] Munya did as asked, and the empress consented to meet with Felix that afternoon. Just as he was leaving, however, the telephone rang; it was Anna Vyrubova: She announced that Alexandra had changed her mind: If Felix had anything to say to her, he should submit a letter explaining Rasputin's disappearance.

Returning to the Moika Palace, Felix found an automobile waiting to take him to see General Balk, the prefect of police. After again repeating the story of the dog having been shot, the prince was informed that the empress had ordered a search of the Moika Palace. "My wife," Felix declared angrily, "is a niece of the Emperor. Members of the imperial family and their residences are inviolable, and measures against them cannot be taken except by order of His Majesty the Emperor himself."[3] With this, Felix dismissed the officer.

But it was too late to stop the investigation. Felix quickly learned that all of his servants had been interrogated while he was out. A full search of the Moika Palace had also been started, and from the amount of blood found in the cellar, on the staircase, in the courtyard, and in the entrance hall, the police were left with little doubt that someone had indeed been killed there. When Felix heard that the police had traced the trail of blood, he made plans to leave Petrograd for the Crimea to join his family. He had a few suitcases packed and, along with three of his brothers-in-law and Capt. Oswald Rayner, an attaché at the British embassy, set off for the train station. Upon his arrival, however, he found a group of officers waiting to take him into custody. "By Her Majesty's orders you are forbidden to leave Petrograd," one of them announced. "You must return to the Palace and remain there until further instructions."[4] Under police escort, Felix drove to his father-in-law's palace, where a twenty-four-hour guard was posted.

The following morning, Felix moved into the Belossielsky-Belossievsky Palace, where Grand Duke Dimitri lived. The guard posted at Grand Duke Alexander's palace followed him, and at noon they were supplemented by a police deputation which arrived to put Dimitri under house arrest, on orders of the empress. When he learned of this development, Dimitri was furious: Only the tsar could, by law, order the arrest of a member of the imperial family. Felix and Dimitri had no choice but to wait and worry.

Not content with the police inquiries, the empress ordered Alexander Protopopov to begin a full investigation. To her absent husband, Alexandra wrote:

> My Own Beloved Sweetheart:
>   We are sitting together—you can imagine our feelings—thoughts—Our Friend has disappeared.
>   Yesterday, Anna saw him and said Felix asked him to come in the night, a motor would fetch him, to see Ir-

ina. A motor fetched him (a military one) with two civilians and it went away.

This night, big scandal at Youssoupov's house—big meeting, Dimitri, Purishkevich, etc., all drunk—police heard shots, Purishkevich ran out screaming to the police that Our Friend was killed. . . . Our Friend was in good spirits but nervous these days. Felix pretends he never came to the house. . . . I shall still trust in God's mercy that one has only driven him off somewhere. Protopopov is doing all he can. . . . I cannot and won't believe he has been killed. God have mercy, such utter anguish (am calm and can't believe it). . . . Come quickly. . . .

Felix came often to him lately.[5]

It had been less than twenty-four hours since Rasputin's disappearance, but the empress already possessed the main details of the crime. The tsar immediately answered, "Am horrified and shaken. In prayers and thoughts I am with you. Am arriving tomorrow at five o'clock."[6] But the atmosphere at headquarters was far from sad: Celebratory toasts were exchanged, officers congratulated each other, and even the tsar seemed relieved that the Rasputin affair might have come to an end. Pierre Gilliard, the tsarevich's tutor, accompanied the tsar back to the capital. On arriving at Tsarskoe Selo, he noted the empress's "agonized features" and "inconsolable grief . . . her idol had been shattered. The only person who could save her son was killed. Any misfortune, any catastrophe, was now possible that he was gone. The time of waiting began, that terrible waiting for the disaster which could not be escaped."[7]

By nightfall on the day after the murder, all of Petrograd knew of Rasputin's disappearance. Under heavy censorship, the press still could not refer to Rasputin by name. Thus, one highly cryptic account read:

A certain person visited another person with some other persons. After the first person vanished, one of the other persons stated that the first person had not been at the house of the second person, although it was known that the second person had visited the first person late at night.[8]

Another equally evasive account conveyed the drama of the event:

> A heavy frost. The waters of the capital are held by ice, silent, dusted with snow are the gardens. But over the still capital hover strange nightmares. In the depths of the night shots ring out in a dead garden, secret cars hurry across the city carrying corpses and live men. . . . Fantasic nightmares weave a poisonous fog and turn into horrid reality.[9]

This same edition was also the first newspaper to connect the disappearance of Rasputin with the mysterious events at the Moika Palace the evening before. "It was dark upstairs, and the darkness of the wide window was just as secret and intriguing as the riddle of the secret events that have been occupying all our minds," the paper declared.[10] Only the *Stock Exchange News* defied the restrictions, announcing "Death of Gregory Rasputin in Petrograd," at the bottom of page 2 in bold typeface. "This morning at 6 o'clock," the paper declared, "Gregory Efimovich Rasputin suddenly passed away at one of the most aristocratic houses in the center of Petrograd after a party."[11] Within an hour, copies of this newspaper were either sold out or had been confiscated by the police.

Given the halfhearted attempts at secrecy, Purishkevich's repeated confidences to others prior to the crime, and both his and Felix's spontaneous confessions the night before, it is not surprising that most of Petrograd knew the general details of Rasputin's murder within hours of its completion. No one seems to have expressed much surprise. The feeling of elation over the alleged murder, however, was tempered by a growing fear on the part of the conspirators. Purishkevich, hearing of the guard ordered by the empress to keep watch on both Felix and Dimitri, left the capital for the front on 18 December, escorted by friendly security agents of the military police. Then, suddenly, the story disappeared from the pages of Petrograd's newspapers as everyone waited for the next development: the discovery of the body.

On 18 December 1916, investigators discovered a trail of blood on the Petrovsky Bridge; upon further examination, they found a boot lying beneath an arch next to a hole in the frozen river. Rasputin's daughters tearfully identified the boot as having belonged to their missing father. The police also apparently managed to isolate and trace a set of distinctive tire tracks which led across the frozen city from the snowy courtyard of the Moika Palace to the edge of the Petrovsky Bridge. The two locations, both stained with blood, were now linked.

Divers began an immediate search of the Neva. The next day, 19 December, they finally located the corpse some six hundred feet downriver. Using grappling hooks, they pulled it to the surface. Rasputin had evidently been alive at the time he was bound with rope, for he had made an attempt to raise his arms as if to free himself. Both forearms were contracted toward his upper torso. He still wore his black trousers and white silk peasant blouse, though the later was torn and stained with blood. His eyes were open and staring. Officials quickly covered his body with a blanket, loaded it into an ambulance, and drove it to the Chesme Workhouse just outside the capital, on the road leading to Tsarskoe Selo.

The body was frozen solid, and officials had to wait a full day before conducting the autopsy. Maria Rasputin, then eighteen years old, came to the workhouse to identify her father. She later wrote: "The face was almost unrecognizable: clots of dark blood had coagulated in the beard and hair; one eye was almost out of its socket and on the wrists were deep marks left by the bonds that my father had succeeded in breaking in his death struggle, probably when, reanimated by the sudden shock of the freezing water, he had made a supreme effort to escape from his prison of ice."[12]

Professor Kossorotov began a formal autopsy on 20 December. He found that Rasputin had been shot three times, once in the head and apparently twice in the back—wounds which closely match those described by both Felix and Purishkevich.

In addition, the head and upper body had been horribly battered, wounds possibly inflicted during Youssoupov's beating. Rasputin's arms also bore apparent stab wounds, which appeared to be defensive in nature. The lungs were found to contain water, suggesting that the peasant had still been alive when he was thrown into the Neva and that he had drowned. This was certainly a devastating piece of news to Rasputin's most hysterical devotees; according to the traditions of the Russian Orthodox Church, no potential saint could die by drowning. The persistent legend that Rasputin had freed one of his hands and made the sign of the cross before his death rests entirely on the evidence of his daughter Maria. Certainly, his right arm was raised at the elbow, but this may have been nothing more than an attempt to escape his bonds.

The autopsy remains one of the most controversial and mysterious elements in Rasputin's murder. Although virtually every writer and historian on the subject makes reference to its findings, no one has yet been able to produce the actual document. When Empress Alexandra learned that Professor Kossorotov had taken it upon himself to conduct a postmortem examination, she gave orders that the investigation be stopped at once, saying, "Just leave the body of Gregory Efimovich Rasputin in peace."[13] Kossorotov's findings thus remain incomplete. It is therefore impossible to settle once and for all such legendary and important questions as the issue of Rasputin's raised hand or his alleged castration.[14]

The empress asked a nun named Sister Akulina to prepare the body for burial. She washed the corpse and dressed it in a white shroud. Finally, Rasputin's body was placed in a plain, polished-oak coffin, purchased by Alexandra. An Orthodox cross decorated the top of the casket. The coffin was placed in the workhouse chapel, where the Orthodox liturgy for the dead was sung in the presence of Rasputin's daughters and several of his followers, including Anna Vyrubova.

Rasputin was buried on 21 December. At first, arrangements were made to transport the body back to Pokrovskoe in Siberia, but Protopopov, the minister of the interior, feared that such a move would attract crowds and attention. Instead, Anna Vyrubova suggested that the peasant be buried beneath the center aisle of a new church she was building in the park at Tsarskoe Selo. Rasputin's family—his wife, Praskovie, and two daughters, Maria and Varvara—attended the short service. Lili Dehn, a friend of the empress's, recalled:

> It was a glorious morning. The sky was a deep blue, the sun was shining and the hard snow sparkled like masses of diamonds. My carriage stopped on the road . . . and I was directed to walk across a frozen field toward the unfinished church. Planks had been placed on the snow to serve as footpaths and when I arrived at the church I noticed that a police motor van was drawn up near the open grave. After waiting several minutes I heard the sound of sleigh bells and Anna Vyrubova came slowly across the field. Almost immediately afterwards a closed automobile stopped and the Imperial Family joined us. They were dressed in mourning and the Empress carried some white flowers; she was very pale but quite composed although when the oak coffin was taken out of the police van I saw her tears fall . . . and the burial service was read by the chaplain and after the Emperor and Empress had thrown earth on the coffin, the Empress distributed her flowers between the Grand Duchesses and ourselves and we scattered them on the coffin.[15]

Before the coffin was closed, Alexandra placed two objects on Rasputin's chest. One was an icon, signed by herself, her husband, and their children.[16] The other was a letter, written by the empress herself: "My Dear Martyr, Give me thy blessing that it may follow me always on the sad and dreary path I have yet to follow here below. And remember us from on high with your holy prayers. Alexandra."[17]

Rasputin remained in his grave for less than three months. A week after the Revolution, in March 1917, a group of drunken soldiers broke into the unfinished church and disinterred the body. When the coffin was opened, Rasputin's face had turned black and the body smelled horrible. The icon laid on Rasputin's chest by the empress was stolen; subsequently, it was sold to an American collector. The soldiers apparently battered the rotting corpse and defecated on it. According to at least one source, the soldiers used a brick to measure Rasputin's penis, which, if true, would disprove the castration story.[18] The men put the corpse into a packing case and transported it to the old imperial stables in the Pargolovo Forest nearby. A funeral pyre was hastily constructed out of pine logs and the body placed on it and drenched with gasoline, then set ablaze. For over six hours, the fire burned as groups of terrified peasants watched from the forest. When it was over, the soldiers gathered up what remained and buried it in the snow, casting the ashes into the icy wind. It all happened as Rasputin had once predicted: After his death, he said, his body would not be left in peace but burned and his remains carried away by the wind.

18

The Reaction

News of Rasputin's death caused a spontaneous eruption of joy among the citizens of Petrograd. At the Cathedral of Our Lady of Kazan, crowds surged forward to light candles before the icon of St. Dimitri, and photographic shops quickly sold out of pictures of Prince Felix Youssoupov, Grand Duke Dimitri, and Purishkevich. One visitor to Petrograd at the time noted, "The very cabmen in the street are rejoicing over the removal of Rasputin and they and many others think that by this the German influence has received a check."[1] At the theaters, crowds lustily sang the national anthem, men walking down the Nevsky Prospect embraced each other, and champagne flowed freely in the clubs and palaces lining the Neva. The reaction abroad was just as jubilant: The *Times* of London printed photographs of Felix and Irina with the caption "The Saviours of Russia."

The Russian peasant, however, found no glory in Rasputin's murder. One man, returning to the capital from the provinces, reported to the French ambassador, "To the *moujiks*, Rasputin has become a martyr. He was a man of the people, he let the Tsar hear the voice of the people; he defended the people against the court folk, the *pridvorny*. So the *pridvorny* killed him. That's what's being said."[2]

Surprisingly, the most violent reaction came from members of the imperial family who had for so long clamored for Rasputin's murder. Felix's father-in-law, Grand Duke Alexander Michailovich, was less than enthusiastic about the assassination. "Rasputin alive was just a man," he wrote, "known to everybody as a drunken peasant. . . . Rasputin dead stood a chance of becoming a slaughtered prophet."[3] The tsar's own sister, Grand Duchess Olga Alexandrovna, later said: "There was nothing heroic about Rasputin's murder. It was ... premeditated most vilely. Just think of the two names most closely associated with it even to this day—a Grand Duke, one of the grandsons of the Tsar-Liberator, and then a scion of one of our great houses whose wife was a Grand Duke's daughter. That proved how far we had fallen."[4]

It so happened that the British embassy in Petrograd, at the invitation of Grand Duke Dimitri Pavlovich, had set up the Anglo-Russian Hospital in the first floor rooms of the Belossielsky-Belossievsky Palace. Lady Sybil Grey, daughter of Earl Grey, ran the hospital which treated British and Russian officers wounded at the front. Lady Sybil, living one floor beneath the two most prominent of Rasputin's assassins, was privy to all of the important gossip and latest developments in the case. In a candid letter to her brother-in-law, she reported:

> I wouldn't be out of Russia for anything now. It is curious isn't it that things of immense moment and importance can only be accomplished by intrigue and murder. Can you imagine Tecks, Connaughts, etc., doing the like in England. But the funny thing is that here one fits into the atmosphere to such an extent that one realizes that it was the only thing to be done and that it was right and one thoroughly approves of the thing itself although perhaps not of the way it was carried out.[5]

Felix himself was quickly caught up in his newfound fame. He had almost certainly expected as much. Dimitri Pavlovich's sister Grand Duchess Marie Pavlovna wrote that he seemed "intoxicated by the importance of the part that he had played and saw in it a great political future."[6] He received hundreds of letters and telegrams congratulating him on his action. One letter, intercepted by the Okhrana, came from Lower-Novgorod:

> What was done was what the people thirsted for. The rot has been uncovered, the first vermin has been disposed of. Grishka is no more, only his stinking body which pre-

sents no danger remains. . . . But there are still many dark forces partaking with Rasputin, building their nest in Russia in the person of the Tsarina and other trash and degenerate animals of human refuse.[7]

Unlike Felix, Dimitri Pavlovich was soon overwhelmed with a tremendous sense of guilt. At first, when confronted by his father, Grand Duke Paul Alexandrovich, Dimitri swore on an icon and a photograph of his late mother that he had not killed Rasputin.[8] He explained to his sister, however, that by killing Rasputin he had hoped "to urge action, by example of action, all in one decisive stroke."[9] Eventually, in exile, however, Dimitri realized the utter futility of having participated in the murder— in the words of a member of the Duma, "What was the use in killing the snake after it had already struck its poisonous blow?"[10] Grand Duchess Marie Pavlovna later wrote:

> His death came too late to change the course of events.
> His dreadful name had become too thoroughly a symbol
> of disaster. The daring of those who killed him to save
> their country was miscalculated. All of the participants in
> the plot, with the exception of Prince Youssoupov, later
> understood that in raising their hands to preserve the old
> regime they struck it, in reality, its fatal blow.[11]

The question of punishment loomed large. Nicholas II was in an extremely difficult position. He could not be seen to condone such a public murder, especially in light of the participation of members of his own family. The conspirators were hailed as heroes; to punish them, the tsar would be forced to ignore the enormity of public opinion.

In the end, Nicholas dealt with the conspirators as if they had committed two different crimes. Purishkevich, who had quickly fled to the front when he learned that Felix had been placed under house arrest, presented the greatest challenge. Along with Felix Youssoupov, he was obviously the conspirator most responsible for Rasputin's murder. But fate worked to Purishkevich's advantage: He was a popular member of the Duma who had participated in what was believed to be a patriotic act and who now sought refuge among the troops at the front, where his deed instantly won him admiration. Not even Nicholas II dared touch the deputy, and Purishkevich escaped retribution. Nor did either Dr. Stanislaus Lazovert or Lt. Ivan Sukhotin suffer any formal punishment. Like Purishkevich, they were simply allowed to go free.

Such generous treatment, however, did not extend to either Prince Felix Youssoupov or Grand Duke Dimitri Pavlovich. They were the most visible of the conspirators, and in this case their recognition would count against them. Both Nicholas and Alexandra regarded their participation in the murder as a crime against the monarchy itself. Although public opinion held that the two men were patriotic heroes, neither the tsar nor the tsarina was inclined to share this view. Confined to their palaces, Felix and Dimitri could only wait and hope that their punishment would be moderate. Unfortunately for them, the tsar was not in a generous mood. That members of his own family had participated in the crime seemed to weigh more heavily on his mind than the fact that Rasputin himself had been killed. "I am filled with shame that the hands of my kinsmen are stained with the blood of a simple peasant," he said.[12] "A murder is always a murder," he announced.[13] When Felix's father-in-law pleaded with Nicholas for leniency, the tsar replied testily, "A very fine speech, Sandro. Are you aware, however, that nobody has the right to kill, be it a Grand Duke or a peasant?"[14]

In another plea for leniency, Grand Duchess Elizabeth, Felix's mentor, wrote a long letter to her brother-in-law the tsar:

> When I am vexed that faith is not readily placed in what I wish to say in God's name, I retire alone, and pray to God . . . dearest Nicky. I can't understand your silence, you all my dear ones show me . . . but I never lied to you, perhaps have been at times rough but always straight forward. . . . I spoke with Alix all my fears, my anguish with which my heart was overwhelmed: big waves seemed to be rushing over us all. In despair I flew to you, I love you so truly, to warn you that all classes, from the lowest to the highest, even out at the war, are at their wit's end. She told me not to talk to you as I had written and I left with

the feeling will we ever meet as now—what dramas may
come to pass—what sufferings are in store. . . . Arrived
here the news that Felix killed him, my little Felix I knew
as a child, who all his life feared to kill, who did not wish
to become military so as never to have the occasion to
shed blood—and I imagine what he must have gone
through to do this, and how moved by patriotism he decided to save his sovereign and country from what we all
were suffering. I telegraphed to Dimitri not knowing
where the boy was—but got no answer and since then all
is in a kind of silence . . . crime remains crime, but this
one being of a special kind, can be counted as a duel and
it is considered a patriotic act and for these deeds the law
I think is alternating. Maybe nobody has had the courage
to tell you now, that in the street of the towns people
kissed like at Easter week, sang the hymn in the theatres
and all moved by one feeling—at last the black wall between us and our Emperor is removed, at last we will see,
hear, feel him as he is and a wave of pitying love for you
moved all hearts. God grant that you may know of this
love and feel it and not miss this great movement as the
storm is still and thunder rolls afar. . . . Your heart must
be so heavy in spite of your deep faith in God, yet your
heart must ache and maybe a doubt of the truth of the position knocks at the door of your brain, don't shut the
door, open it clearly and let the bright wisdom from
above enter for the welfare of all. . . . During the time of
black clouds . . . may in the new year of 1917 the clouds
be lifted, the sun shine in all beloved Russia, victories in
the interior and exterior bring a glorious peace to you, our
beloved Sovereign and all, all your subjects of which I am
one—God bless you, God help you.

Your faithful sister,
Ella.[15]

In spite of the numerous pleas, punishment was swift in
coming. Both Felix and Dimitri were sentenced to exile, Felix to
Rakitnoe, his estate in central Russia, and Dimitri to Kasvin, on
the Persian front, with the army. Youssoupov's exile amounted

to little more than temporary discomfort; but Dimitri, in an already precarious state of health, faced very real dangers on the Persian front, where disease, mutinous attacks, and food shortages were all commonplace. On his behalf, sixteen members of the Romanov family addressed a petition to the tsar:

Your Majesty:
    We, all, whose names you will find at the end of this letter, implore you to reconsider your harsh decision concerning the fate of Grand Duke Dimitri Pavlovich.
    We know that he is quite ill and unnerved by all he has gone through. You, who were his guardian and supreme protector in infancy and boyhood, well know how deeply he loved you and Our Country.
    Most heartily do we implore Your Majesty, in consideration of his weak health and his youth, to allow the Grand Duke to go and live on his own estates, either at Oncova or at Ilinskoe.
    Your Majesty must know the very hard conditions under which our troops have to live in Persia—without shelter and the constant threat to health and life.
    To have to live there would be, for the Grand Duke, almost certain death, and in the heart of Your Majesty surely a feeling of pity will be awakened toward this young man who from childhood had the joy of living in your home, and whom you loved and to whom you used to be like a father.
    May God inspire you and guide you to turn wrath into mercy!
        Your Majesty's most loving and devoted,
                Olga, Queen of Greece
                Marie, Grand Duchess Vladimir
                Cyril, Victoria, Boris and Andrei
                Paul Alexandrovich
                Marie Pavlovna
                Elizabeth, Grand Duchess Constantine
                Ivan, Helene, Gabriel, Constantine
                    and Igor
                Nicholas Michailovich
                Serge Michailovich

The tsar returned the petition to the family. At the bottom, he had written a short note: "Nobody has the right to kill on his own private judgement. I know that there are many others besides Dimitri Pavlovich whose consciences give them no rest, because they are compromised. I am astonished that you should have applied to me. Nicholas."[16]

The Romanov appeal on Dimitri's behalf represented a final breach between Nicholas and Alexandra and their family. Rasputin's murder had clearly been a political act: against the peasant; against his influence over governmental affairs; and perhaps most importantly, against the empress herself, who was widely held responsible for the disintegration of the Russian government. The support of these aunts, uncles, and cousins in favor of Dimitri amounted to a rejection of Nicholas II. The tsar's response to their plea was a complete repudiation of family solidarity. The conspirators had committed Rasputin's murder to save the monarchy; instead, the peasant's death only further isolated Nicholas and Alexandra not only from public opinion but from their own family as well.

On 21 December—the same day that Rasputin was buried at Tsarskoe Selo—Felix and Dimitri left Petrograd. At eleven-thirty that night, Grand Duke Alexander Michailovich drove his son-in-law to the railway station; the platform was dark and deserted, guarded by members of the police. Just after midnight, Felix's train steamed off into the night, carrying him away from the capital. Writing in his diary about the two exiles, the Honorable Bertie Stopford said, "I feel Felix is so clever he will get all he wants, whereas the other boy is always hopeless and desolate; he had *une crise de nerfs* and completely broke down in the train next day in his famished condition."[17]

19

Predictions Fulfilled

F ELIX'S JOURNEY TO RAKITNOE took two days. He was accompanied on the train by Captain Zenchikov, one of his instructors from the Corps des Pages in Petrograd. A second, less welcome presence was a certain man named Ignatiev, the assistant director of the Okhrana, who had been detailed by the tsar to keep watch over Felix. Because members of the imperial family had intervened on behalf of both Felix and Dimitri, Nicholas II believed that the conspiracy's roots might lead to a plot against the throne. He feared Felix and those who regarded his action as a great heroic deed enough to keep track of all of his movements, meetings, and correspondence once he was away from the capital.

The train journey to Rakitnoe was an unpleasant one. There was no food, and the compartment occupied by the prince had only occasional heat. The spur of track had not been maintained, and the constant jolting kept Felix awake for much of the trip. By the time the train pulled into the small station near Rakitnoe, Felix was completely exhausted.

Nicholas II had chosen Rakitnoe due to its location in the middle of Kursk Province. Unlike the other Youssoupov estates outside Moscow or in the Crimea, it was almost entirely isolated from those of other aristocrats. The tsar did not want Felix to have any contact with potential conspirators. To this end, the Okhrana agents from Kursk monitored the prince's mail, kept track of his daily movements, and diligently reported their findings back to Petrograd.

Irina and Felix's parents, informed of his forced exile, had rushed from the Crimea to await his arrival from the capital. Reunited, the family spent their days at Rakitnoe under Okhrana supervision, taking long carriage rides in the day and reading at night. While the tsar and his agents were on constant alert over Felix's latest activities, they need not have worried. Having made his decision to kill Rasputin, he had undertaken the one and only political act of his life. He fully expected that members of the Russian government and even the tsar himself would respond to the peasant's death with action and insight. When this did not occur, Felix finally abandoned all interest in Russian politics.

It took only ten weeks from the time of Rasputin's death for the Romanov dynasty to fall. The peasant had often said to the empress, "If I die or you desert me, you will lose your son and your crown within six months."[1] The conspirators had hoped that by removing Rasputin and his influence, Alexandra would retreat from politics altogether. What they failed to understand was that the force which drove the empress in her struggles with the ministers had never come from the peasant but rather from the concern over the future inheritance of her only son. Rasputin might be gone, but the autocracy remained. While it did, Alexandra would continue to fight for its survival.

The majority of the Romanovs also hoped that Rasputin's death would lead to the empress's withdrawal from political affairs. With just such a goal in mind, Felix's father-in-law Grand Duke Alexander Michailovich visited the Alexander Palace at Tsarskoe Selo shortly after Rasputin's murder. The empress received him from her bed, where she lay dressed in a white négligé. The grand duke stated his case bluntly: "Nobody knows better than I your love and devotion for Nicky, but yet I must confess that your interference with affairs of state is causing harm both to Nicky's prestige and to the popular conception of a sovereign." He said that although for "twenty-four years" he had been the empress's "faithful friend," he had to "point out to [her] that all classes of the people are opposed to [her] policies." He asked, "Why can you not concentrate on matters of peace and harmony? Please, Alix, leave the cares of state to your husband."

At this the empress blushed but said nothing. The grand duke continued: "The granting of a government acceptable to the Duma and coming at this dangerous moment would lift the responsibilities from Nicky's shoulders and would make his task easier. . . . Please, Alix, do not let your thirst for revenge dominate your better judgement."

"All of this talk is ridiculous," the empress replied. "Nicky is an autocrat. How could he share his divine rights with a parliament?"

"You are very much mistaken, Alix," the grand duke shouted, referring to the creation of the Duma. "Your husband ceased to be an autocrat on 5 October 1905!"

In a last bid for her attention, the grand duke bellowed: "Remember, Alix, I remained silent for thirty months! For thirty months I never said as much as a word to you about the disgraceful goings on in our government, better to say *your* government!" He bellowed that although the empress might be "willing to perish," she had no right to ask the entire country "to suffer from your blind stubborness! No, Alix, you have no right to drag your relations with you down a precipice! You are incredibly selfish."

"I refuse to continue this dispute," the empress declared. "You are exaggerating the danger. Some day, when you are less excited, you will admit that I know better."[2] With this she dismissed the grand duke.

Other members of the imperial family decided to act on their own. Grand Duchess Vladimir, one of the empress's most dedicated enemies, aggressively plotted the removal of her nephew from the Russian throne. After the empress and the dowager empress, the Grand Duchess ranked as third lady in the land. Her ambitions, jealousies, and intrigues had caused many family quarrels among the Romanovs. Her three sons, Cyril, Andrei, and Boris, all lived scandalous lives. Cyril, the eldest, had wed the empress's former sister-in-law Victoria Melita without the tsar's permission, been stripped of his offices and honors, and banished from the country. Although both he and his wife eventually returned to Russia and their marriage received imperial recognition, they remained hostile to the sovereigns. Andrei openly lived with the tsar's former mistress, ballerina Mathilde Kschessinska, and had fathered her child. The youngest, Boris, had once proposed marriage to the tsar's eldest daughter Olga, only to be rejected out of hand by the empress. As a result, Grand Duchess Vladimir never forgave Alexandra.

Grand Duchess Vladimir launched a plan to place Cyril on the throne. She believed that Tsarevich Alexei could be removed from the succession by reason of his ill health and that the tsar's brother Michael would also be excluded by virtue of the morganatic marriage he had contracted with a twice-divorced commoner named Nathalia Cheremetievskaia. Cyril, a commanding officer in the Garde Equipage, drew soldiers from this regiment—many of whom had served aboard the imperial yacht—into the plot. They planned to seize the Alexander Palace one night, force the tsar to abdicate for himself and his son, and proclaim Cyril emperor. They made no secret of the plot. Maurice Paléologue wrote:

> Yesterday evening Prince Gabriel Constantinovich gave a supper for his mistress, formerly an actress. The guests included Grand Duke Boris . . . a few officers and a squad of elegant courtesans. During the evening the only topic was the conspiracy—the regiments of the guard which can be relied on, the most favourable moment for the outbreak, etc. And all this with the servants hovering about, harlots looking on and listening, gypsies singing and the whole company bathed in the aroma of *Moët et Chandon Brut Imperial* which flowed in streams.[3]

There is evidence that other members of the Romanov family had their own plans; but in the end these palace plots came to nothing: The citizens of Petrograd took matters into their own hands. On 23 February 1917, stores in the capital ran short of black bread, the daily staple for most of Petrograd's workers. During the war food shortages had become commonplace, and increasing inflation made it difficult for many families to feed themselves. By 1917 food supplies to the capital had all but stopped, as everything was diverted to soldiers at the front. Those who could afford to pay the exorbitant prices did so; others went hungry.

By coincidence, 23 February happened to be International Women's Day and the Socialists were in the streets demonstrat-

ing against the war and the monarchy. In addition, thousands
of factory workers had gone out on strike a few days earlier.
These three groups—the hungry, the revolutionaries, and the
workers—all came together on Petrograd's streets that day out
of circumstance. Riots quickly broke out, demonstrators were
arrested, and small groups shouted, "Down with the autocracy!"
The Revolution had begun.

It was a popular revolt, and within days thousands of people took to the streets, waving red flags and singing the "Mar-
seillaise." The government ordered the schools closed, a foolish
action that added hundreds of angry students to the mobs.
Streetcars and taxicabs ceased to operate. The imperial cabinet
cabled the tsar at headquarters with an urgent request that he
return to the capital at once and create a responsible government.
Nicholas, knowing only the barest of details, telegraphed to General Khabalov, military governor of Petrograd: "I order that the
disorders in the capital, intolerable during these difficult times
of war with Germany and Austria, be ended tomorrow. Nicholas."[4]

General Khabalov responded by turning his troops out into
the streets. They were among the worst in the country—men
who had been rejected for duty at the front. The capital continued to riot as these soldiers patrolled the streets. Hundreds of
demonstrators were shot, bringing more protests, more calls for
revolution. On Sunday, 26 February, Michael Rodzianko, president of the Duma, cabled the tsar: "Situation serious. Anarchy
in the capital. Government paralyzed. Transport of food and fuel
in full disorder. Popular discontent growing. Essential immediately to order persons having the confidence of the country to
form a new government. Delay impossible. And delay deadly. I
pray to God that in this hour the blame does not fall on the
crown."[5] On receiving this telegram, the tsar angrily told General Alexeiev, his chief of staff, "That fat Rodzianko has sent me
some nonsense which I shall not even bother to answer."[6]

By Monday, 27 February, most of the tsar's famous guards
regiments—including the Volinsky, the Preobrajensky, the Litovsky, the Semanovsky, the Ismailovsky—had mutinied and
joined the Revolution. There was no turning back. The Duma
met and took decisive action: on their own authority: They dis-

solved the imperial government and created a new, provisional government, with full powers, in its place. The opposition—General Khabalov and those soldiers still loyal to the tsar—lodged themselves in the Winter Palace. Across the Neva River, revolutionaries trained the guns of the Fortress of Saints Peter and Paul on the palace's three-city-block façade; they gave Khabalov and his men twenty minutes to clear out. The general had no choice. He gave up, and the resistance went with him. The imperial government had fallen.

Anarchy erupted in Petrograd. Mobs stormed offices and prisons, setting them ablaze. In Kronstadt sailors murdered all of their officers, shooting one and throwing a second, unharmed, into the grave alongside the corpse, to be buried alive.[7] Many of the opulent palaces of the capital fell victim as well. Mathilde Kschessinska managed to escape from her mansion just in time; a violent mob surged through the house, breaking windows, smashing furniture, smearing the walls and carpets with ink, and filling the bathtubs with cigarette butts.[8]

On Wednesday, 2 March 1917, Tsar Nicholas II abdicated from the throne. Although the revolt in Petrograd involved only a small fraction of his subjects, his entire government had fallen, and after years of fighting World War I, the tsar lacked the inner strength to plunge his country into a civil war. At first, he abdicated only for himself; for a few hours, Alexei, aged twelve, held the title of tsar of all the Russias. Then Nicholas changed his mind, abdicating for his son as well, a move which, legally, he could not do. The tsar realized that after the revolution he and his family would probably be exiled, and he did not wish to be separated from his ailing son.

The crown fell to Grand Duke Michael, the tsar's brother. The revolutionaries in Petrograd, however, could not be appeased by replacing one Romanov with another. Under intense pressure, Michael declared that he would not assume the throne unless called upon to do so by a parliamentary vote. No such vote ever took place, and Michael never reigned. The Romanov dynasty had come to an end.

News from Petrograd filtered slowly into Rakitnoe. With the fall of the imperial government, the Youssoupovs decided to

return to the capital. As Felix's exile rested solely on the authority of the tsar, there was now no longer any restriction to keep
him in the country.

The Youssoupovs arrived in Petrograd on 19 March 1917,
two weeks after the uprising had ended. Immediately Felix made
contact with his old friends and took advantage of his popularity. He never seems to have questioned the role he may have
played in helping to accelerate the downfall of the Romanovs,
and he clearly believed that capital could be made from his role
in Rasputin's murder. He reserved his most vehement hatred for
the imperial family. To Bertie Stopford he complained that the
former tsar and his family should be exiled from Russia as soon
as possible and be imprisoned for the security of the country;
otherwise, he told his friend, "there would always be the fear of
their correspondence with Germany."[9]

Grand Duchess Marie Pavlovna, Dimitri's sister, later recalled of Felix: "At the time he was seriously imagining himself
an historic figure of considerable importance and all he did was
calculated to enhance this position. He cherished the hope of
playing a political part in Russia, basing his calculations on the
notoriety, mistaken for popularity, which came to him through
Rasputin's murder. His desire to be talked about at all costs
made no discrimination as to method or manner."[10]

Despite Marie Pavlovna's scorn, there was clearly some basis for Felix's perception. One day Michael Rodzianko called on
Felix at the Moika Palace and informed him, "Moscow wishes
to proclaim you emperor. What do you say to that?" This offer
came as no surprise to the prince; the immense public attention
he had attracted by killing Rasputin itself suggested the possibility of some political future. Grand Duke Nicholas Michailovich, one of Irina's uncles, urged him to accept: "The throne of
Russia is neither hereditary nor elective: it is usurpatory. Take
advantage of the circumstances. You hold all the trumps. Russia
cannot go on without a monarch, and the Romanovs are discredited; the people don't want them back."[11]

There is a chance that had Felix accepted, he might have
succeeded; certainly, among much of the general public, he already possessed the stature of a popular leader. With his sense

of destiny and air of self-importance, Felix no doubt found the offer a tempting one. But Russia was still in a state of upheaval, and there was no guarantee that if he accepted, Felix might not suffer the same fate as his uncle, the tsar. The prince might have relished the ceremonial side of the monarchy, but the thought of bearing the ultimate responsibility for the empire, tottering on the edge of ruin and embroiled in a devastating European war, was too much. While those who promoted his elevation to the throne may have looked to Felix as something of a popular figurehead, he himself was under no illusion as to the terrible, crushing weight of the office and the responsibilities which accompanied it. Nicholas II had not been able to save his throne, and Felix himself certainly was no more resolute a man. Then, too, Irina had no wish to see herself as empress; her dedication to her country did not extend to the sacrifice of her personal life. In the end, Felix declined the offer.

Eventually, the uncertain and volatile atmosphere of Petrograd became too heated for the Youssoupovs, and they traveled south to the Crimea. Felix's parents divided their time between Koreiz and Kokoz, while Felix and Irina stayed with her parents at Grand Duke Alexander Michailovich's estate of Ai-Todor on the Black Sea.

Many of the Romanovs had, by this time, already established themselves in their Crimean estates. At Ai-Todor, Dowager Empress Marie Feodorovna arrived on 12 March to join her daughter and son-in-law. Following the Revolution most of the Romanovs were arrested by the provisonal government, ostensibly for their own protection. In Petrograd the former tsar and his family had all been imprisoned in the Alexander Palace at Tsarskoe Selo. One day, at Ai-Todor, a man bearing the title of special commissar of the provisonal government arrived and announced that henceforth the Romanovs should consider themselves restricted to the confines of the estate. A detachment of soldiers was detailed to guard the house and allowed to enter any of the rooms at all times of the day and night. All correspondence entering and leaving the estate was subject to examination, and the Romanovs were permitted to speak only in Russian. Visitors to Ai-Todor could enter and leave only after they had been thoroughly searched. In addition, candles and kerosene were strictly limited out of fear that the prisoners might attempt to signal to boats in the harbor.

On the night of 22 April, upon the orders of the provisonal government, a group of soldiers broke into the house to conduct a surprise search. Grand Duke Alexander Michailovich awoke to find a gun pressed to his head. "Not a move or I'll shoot you on the spot," the soldier threatened.

"What is it you want from us?" Grand Duchess Xenia asked. "If you are after my jewels you will find them in the little table in the corner."

"No such luck," one of the men answered. "We are after you aristocrats. Your game's up. The whole house is surrounded. We are representatives of the Sevastopol Soviet. I would advise you to obey my orders."[12]

The soldiers moved on to the dowager empress's bedroom; they found the old lady sitting upright in her bed, eyeing them curiously. They ordered her to dress at once and submit to a search. All of her personal correspondence—letters and diaries—was thrown into a sack, along with her family Bible, which she had brought with her from Denmark upon her marriage.[13] Then, just as suddenly as the men had come, they left Ai-Todor.

A few days later, the president of the naval court-martial of Sevastopol arrived at Ai-Todor to apologize for the search; however, the apology took the form of an interrogation of members of the Romanov family. At the end of this session, all of them were asked to sign statements as to what had taken place. When the dowager empress was asked to sign, she was told to do so as "the ex-Empress Marie." Instead, she signed "the widow of Emperor Alexander III."[14]

Felix and Irina had not been arrested along with others in the family. They decided to return to Petrograd to ask the provisonal government to intervene. Irina applied for an appointment with Alexander Kerensky, the minister of justice. He agreed, and she went to see him in his new offices in the Winter Palace. A few old servants recognized her as she entered and bowed in respect. Kerensky had lodged himself in the study of Alexander II, Irina's great-uncle. Kerensky greeted Irina with some embarrassment and invited her to sit down; she immediately selected the tsar's armchair, forcing Kerensky into a seat reserved for visitors. Irina began describing the search at Ai-Todor. Kerensky protested that it was not his responsibility, but Irina continued on with her arguments until the minister promised to look into the matter. Hearing this, Irina rose from her chair and left the room, concluding the interview. It was a rare burst of willpower from a woman not known for displays of self-possession.[15]

Felix and Irina remained in Petrograd for several months. Although the Revolution had swept the Romanovs from the throne, the Youssoupovs carried on in their aristocratic manner, hosting dinner parties for their friends where the guests were still attended by footmen in livery. On some evenings he entertained friends in the cellar room below his study, where he had killed Rasputin; everything had been left exactly as it had been that night, and Felix took a perverse delight in leading his nervous guests around the room, pointing dramatically from spot to spot as he happily chatted about the crime and how it had transpired.[16]

A visiting American lady, Rheta Dorr, made her way to the Moika Palace to personally interview Felix. The prince readily welcomed her. Although she had heard the tale of Rasputin's murder from other sources, it was Felix himself who brought the subject up. "I don't want to be forever remembered for—for just one thing," he complained to her. Instead, he discussed his ideas for the future, which involved funding a series of schools for uneducated children in both Moscow and Petrograd: "My wife and I want to do something for Russia, something really worth while. . . . I want to do something constructive. Of course, as things are now, there is nothing constructive to be done. Besides, my wife is a Romanov, and naturally. . . . But when the time comes, if it ever does, when Russia is normal again, why shouldn't the contribution I make be to the education of children?"[17]

As the weeks passed, however, the situation in the capital grew more uncertain: There were constant strikes and riots, the electricity was often cut off, and so was the water supply. Food rationing was put into effect. Conditions were ripe for another upheaval, and the Youssoupovs were in Petrograd when the first Bolshevik uprising took place in June.

On 22 June 1917, the Bolsheviks made a bid for power. Count Alexei Bobrinsky later recalled:

> All seemed quiet on that particular morning; the streets were rather empty as I hired a cab to take me from our house to the Finland Railway Station. . . . As my cab was getting near the Liteiny Bridge, which we were to cross in order to get to the station, I saw a considerable crowd marching from the Finland side toward the bridge. I also heard a few distinct rifle shots. My driver did not like the situation at all and turning toward me, said, "Well, sir, I shall go no further. I have had enough trouble through all of these demonstrations—I am not going to expose myself and my old horse to new dangers. People have gone quite crazy. . . . " On my way I saw many excited workmen, some with rifles in their hands. They were going towards the Liteiny Bridge with the intention of marching against the Provisional Government. Three artillery salvoes thundered out as I was about to take the train. . . . As I learned afterwards it was the Guards' Artillery Battalion, under Lieutenant Rehbinder, which was loyal to Kerensky and which tried to displace the communist demonstration. The effect of these three salvoes was very great. Not only did they dispense the disorganized workers on the Liteiny Bridge but the sound of the cannonfire created a panic in the streets leading to the Duma where other demonstrators were forming their processions. These three salvoes saved Kerensky and his government from ruin.[18]

Before he left Petrograd, Felix managed to retrieve two of his most important paintings in the Moika Palace: *The Man With the Large Hat* and *The Woman With the Ostrich Fan*, both by Rembrandt. The canvases were unframed and rolled so that he could carry them back to the Crimea. He also visited the Anichkov Palace, where he slashed a large portrait of Alexander III from its frame and rolled it with the Rembrandts; he later gave it to the grateful dowager empress.

Other objects presented more of a problem. Felix divided up the jewels belonging to his wife and his mother, along with various *objets d'art*. He then concealed them in a number of secret rooms in the basement of the Moika Palace. One room, constructed to be fireproof, was reached through a secret door built into the back of a bookcase; another cache was concealed in a false ceiling. Other jewels were hidden in a secret room in the Moscow house. A few months later, Felix asked Robert Bruce Lockhart to make a search of the Moika Palace for jewels. In turn, Lockhart asked a friend of his, Galina von Meck, to make discreet inquiries. She later wrote:

> I knew the house to be a labyrinth of passages. I thought it unlikely that anyone could hope to find anything concealed there on a mere superficial examination. However, to please Lockhart, I visited the house. It was empty at the time. I told the caretaker that I had come from one of the offices to see if the building was worthy of taking over. He showed me round and I noticed that, in one of the passages, the wall seemed to have been replastered and painted fairly recently. Shortly after, the building was taken by a government office, and, as far as I was concerned, that was the end of the matter. But later we heard that the jewelry was found when the house was under repair, and it was confiscated by the government. So Mr. Lockhart had been right after all.[19]

Although he returned later to St. Petersburg, Felix was never able to recover any of this hidden treasure. Left in the Moika Palace were five secret rooms filled with treasures—forty-seven thousand different items, including 1,182 pictures, 100 packages of silver, 184 musical instruments, antique sculptures, snuffboxes, coins, weapons, jewels, and tapestries.[20] The Soviet government later divided it all up, sending pieces off to Moscow and keeping some in Petrograd. The jewels walled up in the Moscow house remained hidden until a 1925 restoration by the

Soviet government. Felix had erected a false wall beneath the main staircase there, enclosing a cloakroom. The Bolsheviks searched for the hidden cache for many years before an acquaintance of Felix's revealed that there had once been a room below the stairs. The Soviets tore out the wall. In the secret room they found 255 diamond brooches, 13 tiaras, 42 bracelets, and 462 pounds of assorted *objets d'art*, including trinkets by Fabergé and gold dinnerware.[21] By this time, Felix and Irina were living in exile in Paris, selling off pieces of her jewelry that they had managed to smuggle out of the country.

Felix had just arrived back in Petrograd from Moscow when, on 26 October 1917, the Bolsheviks, under Lenin, finally triumphed over Kerensky's provisional government. Although the coup d'état took place without much resistance, the days which followed it were filled with the beginnings of the Red Terror. Groups of drunken soldiers burst into many houses murdering the owners and stealing their possessions. Felix never knew if the Moika Palace would be their next target. Shooting echoed through the streets at all hours of the day and night. One night he saw a detachment of soldiers assault an elderly general walking beside the Moika Canal; when they had finished, Felix rushed out and found the man lying in a pool of blood on the sidewalk, his eyes gouged out.[22]

The Bolsheviks soon sent a patrol of soldiers to the Moika to inspect the house; Felix knew that within a few days they would probably return to arrest him. In a panic, he managed to get hold of a set of false identity papers on the black market and boarded a train for Kiev. This proved less than reassuring: On the streets, Felix dodged bullets as rival factions battled for control of the town. He was forced to return to Petrograd but almost immediately left the city aboard a train for the Crimea. He would never set foot in Petrograd again.

20

Escape

ALTHOUGH THE CRIMEA HAD SEEMED a safe haven
in the early days of the Revolution, by the time Felix returned in
the fall of 1917, the political situation was grave. As long as Kerensky had remained in power, the Romanovs had been reasonably secure. Now, with the arrival of Lenin, they faced the very
real possibility of being rounded up and taken away. The Yalta
Soviet was calling for their immediate executions, while the more
moderate Sevastopol Soviet believed that they should wait for
instructions from the government before acting. These two
groups—Yalta and Sevastopol—fighting for control of the Crimea, used the Romanovs as pawns in the deadly struggle for
power.

In the end, the Sevastopol Soviet decided to take matters
into their own hands; unwilling to answer to the government in
the event that their comrades at Yalta took drastic action, the
Sevastopol Soviet moved the prisoners to the estate of Grand
Duke Peter Nicholaievich at Dulber, just down the coast from
Ai-Todor. Dulber had the advantage of being surrounded by
high stone walls, which made it easy to defend. Machine guns
were mounted on the roof of the house, and those imprisoned
at Ai-Todor were transferred in secret to their new place of con-
finement.

Because Irina had married Felix morganatically and thus
removed herself from the line of succession to the Romanov
throne, she was allowed, along with her husband, to remain free.
Felix and Irina took up residence with his parents at Koreiz. But,
even though not under arrest, the Youssoupovs faced the same
uncertainty as her imperial cousins. "We were never sure, on

going to bed at night, of waking up alive in the morning," Felix wrote.[1]

In March 1918, Lenin signed the Treaty of Brest-Litovsk with Germany, ending Russia's participation in World War I. The Germans received stunning concessions from the embattled Bolsheviks, including the ceding of most of the Ukraine and the Crimean peninsula. The German army moved swiftly into these new territories and released all of the imprisoned Romanovs on the personal instructions of the Kaiser. Even though they were free to leave the country, few of the family considered this an option. The Civil War between the Bolsheviks and the monarchist White Army was raging all across the country, and no one expected that the Communists would triumph. To most of the Romanovs, it was only a question of time before their family was restored to power.

But circumstances decreed otherwise. By the summer of 1918 the Bolshevik regime again held captive all members of the Romanov family that they could imprison. In August of the previous year, the former tsar and his family had been exiled to Siberia by Alexander Kerensky. At first, they lived relatively comfortably in the small provincial town of Tobolsk; then, in April 1918, they were transferred, at Moscow's insistence, to the Ural Mountain mining town of Ekaterinburg and imprisoned by the Ural Regional Soviet in a house formerly belonging to a merchant named Ipatiev. Soon enough, the grim news filtered to the Crimea: On the night of 16 July 1918, Nicholas II; his wife, Alexandra; Tsarevich Alexei; and their four daughters—Olga, Tatiana, Marie, and Anastasia—along with those servants remaining with them, had all been shot by a firing squad on Lenin's orders.

In the summer of 1918, the Bolsheviks launched a systematic execution of other members of the Romanov family under their control. At about the same time as the Ekaterinburg murders, Grand Duchess Elizabeth Feodorovna, Grand Duke Serge Michailovich, Princes Ivan, Igor, and Constantine Constantinovich, and Grand Duke Paul's second son from his morganatic marriage, Prince Vladimir Paley, were all killed in the Siberian town of Alapayevsk. The tsar's brother Grand Duke Michael Alexandrovich was also shot by the Bolsheviks. Six months later, four Romanov grand dukes—Paul Alexandrovich, Nicholas Michailovich, George Michailovich, and Dimitri Constantinovich—were all executed in Petrograd on Lenin's orders.

The Romanovs in the Crimea were safe—at least for the moment. But, in November 1918, when World War I ended, the German occupying forces abandoned the Crimea, and once again a struggle for power began. Control of the Crimea passed nominally to the Volunteer Army, an organization composed chiefly of former tsarist officers and those dedicated to the overthrow of the Bolshevik regime. As the official governing body, the Volunteer Army proved highly ineffectual, and revolt quickly followed. In February 1918, the native Crimean Tartar population had attempted to stage a coup. They failed to win popular support, however, and hundreds of people were massacred. The Black Sea Navy mutiny followed. Most of the officers were killed, hacked to pieces, burned alive in the ships' furnaces, or thrown into the water with iron bars tied to their legs. In Sevastopol the sailors massacred hundreds of men, women, and children they suspected of being White Army sympathizers.

At the beginning of 1919 the Allied High Commission in Constantinople divided up the responsibilities of governing the Crimean peninsula among themselves for the duration of the Civil War. The French navy was put in charge of the entire Crimean coastline. However, by March, the French fleet at Sevastopol had mutinied and demanded that their commander return them at once to their country. At this time, the Bolshevik forces were rapidly gaining ground in the Crimea. Although the Allies extracted a promise from the French High Command that they would remain in place, the French navy secretly began to evacuate their forces from the Crimea.

The Romanovs were once again in imminent danger of being taken captive by the Red Army. At this moment, the British royal family intervened. King George V was a first cousin of both Tsar Nicholas II and Empress Alexandra; his mother, Queen Alexandra, was a sister of Dowager Empress Marie Feodorovna. After the Revolution there had been every expectation that the imperial family would be exiled to England. At first, the king and the British government extended the invitation to the Romanovs, but as the weeks passed, King George V, fearing for the security of his own throne, forced his government to rescind its offer of asylum. Now, in 1919—after hearing of his cousins' murders in Ekaterinburg—King George bowed to pressure from his mother, Queen Alexandra, and caused his government to dispatch a British warship, HMS *Marlborough*, to rescue the Romanovs left in the Crimea.

HMS *Marlborough* was an Iron Duke–class dreadnought which had been involved in the Battle of Jutland. Her commander, C. D. Johnson, C.B., M.V.O., D.S.O., carried a personal letter from Queen Alexandra to her sister Marie Feodorovna urging her to leave Russia before it was too late. Barely a month earlier, the dowager empress had refused a similiar offer from Capt. Bertram S. Thesiger, C.B., C.M.G., commander of HMS *Calypso*, with the explanation that in spite of the growing Bolshevik threat, the continued presence of the Romanovs in the country provided a stabilizing influence.[2]

When HMS *Marlborough* steamed into the harbor at Sevastopol, her crew saw firsthand the mute evidence of the precarious political situation. The French battleship *Mirabeau* lay abandoned, having run aground, while the Russian battleship *Imperatritza Maria* had capsized and been left to the sea. Bodies of officers—victims of the Black Sea Fleet mutiny— bobbed in the water. The streets of both Sevastopol and Yalta were littered with debris and makeshift barricades, while the buildings were scarred with bullet marks.

On the morning of 7 April 1919, HMS *Marlborough* sailed to Yalta, and Captain Johnson presented the dowager empress with the letter from her sister the queen. At first, Marie Feodorovna absolutely refused to leave the country; however, after some urging, she agreed to accept the British offer as long as all of those remaining in the Crimea who wished to leave could do so as well. This presented immense difficulties; King George V had dispatched the battleship to collect his aunt and did not expect to take responsibility for the remainder of his Romanov cousins. Captain Johnson eventually decided that the only way to rescue the dowager empress was to take them all away and face the consequences later.

For two days, HMS *Marlborough*'s crew readied the ship to receive the would-be exiles. All of the officers' cabins at the rear of the ship were vacated to make room for the Romanovs. Captain Johnson's quarters were prepared for the dowager empress. Members of the imperial family spent their days packing steamer trunks; one of the greatest myths surrounding the exile of the Romanovs is that they managed to take nothing with them when they left Russia. In two days, however, as HMS *Marlborough* lay anchored, over two hundred tons of luggage were loaded on board the ship.

The dowager empress did not wish to embark at Yalta, so a makeshift pier was hastily built in the harbor below the Youssoupov estate at Koreiz, and all of the Romanovs made their way there to board the ship. On 11 April 1919, HMS *Marlborough* left Yalta with eighty-five passengers, including the dowager empress; her daughter Grand Duchess Xenia Alexandrovich; Princes Feodor, Nikita, Dimitri, Rostislav, and Vassili Alexandrovich; Grand Duke Nicholas Nicholaievich and his wife, Anastasia; Grand Duke Peter and his wife, Militza; their children Marina and Roman; Felix, Irina, and their daughter, Irina; and Felix's parents. As the ship steamed out of Yalta harbor, the passengers gathered on the deck, gazing at the receding coastline. The dowager empress stood alone, tears in her eyes as her imperial guard solemnly sang "God Save the Tsar." It was to be the last time that the Russian imperial anthem was sung to a member of the imperial family within the boundaries of the former empire for three-quarters of a century.

The voyage to Constantinople took two days. Those on board resembled the survivors of a shipwreck—bewildered, uncertain, dejected. The dowager empress, aged seventy-two, remained in her cabin for most of the voyage; she felt the catastrophic effects of the Revolution keenly, having lost two of her children to the Bolshevik firing squads. Not surprisingly, Felix regarded it all as something of an adventure. He quickly became the most popular passenger on the ship. He regaled the sailors on board with his lurid tale of murdering Rasputin and often played the balalaika and sang Gypsy songs to entertain them. Of Irina, one of the officers wrote that she "appeared shy and retiring at first, but it was only necessary to take a little notice of her pretty, small daughter to break through her reserve and discover that she was also very charming and spoke fluent English."[3]

At Constantinople a number of the passengers from HMS *Marlborough* disembarked and transferred to HMS *Lord Nelson*, including Grand Duke Nicholas Nicholaievich and his wife. With them, they took over two hundred trunks filled with silver and gold plate, furniture, paintings, and jewelry.[4] The rest of the passengers continued on in HMS *Marlborough* to Malta, where they transferred to the other ship. The dowager empress did not want to change ships, but the British government needed the bigger ship for duty immediately, so Marie Feodorovna reluctantly moved to HMS *Lord Nelson*—along with her daughter Xenia and her grandchildren Feodor, Nikita, Dimitri, Rostislav, and Vassili—to continue the voyage to England.

All of the other passengers on HMS *Marlborough* were forced to disembark at Malta. The British government made it quite clear that although it would be happy to rescue members of the imperial family who remained in the Crimea, it would only offer asylum to the dowager empress, her daughter Xenia, and her children. Felix and Irina were not among those welcome to take up residence in England; they were not barred from entering the country, but the implication was clear that it would be best if they found another place of residence. In these early days following the Revolution, it was by no means certain that the fever for political change which swept the Romanovs, the Hapsburgs, and the Hohenzollerns from their thrones would not eventually have the same effect in Great Britain. The British government did not wish to be thought of as providing a center for an exiled tsarist government, nor was King George V personally willing to assume the responsibility of looking after his numerous dispossessed relatives.

In April 1919, Felix and Irina, along with four-year-old Bebé, entered into a life of exile. He, the wealthiest man in Russia and she, the favorite niece of the last tsar, now faced an uncertain future. They left Malta for Italy, sailing into the unknown.

PART FOUR

The Aftermath

21

Exile

For the first few months of their European exile, Felix and Irina set up temporary residence in the Hotel Vendôme in Paris. They left their daughter with Felix's parents, who had taken a villa near Rome, until permanent arrangements could be made. At the beginning of World War I, the Youssoupovs, like many other great Russian families, had followed the tsar's patriotic lead and repatriated their foreign investments, including bank accounts and industrial stocks, in Europe, South America, and the United States.[1] Fortunately, however, Felix had kept a number of valuables in Europe where they remained untouched by the Revolution. He owned a villa in Switzerland. In Paris, he found one of his automobiles still carefully looked after in a garage where he had deposited it on his honeymoon. One afternoon, he was visited by a banker who brought with him a bag of diamonds Felix had left with him before the war. Most importantly, Felix still held ownership of his flat in London, which he had leased during the war. This allowed him and Irina to live in England on a permanent basis as British taxpayers.

Although the British government had made its feelings known about members of the Romanov family coming to the country to take up residence, Felix decided that this was precisely what he and Irina would do. He was never barred from the country, as others were, perhaps because King George V had already granted asylum to his mother-in-law and her sons or perhaps because he was solvent enough to support his family.

The flat at 15 Parkside Street in Knightsbridge soon became a center for Russian émigrés living in London. They lived lavishly, at Felix's expense, enjoying dinner parties and dances. Felix often entertained his guests with tales of Rasputin's murder. Not surprisingly, the story became more dramatic with time and made quite an impression on his visitors. After one particularly grisly evening, the duchess of Portland remarked, "I felt I was there," in hushed, somber tones.[2] According to Grand Duchess Marie Pavlovna, Irina disliked all of this, looking like "a spectator and to all appearances an unconscious one."[3]

Exile seems to have had little effect on Felix's style of living—at least in the beginning. Grand Duchess Marie Pavlovna later recalled, "He was fond of wealth and realized its value chiefly on account of the power that it gave him over the human soul. He was made up of contrasts. He spent nothing on himself; his wife would hardly ever have a new frock, and their automobile was a pre-war, high-wheeled and dilapidated Panhard. Yet their house was still full of innumerable and useless servants."[4]

Felix often lodged his friends in the flat while they looked for work. For most of the Russian exiles, this proved a long and difficult process, since they had never held proper jobs and had been trained only as officers and to supervise the running of their various estates. Felix's cousin, Serge Obolensky, lived at the flat for several months. With him, Serge brought his chef, Vassili. By this time—Felix was thirty-two years old—both the prince and his cousin were going prematurely bald. Always vain, Felix hired a barber to come to the flat and give both himself and his cousin daily scalp massages. Serge claimed that his chef could do the job for them just as well, so Felix dismissed the barber. This, however, proved less than successful: "He always makes me feel he's pounding a cutlet," Felix complained after one of these treatments, and soon Vassili returned to his post in the kitchen.[5]

On weekends, Felix and Irina went to house parties in the country given by their friends. They moved in fashionable circles whose members included King Manuel of Portugal, Mrs. Hwfa Williams, Freda Dudley Ward, Lady Juliet Duff, and Duff and Diana Cooper. But Felix did not concern himself only with the pursuit of pleasures; he saw the need for organizing a center for Russian exiles and threw himself into the work. He set up the center in a house on Belgrave Square loaned to him by the owner and arranged for charity evenings and fund-raisers. He and Irina also presided over a 1919 benefit auction and charity bazaar for the White Army, which, at the time, was still waging a violent fight against Lenin's troops in Siberia and the south of Russia. They appeared elegant yet ill at ease at their booth, Felix in proper morning dress and Irina in a formal black velvet dress with a fashionable toque. They sold some handmade things—watercolors painted by both of them, small Orthodox crosses, some china figurines which they had discovered in their London flat, as well as used books and some inexpensive pieces of Irina's jewelry.

Felix could afford to be generous—for a time. He had a number of assets rather than cash available to him. But eventually the expense of maintaining his pre-Revolutionary lifestyle caught up with him, and he and Irina were forced to make cuts in their extravagant habits. Misfortune also played its part: One night, after a party at their Knightsbridge flat, Felix discovered that the bag of diamonds which had been returned to him from his Paris bank was missing.

The jewels had disappeared from a locked desk drawer in Felix's study. Nearly a hundred loose diamonds as well as a string of black pearls had been taken. The story immediately captivated the press. Newspapers hinted that the jewels had been part of the Russian crown regalia which Felix had somehow managed to smuggle out of the country. To squash these rumors, Scotland Yard issued an official statement:

> The diamonds reported as having been stolen were the absolute property of Prince Felix Youssoupov himself. They had been in the family for many years, and had nothing whatsoever to do with the late Tsar's jewels.[6]

Felix went to Sir Basil Thomson, the commissioner of police, and asked him to investigate the matter. Sir Basil suggested that the prince make out a list of those guests who had been present the night that the jewels disappeared; Felix could not do this principally because he did not know the names of everyone who had been at the flat and also because he was reluctant to involve his friends in a police investigation.

The jewels were eventually recovered. There is, however, some disagreement as to the manner of their reappearance. According to Serge Obolensky, Felix, by working through a list of his guests that evening, eventually determined the identity of the thief. He then invited the suspect to another party, led him into his study, opened the empty drawer where the jewels had been kept, pointed inside, and walked out of the room. Soon enough, the bag of diamonds reappeared.[7]

Felix's own version was quite different. One night, he wrote, he had a dream in which he saw the thief taking the jewels. He claimed it had been one of the poorer refugees whom he had once helped. According to the prince's account, he asked the suspect to the flat and showed him the drawer. Immediately the man confessed that he had taken the diamonds and intended to sell them to provide for his family. Felix, knowing that the man was destitute, let the matter drop.[8]

There is no use in trying to determine which version is the correct one. On 26 November 1919, the *Star* reported:

> The disappearance of diamonds worth £15,000 from Prince Youssoupov's flat has taken a further turn but elucidation seems to be as far off as ever.
>
> It is reported today that the diamonds said to have been missing since before 15 October have been found, but the *Star* is informed that the police have no knowledge of this discovery.
>
> There is no reason to believe that a forcible entry to the flat was effected and at the flat a *Star* reporter was told that there were "no missing jewels." The report that the jewels, nearly a hundred cape diamonds, were missing, followed an after-dinner party.[9]

Increasingly, life in England became difficult for the Youssoupovs. Aside from Irina's mother and brothers, none of their closest relatives were allowed entry. Irina's father had applied for asylum and been rejected. Certainly political worries figured in the decision, but the grand duke openly kept a mistress in the south of France and also made repeated pronouncements against

British foreign policy—the latter obviously influencing the government in their decision to reject his request. They reported:

> All of this makes the Foreign Office think that the arrival
> in London at this particular moment of a member of the
> Russian Imperial Family would be liable to cause a whole
> lot of unhealthy agitation and malicious rumour.[10]

So the grand duke returned to his French mistress, leaving his wife and sons in England.

Felix and Irina eventually settled in Paris. He bought a house on the rue Gutenburg near the Bois de Boulogne, moving the furniture from their London flat to Paris. Soon the house was filled with exiled relatives, dispossessed friends, and curious hangers-on. Here the Youssoupovs lived during the turbulent 1920s.

Paris was a natural choice for them. Following the Revolution it quickly became a center for Russian exiles. Many aristocratic Russians already had homes and stables there. The wealthier of the exiles lived in the 16th Arrondissement—Auteuil and Passy; those not as fortunate took up residence in the 15th Arrondissement. These sections of Paris boasted their Russian cafes, shops, and meeting halls. In the 1920s, three separate Russian language newspapers were printed daily in Paris. Paris, too, was a natural destination due to the language factor; while members of the aristocracy all spoke French—the official language of the Russian court—few of them could manage in English. In spite of his time at Oxford, Felix's English left much to be desired; Irina's grasp was much better. The surroundings of the French capital, the atmosphere of an exiled court, the thousands of émigrés who lived here—all made Paris a comfortable substitute for St. Petersburg for the Youssoupovs.

Life in the Paris of the 1920s proved a curious adventure for most of the Russian exiles. Grand Duke Alexander wrote:

> There did not seem to be any point in looking for a job or
> settling down, when in another month or so "order" was
> to be restored in Russia. And so they sat on the terraces of

the cafes and around the green tables in the clubs, wondering in what condition they would find their estates and trying their luck at baccarat. . . . The luck was usually bad and was eating up whatever jewelry or money they had managed to bring with them, but there always remained Paris, the city that accepted everyone who understood that life was short and real enjoyment rare.[11]

Grand Duchess Marie Pavlovna explained:

All our conversations still turned around one subject—the past. This past was like a dusty diamond which we held to the light in the hope of seeing the sun's rays play through it. We spoke of the past, we looked back to it. And speaking of the past we sought for no lessons but tirelessly and aimlessly went over old ground seeking whom to blame for what had befallen us. Our future as a whole we could not imagine, while our return to Russia, of which we were then certain, we pictured only under very definite auspices. We lived side by side with life but were afraid of meeting it; drifting on its surface we avoided penetrating deeper into the reasons and meaning of things, afraid to be faced with our own deficiencies.[12]

Another exile remembered the cafés as settings for armchair warfare:

People would be eating in front, while at the back there would be a room where old Russian generals would be drinking vodka and eating the restaurant's food, talking politics and fighting battles. "Now, if I'd put my cavalry *there* and my guns *there* . . ."—it was a stock joke.[13]

Times were hard for most of these exiles. Very few had any real training. Officers who had served in the elite Guards Regiments often joined the French Foreign Legion; émigré princes, used to the finest things in life, took their knowledge of wine, food, and expensive motorcars and became waiters, chauffeurs, and sales representatives. Their wives and daughters—having never worked in their lives before the Revolution—took positions as maids, cooks, and waitresses. One exiled countess recalled:

> My husband got a job with the Guaranty Trust Bank. First he was a cashier, then a sorter. After that he was with the Listerine Company. To get into these firms, you had to know somebody already there. We were very poor; my husband was earning 600 francs a month—much less than our friends driving taxis were getting. He would work from 6PM to midnight because it paid better. When he bought his first pair of shoes in France—that was years after we arrived there—we looked at them for weeks before he put them on.[14]

Then there were the most famous of the working exiles— the Russian dustmen of Cannes:

> They were very elegant and glamourous in their military tunics. Everyone loved them. I knew an English woman who lived below a Russian colonel who was working as a dustman, and he used to give her copies of the *Tatler* every week. She asked him why on earth he got the *Tatler*—"Oh, to keep track of my friends."
>
> Some of the French whom Russians had known before the war were very kind. My husband went instinctively to the Hotel Maurice when he arrived. After three days he realized they were charging him the same price they had in 1914, despite the fact that in the meantime inflation had made that sum almost ridiculous. He couldn't pay the real price, so he left. Another friend went to Duse to get some new shirts and he told them he owed them money from before the war. They told him they'd torn up all those bills. Nor did they want him to pay for the new shirts—he'd been a good customer in the past.
>
> Russians adapted very quickly, but few made fortunes. They're very bad at money. But they soon found

jobs: couture for the women, nursing, embroidery. The
men started driving taxis, acting as guides for American
tourists— anything. . . . [15]

These émigrés kept the memory of imperial Russia very
much alive, and they raised their children accordingly. One child
who grew up in exile recalled:

> I had always dreamt of Russia. All my generation was
> brought up like that. We lived Russia, dreamed Russia,
> working and sleeping. . . . It was, to some extent, un-
> real. . . . But it was unreal like a lost paradise. Everything
> that our parents remembered about Russia was beautiful,
> great, virtuous, glorious, honourable. . . . The dark side,
> the unattractive grey things, had somehow vanished from
> their minds. We, too, were brought up with this dream;
> we learned the language, the history, the geography, the
> literature, the culture of Russia and we lived within that
> culture. I remember, when I was about fifteen years old,
> someone asked me why I didn't want to become a French
> citizen, and I replied that I wanted to remain Russian
> and that I would prefer to die in Russia than to die
> abroad. . . . [16]

The sense that someday order would be restored in their
country was very real to most of these exiles. One of Felix's cousins recalled, "My uncle, to the end of his life, kept a suitcase
under the bed so that he would be able to go back quickly. A
friend of mother's always refused to tidy up her house—'What's
the point? We'll be going back soon. . . . ' "[17]

For the Romanovs, who were trained only to be a ruling
family, life was particularly hard. Felix's father-in-law later recalled the efforts of Marie Pavlovna and her brother Dimitri Pavlovich:

> There was a young Grand Duchess who fancied she could
> make her living as a dressmaker in London. She rented a
> small flat and began designing her own fashions. People

came in droves, looked at her models and said that she was a "real sport," a "truly brave little woman." While they themselves were not in the market for new dresses just then, they felt certain that they would be able to recommend the industrious Grand Duchess to their numerous friends. Weeks went by. The rent had to be paid. The adorable, cute models remained unsold. Something had to be done right away. The Grand Duchess swallowed her pride and confided her difficulties to a member of the Royal Family. She hated to do it, but was immensely relieved to hear that aid would be forthcoming at once. Next morning, a gold-braided messenger rang her bell. A letter for Her Imperial Highness. The envelope was thick and sealed. Its appearance suggested money. "Lord be praised!" said the Grand Duchess and opened it with trembling hands. There is no end to the variety of ways in which an order can be issued to a bank for the payment of a sum of money and at first she thought that the three sheets of vellum paper contained instructions to be followed by her. She read the letter carefully. She saw names, names, names: twenty-four names of the ladies who would be likely to become her clients.

Then, there was a young Grand Duke who came to the conclusion that the choice of one's profession should be based on one's past performances as an amateur. His mind drifted toward the city of Rheims, with its miles of cellars laden with champagne. "The cursed stuff cost me so much money before," said the young Grand Duke, "that surely it ought to support me now. With all due modesty, I do maintain that I know more about the vintages of champagne then even the widow Cliquot herself." So he went to Rheims and spent a whole week in the profound business of tasting the various Vintages. . . . He chose a well-known brand and signed an agreement with its manufacturers.[18]

The grand duke went on to describe the difficulties which he himself experienced in trying to remain solvent:

Stocks and bonds? I had bunches of them left in my safe deposit vault in St. Petersburg but even the Bolsheviks who stole them could not have disposed of them at any price because the concerns that issued the stocks had been destroyed by the Revolution. Oil lands? Copper? Manganese? Real estate? I had all of that but there was no way to persuade a tailor of the Rue de Faubourg St. Honore that he should exchange a pair of Hennel trousers for the deed to my apartment houses in St. Petersburg, or to my oil lands in the Caucasus.[19]

Marie Pavlovna later wrote:

Never before had I carried money or written out a check. My bills were always paid by someone else. . . . I knew approximately the price of jewels and clothes but had not the slightest idea about how much bread, meat, milk ought to cost. I did not know how to buy a subway ticket: I was afraid of entering a restaurant alone; I would not have known how and what to order there and what to give as a tip. Although I was then twenty-eight years old, in practical matters I was a child and had to learn everything from the beginning, just as a child has to learn to cross a street before it can go to school alone.[20]

What the Romanovs did have were their assets in the West and what they had managed to bring out of the country with them, most particularly, jewels. Grand Duke Alexander Michailovich admitted that they made "a series of childish attempts at salesmanship and shrewdness." Too proud to sell the jewels themselves, the Romanovs hired the services of agents who were less interested in getting the full worth of a piece than their commission. When one of these agents brought in a string of pearls which had belonged to Grand Duchess Xenia, the jeweler told him, "As a museum piece it represents a great value. As a piece of merchandise it has practically none. Now that the Romanovs, the Habsburgs and the Hohenzollerns are no more, who could possibly buy it?" In the end, the pearls were sold for less than a fifth of their original purchase price some twenty-five years earlier.[21]

There were other humiliations. Beginning in the early 1920s, the Soviet government commenced the sale of various pieces of jewelry and *objets d'art* confiscated from the collections of the aristocracy and members of the imperial family. These were sold in both London and Paris at bottom-of-the-market prices, but still at an expense too great for the original, exiled owners. One day, a gentleman turned up at Frogmore in Windsor to show some recently purchased pieces of Fabergé to Felix's mother-in-law, Grand Duchess Xenia Alexandrovna. The man pulled out a lavish jade presentation box, crowned with initials set in diamonds, and asked the grand duchess if she could tell him whose initials they might have been. Xenia took the piece from his hand, quickly looked it over, and tearfully declared, "These are mine. This is my property!" The embarrassed gentleman quickly retrieved the piece and placed it back into his case. Xenia sat, stunned, long after her caller had left.[22]

Felix responded in indignant fashion. He learned that a Berlin auction house was to hold a sale of Soviet treasures and quickly got hold of a catalog. As he thumbed through its pages, he found item after item which had come from the Youssoupov collections. Particularly painful was the discovery that all of the furnishings and paintings from his mother's drawing room in the Moika Palace were to be sold to the highest bidder. Felix informed the Berlin police that his personal property was about to be sold illegally at auction, and the authorities raided the firm's storerooms, seizing the pieces in question.

The matter went to a Berlin court and the Soviet government was forced to dispatch a representative to explain the sale. It was, the emissary declared, perfectly within the rights of the Soviet government to sell items which belonged to the Russian state. Felix protested that the items had been seized illegally and that Stalin's government had no authority. Unfortunately for Felix, the German courts eventually agreed with the Soviet position, and the prince suffered the humiliation of reading newspaper accounts of his mother's former possessions disappearing piece by piece into private houses across the world.

Soon their extravagant lifestyle caught up with Felix and Irina, and they, too, were forced to begin the difficult task of selling off pieces of the Youssoupov jewelry. Between 1918 and 1921 many of the Youssoupov jewels left in Russia were sold by the Soviet government on the Paris market. Felix noticed that the Paris firm of Cartier purchased many of them, and in 1922 he first made contact with Pierre Cartier. At the beginning he offered only one item—his mother's necklace of black pearls, which had once belonged to Catherine the Great. The value of the rare jewels—along with the provenance of the piece—allowed Cartier to advance to Felix $75,000. At the same time Felix also deposited with Cartier another necklace of thirty-one pearls. Eventually, Catherine the Great's black pearl necklace was sold to Mrs. Goelet Gerny of Washington, D.C., for $400,000—an immense fortune at the time. Of this sum, Felix received approximately two-thirds.[23]

Later that same year, Felix returned to Pierre Cartier and offered him a number of important pieces: the Ram's Head diamond of 17.47 carats, which had been given to Prince Potemkin by Catherine the Great; the Sultan of Morroco, a steel-colored diamond of 35.67 carats; the Polar Star, a diamond of 41.28 carats; and Marie Antoinette's diamond earrings, weighing 34.59 carats.[24] Immediately, Vincent Astor wished to buy the diamond earrings as a wedding present for his sister Alice, who was marrying Prince Serge Obolensky. But Serge asked him not to: "These jewels were associated in my mind," he wrote, "with bloodshed and tragedy—the duel and death of Nicholas Youssoupov and the Rasputin unpleasantness. The earrings seemed to bring tragedy to whoever owned them."[25] The earrings were eventually bought by Marjorie Merriweather Post, who, upon her death, left them to the Smithsonian Institution in Washington D.C.

The money Felix and Irina received from the sale of these jewels constituted a vast fortune to most people; for the Youssoupovs, however, the hundreds of thousands of dollars that came their way were insufficient, since they continued to live as extravagantly as ever. Although they held still more valuable jewelry, Felix decided to sell his two biggest assets—the Rembrandt paintings he had smuggled out of Russia.

He was introduced to Mr. Joseph Widener, the wealthy American collector, who expressed an interest in purchasing the two canvases. Felix was reluctant to part with the Rembrandts, but he needed the money from the sale. He therefore made a curious arrangement with Widener: for the two paintings, Felix would receive $400,000, but he retained the right to repurchase the paintings at the sale price plus 8 percent annual interest. If Felix could not do so by 1 January 1924, however, they would become the sole property of Widener.[26]

The agreement was signed, and Widener sailed off to America with the two paintings. Within a few weeks, Felix had disposed of, in advance, most of the proceeds from the sale of the Rembrandts in paying off his old debts and donating large sums to various émigré causes. He had still not received the money from Widener; then, one day, a letter arrived from Widener's American lawyers, saying that the prince must sign a second contract promising that if he repurchased the two pictures, he would then keep them for ten years before trying to sell them again. Otherwise, Widener said, the deal was off. Felix, who had already spent most of the money he expected from the sale, had little choice.

Within a year, however, Felix was again in financial trouble. The deadline for buying the two Rembrandts back from Widener was fast approaching. Felix consulted with a team of lawyers, who informed him that the second contract was unlikely to stand up in a court of law; all the prince had to do was come up with the money to repurchase the paintings.

Felix wrote to Widener, asking him to reconsider the terms of the second contract; Widener, however, refused. The prince then tried again, sending a personal letter which was little short of a plea:

> My misfortune and catastrophe are without precedent.
> Millions of my countrymen are suffering and starving.
> This is the principal reason that I signed the contract with
> you and your envoy. I beg you to reconsider the terms of
> the contract, and I must insist that you think about the
> possibility of modifying certain terms. In this matter, be-
> cause I have already signed the contract, I am at your

mercy. I lay the matter at your feet and appeal to your sense of justice and your conscience.[27]

But Widener did not bother to reply. Felix then contacted a shadowy figure named Calousle Gulbenkian, an Armenian oil tycoon living in Paris. All Gulbenkian asked of Felix was that in return for the loan he would be offered first rights to the paintings if Felix decided to sell them. Felix agreed, and Gulbenkian dispatched a check to Widener through an American lawyer. But Widener refused to accept the money. Felix decided to sue.

In November 1923, Felix and Irina set sail on the *Berengaria* for New York to take legal action against Widener. They also came with a number of valuable jewels which they planned to sell in America. This collection included enamel miniatures in diamond frames, snuffboxes and cigarette cases in gold and platinum, jeweled ceremonial daggers, and carved Oriental ruby-and-sapphire miniatures. This last decision was to prove a tragic mistake for the impecunious Youssoupovs.

22

Growing Troubles

THE YOUSSOUPOVS' AMERICAN ADVENTURE proved a disaster from the beginning. When the *Berengaria* moored in New York, an enterprising group of journalists made their way onto the liner and stormed their cabin. Felix had no choice but to answer their questions—not only about the Widener case but also about Rasputin's murder, the Russian Revolution, and the imperial family. Just as the members of the press left, U.S. immigration officials arrived and announced that Felix would not be granted a visa because the laws forbade an acknowledged assassin from entering the country. It took Felix a great deal of explaining to finally convince the officials that he was not a professional murderer and thus not a danger to anyone.[1] Eventually, they relented and allowed Felix to disembark.

But as the Youssoupovs were clearing customs, other officials seized all of the jewelry which they had brought with them to sell on the suspicion that it was part of the Russian crown jewels and was therefore not the sole property of the prince. Felix and Irina both protested vehemently, saying that the pieces in question were their own personal property, but to no avail: The customs officials made out a receipt for the jewels, handed it to Felix, and then took possession of them. It was an inauspicious start to their first trip to America.

Felix and Irina stayed in New York for six months. They first took a suite at the Plaza Annex, where they entertained new acquaintances. They were instant celebrities; at one party, the strain of having such famous guests told on the hostess, who introduced a stunned Felix and giggling Irina as "the Prince and Princess Rasputin."[2] While in New York, they became friends with Elizabeth Shoumatov, a painter of some repute who had fled the Revolution. Irina showed her some of the paintings that she herself was working on. They were grotesque female heads with throats slashed and surrounded by pools of blood. Irina said that she painted these in a trance. When Felix discovered that his wife was displaying her art, he himself jumped into the show, pulling out paintings he had done of Rasputin-like bearded men, their faces set in evil grimaces.[3]

The case against Widener dragged on, with lawyers communicating back and forth. It was an entirely new experience for Felix. He expressed great admiration for America and found the country exciting and pleasantly refreshing; at the same time, he was angered at his powerlessness where his jewels and his legal case were concerned. He could only keep up appearances for so long. Eventually, Felix and Irina were forced to move out of the Plaza Annex and into a small, undistinguished flat. They remained the toast of New York society, but when the parties and dinners had ended, they returned not to luxurious surroundings but to a cold, barely furnished room where they awaited news of the Widener settlement.

One of the peculiar characters who came into the Youssoupovs' circle in New York was a Gypsy singer named Vera Smirnova. As their money ran low, they relied on Smirnova more and more often. She regularly collected leftover bits of food from the nightclub where she entertained, carefully wrapped them up, and took them to the Youssoupovs' flat to provide them with dinner. Felix was so low on funds that sometimes these gifts from Smirnova were the only food which he and Irina had.[4]

No settlement with Widener could be reached, and the prince and princess sailed back to France, having collected their impounded jewels at customs as they left. The affair with Widener was finally settled in 1925. The New York State Supreme Court ruled in favor of the American collector, saying that if the prince were to recover the paintings, he had to do so with his own money, not with funds borrowed for the purpose of redeeming the Rembrandts with the idea of then reselling them at a greater price. Felix was stunned, particularly after having been assured that the second contract was illegal. But the case had ended, and he had lost. The two paintings eventually ended up at the National Gallery of Art in Washington, D.C., donated by Widener.

Felix was still hard-pressed for funds. Again, he went to Cartier with more pieces of jewelry: button pearl ear studs; two teardrop pearls; a necklace of 151 pearls; one of thirty-five pearls; and another necklace of three strands of pearls and seven teardrop pendants.[5] The prince received just over £100,000 for these jewels as an advance; when their sales were realized, further money would be placed in his bank accounts.

He also tried his hand at two business ventures: a dressmaking firm called Irfe, with branches in Paris, Berlin, and London, and a restaurant called La Maisonette. For a time, these businesses prospered, and Felix and Irina once again enjoyed a secure income.

Irfe—from the first two letters in both Irina's and Felix's names—took up where other Romanovs, notably Grand Duchess Marie Pavlovna, had failed. The designs, some executed by Felix and Irina, were modeled by the svelte, shapeless princess, who served as a fashionable example of the flapper chic of the era. An elegant premiere party was planned at the Ritz in Paris. On the scheduled evening, Felix and Irina, impeccably dressed, waited nervously to receive their first guests and clients. But no one appeared. Felix discovered that his butler, André Bull, had forgotten to mail the invitations. A second party was hastily arranged, and members of the Russian exile community thronged to meet with the famous and fashionable prince and princess.[6]

By 1926, Irfe had expanded to branches in Le Touquet and London. Inevitably, however, Felix's bad business sense led him astray, and the operations neared financial collapse. Irfe was saved from total ruin only by the generous financial intervention of his friend Mrs. William K. Vanderbilt.

Marie Pavlovna found all of this rather odd. Herself in dire financial straits, she was amazed at Felix's sheer determination, although, as she noted, he was usually something less than successful:

> Besides distributing money right and left to private individuals he had started one or two organizations for the assistance of the refugees, these along artistic lines. He

preferred to work independently, refusing to allow a routine, never looking for public support. Wishing to have things done according to his own ideas and will he would have nothing to do with committees, nor would he listen to advice. But though he always wanted to dominate, he was not an organizer; he worked at times with feverish energy, yet his efforts were mostly ineffective.[7]

Nevertheless, she greatly enjoyed Felix's company, and the two of them launched a peculiar project: a series of theatrical performances starring Russian exiles. The idea captivated Felix. He seems not to have given much thought to the incongruity of former princes and grand duchesses acting in the works of Chekhov before an audience of the dispossessed. But Felix prevailed, and the performances, intended to help raise funds for various émigré causes, were a success.

The friendship which developed between Marie Pavlovna and Felix was a curious one. Since Rasputin's assassination Felix had been greatly out of favor with her brother Dimitri Pavlovich, who refused to forgive him for breaking the oath of silence that all of the conspirators had agreed upon. Felix seems not to have missed the friendship, so important to him in former days. Marie Pavlovna, longing for companionship in exile, quickly latched herself on to Felix and Irina and became an intimate member of their circle. She shared holidays with the Youssoupovs at their ramshackle villa in Corsica, swimming and boating, all the while reliving the glory of days gone by.

Helene Izvolsky, daughter of Nicholas II's ambassador to France, approached Felix in the mid-1920s with the idea of writing a book about Rasputin and the fall of the Romanovs. She visited him at his house in the Bois de Boulogne and left a memorable account of the occasion:

> On the day of my visit . . . the house was very quiet. The Prince was recovering from an operation and had been ordered to rest. He received me, reclining on a divan, dressed in white silk pajamas. I was struck by the extraordinary beauty of his face. I had not seen him since his wedding day, when he had appeared as a prince charm-

ing. Now he was a mature man and one who had been
through a frightening ordeal. His features had become
even more striking. The large, grey-blue eyes were like
two pools of light, mysterious, hypnotic; the dark eye-
brows straight as arrows, the long eyelashes, the smile on
the thin, slightly twisted lips made him look like an angel
of the Renaissance. His wife Irina entered. The radiant
young bride I had seen in my debutante days was now
austere and melancholy. But she had what Russians call
an icon-like beauty. She stayed only a few moments, shy
and silent as a ghost. . . . When we were left alone, Prince
Felix beckoned me to a chair and offered me a cigarette. It
seemed strange that this beautiful, mysterious creature
should greet me so casually, as if he had known me all his
life. And yet, there was something Satanic about his
twisted smile. He talked for several hours about the assassination, and seemed quite pleased to reminisce, going
over all the horrifying details. In conclusion, he showed
me a ring he was wearing, with a bullet mounted in silver. He explained that this was the bullet that had killed
Rasputin.[8]

It was then, in 1926, that Felix turned his thoughts to the
surest source of income. In the years following the Russian Revolution, many exiled members of the aristocracy and the imperial
family had written memoirs about the collapse of the monarchy.
In nearly all of these books, reference was made to Felix as a
minor character. In addition, several books had been written
about Rasputin, all purporting to tell the truth of the story. Purishkevich's diary had itself been published, which led Felix to
believe that there was no reason why, the pledge to secrecy having been broken, he should not also benefit from a story in which
he had been a major participant. Felix decided that he, too,
should write a book about Rasputin and his murder. Although
he always protested that he did not wish to be remembered for
just one thing, time and time again his murder of the peasant
had saved the day, his notoriety opening doors and giving him
access to finances. Felix saw no reason why others should profit
by his actions and he should not also capitalize on his most fa-

mous act. *Rasputin: His Malignant Influence and His Assassination* was published in 1927 and greeted with a storm of controversy.

The book was chiefly concerned with retelling the story of Felix's acquaintance with Rasputin and the events leading to the murder. As such, Felix naturally tried to present Rasputin in the worst possible light and as deserving of death. When he wrote of the murder, Felix stuck to the orthodox version, which he would repeat over the years, never acknowledging the additional facts about the events that fateful night at the Moika Palace.

Those loyal to the former tsar and his family were less than pleased with the portrayal of the imperial family, particularly with the highly unflattering portrait Felix drew of Empress Alexandra. Supporters of Rasputin considered the book filled with lies and exaggerations and thought that it had been written solely to justify what in their eyes had been an unjustifiable act. Not surprisingly, Felix received threatening letters from both factions. Then there were those, like Grand Duke Dimitri Pavlovich, who were angered that Felix had broken the pledge of secrecy that all of the conspirators had taken that night to remain silent. Over the years, Dimitri Pavlovich privately expressed regret for his involvement in the murder. According to Marie Pavlovna, Dimitri was "revolted" by Felix's actions.[9] The publication of the prince's book caused a permanent rift between the two former friends, and they never again spoke to each other.

The strongest attack came from Rasputin's daughter Maria, then living in exile in Paris near the prince. "To me," she wrote, "it is atrocious, and I do not believe that any decent person could help feeling a sentiment of disgust in reading the savage ferocity of this story. . . ." She took immediate action against both the prince, "who vomited forth the vilest calumnies against my father," and Grand Duke Dimitri Pavlovich by lodging a formal complaint in a Parisian court. Unwittingly, Felix himself had outlined her claim in his own book: Rasputin, the suit declared, had been deliberately lured to the Moika Palace and murdered as part of a premeditated plot. She sought $800,000 in damages.[10]

Felix hired the reknowned Mâitre de Moro-Gaifferri to act as counsel. His new lawyer had already represented one murderer, the infamous "Bluebeard," Henri Landru. Maria's suit rested entirely on the presumption that an essentially political assassination in a foreign court was actionable once the responsible parties admitted their guilt. Through his lawyer, Felix issued a statement declaring that he had been motivated solely for patriotic reasons and that, since his exile, he had seen no information which altered this view. The court, however, refused to hear the case, agreeing with Felix that the killing had been a political act and that the French legal system had no jurisdiction over the internal affairs of imperial Russia.[11]

Although Maria Rasputin's claim was dismissed, it became only one of Felix's legal troubles. Late one night, a distant relative woke the Youssoupovs with the news that the French minister of the interior was about to bring charges against Felix for bank fraud. A number of false Hungarian banknotes had been discovered, and the French government, according to their midnight caller, was set to arrest Felix as a conspirator. Felix was given two Spanish laissez-passer for himself and his valet and warned to leave Paris immediately to avoid compromising Irina.

This news came as a shock to Felix, who protested that he had nothing to do with the Hungarian fraud. Nevertheless, he quickly fled the country and took up temporary residence in Spain. Soon enough, however, he learned that no such indictment had been contemplated by the French government; apparently, the plan had been devised solely to remove Felix from Paris and take advantage of Irina's distress by stealing their valuable collection of jewelry.[12]

A second, even more unpleasant incident soon followed. On 10 January 1928, the White Russian newspaper *Dni* alleged that Felix had been discovered in an unpleasant sexual and financial scandal and been expelled from France. The story strongly implied that this discovery was punishable with a sentence of hard labor. Although no details were given, Felix's reputation was such that everyone assumed he had been caught with a male prostitute.

The accusations, while unfounded, apparently came uncomfortably close to the truth where Felix's sexual activity was concerned.[13] He immediately instructed Mâitre de Moro-Giafferri to lodge a complaint against *Dni* and its publisher, Alexander Kerensky, the former president of the Russian provisional government. In May 1928 a libel suit was brought against *Dni* and several other newspapers which had repeated the story. Under oath, the agents representing the newspapers admitted that they had made a mistake and that there was no evidence to support the assertions. Although Felix needed the money from the settlement, he generously donated the sum to several of his favorite émigré charities.[14]

The end of the 1920s saw the deaths of many of the Russian émigrés who had managed to escape the vengeance of the Revolution. On 11 June 1928, Felix's father died and was buried in Rome. After her husband's death, Zenaide moved in with Felix, Irina, and their daughter; financial hardships had forced the Youssoupovs to sell the house on the rue Gutenburg to a mysterious woman named Mrs Whobee. She had been one of their clients at Irfe, and knowing how desperate their finances were, she had suggested that the Youssoupovs move into a small flat in the gatehouse. This initial noblesse, however, was quickly followed with outrageous demands and tyrannical outbursts. Mrs Whobee was a formidable character, and though she ordered Felix and Irina about like servants, they were in no financial position to refuse.[15]

Emigré politics took a curious turn in the 1920s. The end of the Civil War and the secure establishment of the Bolshevik regime forced many exiled Russians to accept the finality of their position. Nevertheless, several claimants to the old imperial throne began to actively campaign for its restoration. Chief among them was Grand Duke Cyril Vladimirovich, son of Grand Duchess Vladimir. In 1924, Cyril proclaimed himself tsar of Russia. As the most senior surviving Romanov grand duke, Cyril was perfectly within his rights to assume the position of the head of the dynasty and to claim the throne. However, he had incurred the wrath of many members of the Romanov family and Russian émigrés by being the first in the family to publicly break his oath of allegiance to the tsar and lend his support to the provisional government.

The other chief candidate for the throne was Grand Duke Nicholas Nicholaievich, the former commander in chief of Russia's army. However, the grand duke was reluctant to make any claim, and again, there were those who opposed him, holding

Nicholas Nicholaievich responsible for forcing Nicholas II's hand in the granting of the Duma in 1905 and also for urging the tsar to abdicate the throne in 1917. He himself was aware that his position was secondary to that of Grand Duke Cyril.

Grand Duke Nicholas Nicholaievich died in 1929, leaving Cyril Vladimirovich as the sole claimant actively maneuvering for the throne. His wife, Victoria Melita, ambitious for them both, goaded Cyril on and constantly sought out any support for his claims which would lend legitimacy, including that of the fledgling National Socialist German Worker's party under Adolf Hitler. In 1922, Hitler himself was a guest of the Vladimiroviches at their house in Coburg, and Victoria Melita was an enthusiastic participant at early storm trooper meetings throughout the 1920s. Eventually, the majority of the Romanov grand dukes in exile recognized the legitimacy of Cyril's claim, only to later withdraw their support.

On 13 October 1928, Dowager Empress Marie Feodorovna died in Copenhagen at the age of eighty. Her death removed the last of the Romanovs who had once reigned in Russia. The funeral was celebrated with imperial pomp: Nearly all of the surviving Romanovs attended, along with representatives of all of Europe's royal houses. Along with other members of her family, Felix and Irina slowly walked behind her coffin as it was carried through the streets of Copenhagen by officers of her Cossack Guard. Everyone who attended recognized that the dowager empress's death marked the end of an era.

23

Ghosts

THE DEATH OF THE DOWAGER EMPRESS and the en-
suing scramble to claim the former Romanov throne marked ten
years since the deaths of the Russian imperial family on the night
of 16 July 1918. In 1919 an official investigator, Nicholas Sokolov,
was appointed by the White Army to conduct an examination
into their deaths. The results of his inquiry were published in
1924 in a book called *The Assassination of the Russian Imperial Family*. But significant doubts as to the official version of the family's
deaths were raised in 1920 with the appearance of a woman
claiming to be Grand Duchess Anastasia, the youngest daughter
of Tsar Nicholas II.

At the time, Felix, along with other surviving Romanovs,
was caught up in the drama of her claim. Members of his family,
as well as former servants and court officials, visited her
throughout the 1920s; reaction was mixed, with many recognizing her as Anastasia, while others denounced her as a cheap
actress or an adventuress. In the summer of 1927, Felix was one
of those who made the journey to Castle Seeon in Bavaria, where
the claimant, then using the name Fraulein Tchaikovsky, was a
guest of the duke of Leuchtenberg.

It had been twelve years since Felix had last seen Grand
Duchess Anastasia, then a precocious, rather chubby girl of four-
teen. He was now faced with a thin, pale, seriously ill young
woman. According to Felix, Prof. Serge Rudnev, her attending
physician, ran up to the claimant's room to inform her of her
visitor. He then returned to say that she had been delighted,
exclaiming, "Felix! Felix! What a joy to see him again! I will get
dressed and come down immediately. Is Irina with him?"[1]

Felix found "this joy at seeing me again . . . exaggerated."[2]
And it certainly appears to have been, either by Rudnev or, most
probably, by the prince himself. When she learned of her visitor,
the claimant had actually run screaming to the duchess of
Leuchtenberg, "Youssoupov is here! Felix . . . Youssoupov!"[3]
Eventually, Fraulein Tchaikovsky was persuaded to come down
to meet with the prince. They sat in the garden. The entire visit
lasted less than fifteen minutes. Felix made small talk with the
woman in English, Russian, German, and French about his life
in exile and the dress shop he and Irina had begun. After an
uncomfortable period of silence between the two, Felix bid
Fraulein Tchaikovsky farewell and left.

Or did he? According to a story told by the claimant many
years later, not long after returning to her room in the castle,
she looked in her dressing-table mirror only to see Felix standing in the shadows. She turned around and demanded to know
why he was there, but the prince made straight for her, arms
outstretched and hands clutching the air. "I killed Rasputin and
I will kill you for what your mother did to my country!" he is
supposed to have declared. "We will have you out of the
way!"[4]

This story, appearing in an unreliable book, came from
Fraulein Tchaikovsky long after she had begun her descent into
senility. While it is arguable that Felix may have been capable
of a great many things, it is absurd to believe that the Romanov
family would dispatch him to kill the young woman claiming
to be Anastasia, as has been alleged, or that he would have had
the stomach for it. There is no evidence to support the allegation.[5]

Once away from Castle Seeon, Felix denounced her as a
"nervous, hysterical, vulgar and common" woman. He then
wrote a letter to Grand Duke Andrei Vladimirovich, who had
taken a great deal of interest in the case of the unknown
woman:

> *I claim categorically that she is not Anastasia Nicho-
> laievna but rather just an adventuress, a sick hysteric and a
> frightful playactress.*

I simply cannot understand how anyone can be in
doubt of this.

If you had seen her, I am *convinced* that you would
recoil in horror at the thought that this frightful creature
could be the daughter of our Tsar. . . .

These false pretenders ought to be gathered up and
sent to live forever in a house somewhere.[6]

Felix had been asked to see Mrs. Tchaikovsky at the request
of Gleb Botkin, the son of the former court physician, who had
recognized her as Anastasia without hesitation. Following his
visit to Seeon, the prince wrote to the empress's sister Victoria,
marchioness of Milford-Haven, to warn her of Botkin and his
tactics:

Dear Madam,

I am sending you this letter by Mr. Gleb Botkin, son
of Their Majesties' personal Physician. He is quite sure
that the person claiming to be the Grand Duchess Anastasia is speaking the truth and has various documents to
prove it. I hold quite a different opinion, having just seen
her at the Leuchtenbergs' castle near Munich where she is
now living. I cannot understand how anyone can make
such a mistake, since she is very common and has absolutely nothing to remind one of the Grand Duchess. Nor
does she understand a word of English, but answers questions only in German, and not even that unless she is feeling like it. She understands Russian but does not speak it.
I feel such a situation should not be allowed to continue,
and that something should be done about it. This is why I
believe you should see Botkin, since he has all the evidence purporting to show that she is the Grand Duchess
and a lot of people believe it; whereas I myself am sure
that all is untrue.[7]

This was not the end of the Anastasia affair for Felix. During
her first trial in Hamburg in the 1950s to try to prove her identity,
Felix was deposed by the court and gave evidence against her.

After the first verdict against the plaintiff's claim, the case went to court again. Some of "Anastasia's" supporters allegedly approached Felix, who they said offered to testify that he now recognized the woman as the lost grand duchess for a share of her fortune in the Bank of England. Hearing this proposal, Gleb Botkin wrote to a friend:

> The Romanovs are very snobbish to them, Youssoupov is just a commoner. Further, they know as well as I do how completely dishonest and dirty a person he is. Even if we were [to] assume that Rasputin was a horrible villain, his murder as engineered and performed by Youssoupov must still be adjudged as one of the filthiest crimes in history, as well as an act of monumental idiocy. . . . Youssoupov is a self-confessed murderer, perjurer and traitor. As everyone knows, he is also a homosexual, a drunkard and a hooligan. . . . [He] testified under oath that Anastasia is an imposter and that all her supporters are either lunatics or crooks. But now he tells you that he is willing to have Anastasia acknowledged, but only if there is money in the Bank of England and if he is assured of a share of it. . . . This willingness to acknowledge her as the real Grand Duchess in return for a large sum of money would . . . prove him to be a scoundrel. . . . He knows perfectly well that Anastasia is what she claims to be and his fight against her is a crime more horrible and cruel by far than even the murder of Rasputin.[8]

On the whole, however, Felix tended to steer clear of Romanov family politics. His own desperate situation provided him with enough worries. The Depression hit him hard. Irfe went bankrupt, and the Prince was forced to close all the branches of the venture. The Paris restaurant La Maisonette was seized by creditors, who sold the property to pay back debts. Twice, baliffs arrived at his home, threatening to take possession of its contents to settle accounts with those he owed. Still, he was carelessly generous. One day, a destitute refugee arrived at his house and asked for assistance; Felix handed over all of the money he had set aside to pay his creditors. When confronted with a packet of unpaid bills, he merely smiled and said, "It doesn't matter. I have trust in God."[9]

Just as the situation looked hopeless, the specter of Rasputin appeared in the form of a new Hollywood movie about the peasant and his assassination. Public fascination with Rasputin had never abated, and it is not surprising that sooner or later Hollywood would try to capitalize on the drama. By the most extraordinary of circumstances, this film about Rasputin's death also proved to be Felix Youssoupov's financial salvation.

In 1932, M-G-M Studios released *Rasputin and the Empress*, a lengthy, overblown epic about the last days of the imperial regime. It was not the first motion picture to depict Rasputin's life and death, nor would it be the last. Nine years earlier, Felix had been approached by a representative from a Hollywood studio who offered him an enormous sum of money if he would consent to appear, as himself, in a film about Rasputin's murder. Although he desperately needed the money, Felix refused to consider the proposal. This came as an immense shock to the agent. "You, Prince, are an idiot!" he declared when Felix declined his offer.[10] For all of his love of the notoriety which Rasputin's murder had brought him, Felix found the idea of participating in a motion picture about the event too much for his tastes.

Felix's refusal to cooperate, however, did not stop the motion-picture industry: Rasputin's infamous life and legendary death made far too good a story. This eventually led to the production of *Rasputin and the Empress*, starring Ethel, John, and Lionel Barrymore. The film was high melodrama, overacted and brimming with "the most appalling and incredible dialogue" and blatant historical inaccuracies.[11] It opens in the Kremlin's Cathedral of the Assumption during the celebration of the Romanov Tercentenary in 1913. Prince Paul Chegodieff, the main character, played by John Barrymore, has just learned of the assassination of the tsar's uncle Grand Duke Serge. In later scenes, when Prince Chegodieff attempts to comfort the grand duke's daughter, Princess Natasha, played by English actress Diana Wynard, the princess relates her faith in a new miracle worker,

Father Gregory. Although the prince protests vehemently, Princess Natasha continues to defend the holy man.

As the movie progresses, viewers are introduced to the tsar, the empress, and their ailing son. Soon the tsarevich suffers from a severe attack of hemophilia, and Rasputin is called to the palace, where he hypnotizes the boy and arrests the bleeding. Again, Prince Paul protests, but the tsar rejects his pleas and fires him from his post in the Imperial Guards. Throughout the film, Princess Natasha is touted as Prince Chegodieff's true love; to his horror, one day he receives a note from her: "Dearest, I'm no longer fit to be your wife." The prince rushes to his beloved, who tearfully explains that Rasputin has hypnotized her and, while she was in this state, raped her. News of this crime spreads rapidly through the court, and the empress, played by Ethel Barrymore, acknowledges the evil influence of the peasant.

Prince Paul arranges to lure Rasputin to his palace with the help of the imperial court; the royal physician provides him with cyanide to poison the cakes and wine which the prince will serve to the victim. The actual murder scene is a far cry from Felix's version: Once in the cellar of the palace, Rasputin suspects an attempt is being made on his life. He grabs a revolver and then, incredibly, asks the prince for a tour of the basement. While the prince obliges, Rasputin stumbles, and Chegodieff tells him that he has been poisoned. Rasputin shrieks, at the same time aiming the weapon at the prince. Chegodieff manages to wrestle it away from him and beats Rasputin violently over the head with a fireplace poker. But Rasputin is not yet dead; he runs after Prince Paul, and a struggle ensues during which the peasant is hurled into the frozen canal and his head crushed between two blocks of ice. The movie ends on another improbable note, with the imperial family congratulating the prince on his heroic deed and the two lovers, Prince Paul and Princess Natasha, reunited in exile in London.

Critical reaction to the film was mixed. The costumes and sets were surprisingly accurate. But it was considerably dated even when it premiered, and its melodramatic dialogue and fiendish overacting drew howls of laughter from the critics. The *New York Herald Tribune* reported, "It achieves one feat which is not inconsiderable, it manages to libel even the despised Rasputin." The reviewer of the *New York Times* was struck by "the fight between Prince Chegodieff, as Prince Youssoupov is known here, and the 'Mad Monk.' " This line immediately laid out the future case: that Prince Chegodieff was in fact a thinly veiled portrait of Felix Youssoupov. The most damaging portion of the film, however, turned out to be the preface, which flashed on screen before the heavy melodrama began: "This concerns the destruction of an Empire, brought about by the mad ambition of one man. A few of the principal characters are still alive. The rest met death by violence."[12]

The Youssoupovs did not view the film, as it had not yet been released in Europe. But they soon learned of its existence and the general outline of the plot. They contacted the American legal firm of Neufeld and Schlechtev of New York and asked them to intervene on their behalf. The lawyers wrote to M-G-M claiming that the film libeled their clients, since "the incidents surrounding the historic drama and the manner and method of the killing of Rasputin were neither fair nor true."[13] No other complaint was alleged in this first notification. M-G-M replied on 19 January 1933, refusing to discuss the matter.

Nearly two months passed before the next exchange. On 2 March 1933, Neufeld and Schlechtev again wrote to M-G-M, alleging that the character of Princess Natasha was "a thinly disguised impersonation of the real Princess Irina Youssoupov." The lawyers asserted that "the whole world is apprised of the alleged desecration" of Princess Irina. They demanded that M-G-M withdraw the film immediately, issue a worldwide apology to the princess, and make satisfactory retribution to their client.[14]

In the meantime, the film, retitled *Rasputin, the Mad Monk*, opened at the Dominion Theatre in Tottenham Court Road and at the Empire in Leicester Square in London. M-G-M seemed unwilling to address the Youssoupovs' claims and compounded the problem by continuing to actively promote the film. Then, in the summer of 1933, Princess Irina first met the American lawyer Fanny Holtzmann, who effectively took charge of the case and directed the subsequent legal proceedings.

Fanny Holtzmann was then thirty years old. She had met and overcome many difficulties in her struggle to become a member of the bar: She was a woman, Jewish, and headstrong—none of which worked in her favor in the New York of the 1920s. But she quickly made a name for herself and in time became a celebrity.

In the summer of 1933, Fanny Holtzmann happened to be vacationing in the south of France. During her visit she was introduced to Irina. The princess told Miss Holtzmann about the film, protesting that she had never even met Rasputin and that she considered herself libeled by the suggestion in the movie that she had been raped by him. Irina asked the American lawyer if she would be willing to meet with Prince Felix to discuss the matter further, and Fanny Holtzmann agreed.

Felix and Holtzmann met for luncheon at the Ritz. The conversation was difficult: Felix's English was nearly impossible to follow, Holtzmann barely managed in French and could not speak Russian at all. But gradually the prince informed the American of the situation as he saw it. He did recommend, however, that Holtzmann visit Princess Irina's mother, Grand Duchess Xenia, in London, to catch any details she may have missed in the translation.

Holtzmann dutifully went to London. Grand Duchess Xenia had taken up residence along with her sons in Frogmore House, a Georgian mansion below the battlements of Windsor Castle. Xenia spoke at some length about not only the film but Rasputin and the imperial family as well. Referring to her sister-in-law Empress Alexandra, Xenia said bluntly, "That woman made a rag out of Nicky. She was never really one of us. She wouldn't speak a word of Russian unless she absolutely had to."[15]

After this encounter, Holtzmann placed a telephone call to J. Robert Rubin, M-G-M's vice president in New York. "The Princess and her family are very upset, Bob," she told him. "They're determined to press for damages." When Rubin laughed, she continued: "You don't understand, Bob. Royalty looks at these things differently. If I don't take the case, they'll get someone else."

"It wouldn't make any difference if they got God Almighty," Rubin replied. "There is no case, Fanny. The movie is fiction and we're protected by clearances. Anyway, the damn thing stinks. Audiences won't go near it."[16]

Holtzmann arranged to have a private screening of the offending film for both herself and Felix at the M-G-M executive theater in St. Martin's Lane. At the end of the film, Felix turned to the lawyer and exclaimed, "*Voila*! It is clear. *Le Prince, c'est moi, Natasha, c'est Irina!*"[17] Although Holtzmann was not as convinced as her client, she realized that the preface at the beginning of the film had laid out a trap in which M-G-M might be caught: In saying that "a few of the principal characters are still alive," M-G-M effectively discredited their claim that the film was fictional. The principal characters were Rasputin, Prince Paul Chegodieff, Princess Natasha, and the tsar, empress and tsarevich. Everyone knew that Rasputin had been killed, and by 1933 the deaths of the entire imperial family at the hands of the Bolsheviks were accepted historical fact. That left Prince Paul and Princess Natasha; if they were indeed the "principal characters" who were "still alive," they could be none other than Prince Felix Youssoupov and his wife, Princess Irina.

Convinced that a case existed, Holtzmann urged Felix and Irina to follow through with their plans to take legal action. Felix's previous brush with American justice over the Rembrandt paintings had left him bitter, but as long as the movie continued to play in London, legal action could be taken in England, where it was hoped the more respectful attitude of the general public toward royalty would weigh the case in the Youssoupovs' favor. He, therefore, through Holtzmann, made contact with a set of British legal advisers on what action to take.

In New York, legal papers were filed on behalf of the Youssoupovs seeking an injunction against any further public showing of the film. This action was also decided upon in London, but the question brought with it the threat that the British royal family might be unfavorably linked in the mind of the public with their Russian cousins. King George V was not too kindly disposed toward Felix himself, and Holtzmann had to seek an interview with the Lord Chamberlain, the earl of Cromer, to receive royal assent. In turn, Cromer sent her to a meeting with Sir Reginald Poole, a member of the firm of Lewis and Lewis, the king's personal solicitors.

Sir Reginald thought little of the proposed suit. "Not a chance," he told Miss Holtzmann after viewing the film.

"But a woman's chastity—" Holtzmann began.

"We'd be laughed out of court," Poole answered. "The Prince has been married for more than thirty years. It's an awkward business—but they've covered their tracks. No specific identity—just a photograph with a fictional name attached. Rasputin had dozens of women. It could have been anybody."

"I still think it's worth bringing suit, if only to force a disclaimer about any living persons being intended."

"In America, perhaps. In this country, the prospects wouldn't justify the risks of public scandal."[18]

But Holtzmann would not give up so easily. Once again, she telephoned J. Robert Rubin in New York. "Look, Bob, there *is* a case here, but the protocol complications just aren't worth the trouble. I can't afford to spend the next month lunching with the Lord Chamberlain. So here's a simple solution for both of us: Pay the Princess some minimal settlement—say, five thousand dollars—and put in a notice with the credit titles on *Rasputin* that the picture doesn't refer to any living persons."

"Five thousand dollars!" Rubin exclaimed. "You must be out of your mind!"

"It's peanuts to MGM, Bob. But it will cool off the royal hotheads here, and spare both of us a royal headache."

"I can't do it, Fanny. I have to think of our stockholders."

"Which includes protecting them against possible disasters," she answered. "Look—I don't care how much you pay. Make it a thousand, five hundred, even. Just so we can both get off the hook and I don't have to go back to my clients empty-handed."

"I am ashamed," Rubin replied, "that an American lawyer should be so concerned with gaining the goodwill of the decadent Russian aristocracy." At this, Holtzmann hung up the telephone.[19] Her mind was set: she would pursue legal action against M-G-M on behalf of the Youssoupovs.

24

Trial

THE POTENTIAL CASE RESTED SOLELY on the question of whether Irina had been libeled in the film. Felix himself could not press for damages, as the manner of Rasputin's death in the M-G-M film differed greatly from his own published account. There was no legal precedent at the time the case went to trial: Had Irina herself been libeled through the main character of Princess Natasha when the very essence of rape implied that it was an action taken without the consent of the victim? Such complications would make the Youssoupov case an important landmark in legal history.

Suit had not yet been filed in England. Felix, through Holtzmann, therefore contacted Henry St. John Field, a barrister with the firm of Langton and Passmore, who submitted the required forms to begin action. From the outset, M-G-M maintained that the character of Princess Natasha was fictional, not in any way based on the real Princess Youssoupov. The case therefore would be won only after a jury had been convinced that Princess Natasha had been based on Princess Irina.

To represent Irina, Felix hired Sir Patrick Hastings, K.C., a distinguished member of the bar. He would face M-G-M's representative, Sir William Jowitt, K.C. M-G-M demanded that $5,000 bond be posted by the princess as security against costs; Felix and Irina were broke, and the money came discreetly from Buckingham Palace, which also paid for the initial costs of retaining the British counsel.[1]

The trial opened on Tuesday, 27 February 1934, in the Royal Courts of Justice in the Strand. At 10:30 A.M. the case of *Youssoupov v. M-G-M* was called to order. Irina sat on the solicitor's bench, dressed in black. She wore a single strand of pearls round her neck, double pearl stud earrings, and numerous rings. Across her face was a heavy veil. Behind her sat Felix, also dressed in black, with their friends Lady Diana Cooper and Lady Oxford on either side. Presiding over the case was Sir Horace Avery.

Sir Patrick Hastings opened the proceedings. "As you might have heard, this is an action for libel and it is a very unusual case. I think it is probably the first case of its sort that has ever been heard." Hastings went on to explain that if the suit was correct in its action, then the plaintiff, Princess Irina, had been defamed by M-G-M's actions in the film. While he explained that undoubtedly M-G-M would argue that the character of Princess Natasha was fictional, Hastings would also argue that for libel to be actionable it need only be proved that the character of Princess Natasha was based on the real Princess Yousoupov and that members of the general public might reasonably conclude that this was the case after viewing the film.[2]

Hastings then launched into a brief explanation of the film and of Rasputin. He told the jury that Rasputin had been an evil influence at the court of the tsar and that Felix, in a patriotic act, had decided to kill the peasant in the hope that he would remove this malicious presence from the political scene. While the film depicted this event, Hastings continued, the case against M-G-M rested upon the portrayal of Princess Natasha's violation at the hands of Rasputin. Because the plaintiff believed Natasha was based on the real-life princess Irina, the depiction of Natasha as a woman who has been raped by Rasputin and is, in her own words, unfit to be the wife of Prince Paul therefore implied that Irina had, likewise, been intimate with Rasputin.

Pointing at the Youssoupovs sitting nervously on the benches, Hastings proclaimed that they had once owned the largest fortune in Russia but were now penniless, living only with their painful memories, which this film had unfortunately reawakened.

At this point, the barrister began a lengthy analysis of the film and compared it with the known facts of the events it depicted. Prince Chegodieff, in the film, lives in a building called the Moika Palace. "No other Prince had such a palace," he told the jury. "The Moika Palace was the palace of Prince Youssoupov and of nobody else." He detailed the film's depiction of the decision to kill the peasant, saying that Chegodieff decides to lure the peasant to the basement of his palace and poison him. Prince Felix Youssoupov also did this in real life. After the murder, the body is thrown into the river, as Rasputin's body had been. In the film, Prince Chegodieff is exiled by the tsar after the assassination, just as Felix was exiled by Nicholas II. Hastings concluded by asking, "Is anyone going to suggest that Prince Chegodieff, who lives in the Moika Palace by the Moika River, and who kills Rasputin in the cellar of that palace, is a different person from Prince Youssoupov?"

"Yes!" Jowitt interjected.[3]

Hastings ignored the remark and continued by reading out to the jury a list of the cast of the film and their roles. He followed this by reading the preface to the film which referred to the fact that "a few of the principal characters are still alive." Returning to his list, Hastings began to name off each character in the film and to tell the jury whether he or she was dead or alive. The tsar, empress, and tsarevich had all been shot to death in 1918; Rasputin had been killed in 1916. That left the two characters of Prince Chegodieff and Princess Natasha. Hastings turned dramatically to the bench where Felix and Irina sat, pointed at them, and loudly exclaimed, "They are alive and they are there!"[4]

He then turned to the matter of libel. He warned that the lawyers for M-G-M would contend that it was not libel to say that a woman had been raped because such a depiction did not portray consent. To Hastings, this did not matter. If the film showed a woman who, in the eyes of the viewers, had been so utterly degraded by sleeping with a man of such dubious character as Rasputin and if that woman was, in fact, based on the real-life princess Irina, then the implication made was that Irina had, in fact, been so debased by the peasant. Libel was actionable because, regardless of consent, after the fact the character of Princess Natasha considered herself unworthy to marry Prince Paul. Princess Natasha was a niece of the tsar, a princess of Russia. Hastings pointed out that the tsar had only one Russian princess for a niece, and that was Princess Irina Youssoupov. Declaring that no other woman in Russia could have been the basis for the depiction of Princess Natasha, Hastings concluded his opening statement, and the jury was dismissed to view the film in question.[5]

When court reconvened, Irina was called to the witness box by Hastings. He questioned her at some length about Rasputin. She declared that she had never met the peasant. Was there any other palace in St. Petersburg known as the Moika Palace? Irina answered no. Who was the person the public believed responsible for the death of Rasputin? "My husband," Irina answered solemnly.

Hastings turned to the film itself. He asked Irina to recall the scene in which Princess Natasha declares to Prince Paul that she is no longer fit to be his wife. The barrister asked if she understood what the film was implying, and Irina answered that she believed the woman felt too ashamed after having been with Rasputin. Irina's answers were given in a low voice; she kept her head bowed during the examination, eyes directed down. To the jury, it seemed obvious that this was a painful experience for her.

Sir William Jowitt began his cross-examination of the princess. He asked Irina if she really believed that anyone knowing the real circumstances of the death of Rasputin could mistake the fictional character of Princess Natasha with herself, to which Irina replied she believed this was possible.

Jowitt carefully began to hint that Irina had brought the action because the Youssoupovs needed the money. To this suggestion, the princess angrily replied that she was angered with the film's depiction of her as Princess Natasha. What she wanted was not money but a public apology and the film's being pulled from general release. Jowitt tried in vain to shake her on this line of questioning, but Irina would not budge. Finally, he gave up and took his seat. The first day of the trial was over.

On the second day, Irina again took the stand to undergo further cross-examination at the hands of Jowitt. The lawyer turned the focus on Felix. He quoted Maurice Paléologue, the former French ambassador in St. Petersburg, describing her husband as "frail and effiminate." Irina strongly disagreed with the depiction, saying that to her Felix had not appeared like this to her.[6] The questioning was at times brutal, with Jowitt asking repeatedly if Irina considered her husband intelligent, an aesthete, a dilettante, all of which the princess reluctantly agreed to. It was clear that Jowitt was trying to draw a clear distinction between the "frail and effeminate," decadent prince and the character of Prince Paul in the film, who appeared strong-willed and decisive. Jowitt's contention was that the character of Chegodieff was based not on Felix Youssoupov but rather on Grand Duke Dimitri Pavlovich. But when he questioned Irina about this possibility, she replied that Chegodieff had seemed to her much more like Felix than Dimitri.

Jowitt would not give up. He began to go through the film point by point, comparing the character of Prince Paul with both Felix and Dimitri. He then began his examination of Natasha and Irina. But Jowitt's comparisons were so detailed that most of the court—including the witness—seemed lost to the implication.

Hasting's reexamination, by contrast, was short and to the point. His aim was to quickly rack up an undeniable set of similarities between the film's characters and the real-life principals. He asked Irina if the tsar had a niece, as the film showed; Irina again answered yes. Hastings asked who that real niece was; Irina replied that it was she. The lawyer asked if there were any princess other than herself who was the niece of the tsar and who later married an assassin of Rasputin; Irina replied no. He asked if she had ever been engaged to Grand Duke Dimitri; Irina once again replied no. Hastings was satisfied. He dismissed Irina from the witness box.[7]

The next witness for the prosecution was Eugene Sablin, a former member of the imperial diplomatic corps. Hastings asked Sablin who, from general knowledge, was the person most intimately connected with the death of Rasputin. "Prince Felix Youssoupov," the man replied. When Hastings asked Sablin whom he had believed Prince Chegodieff to be a depiction of, the witness answered, "Prince Youssoupov." Sablin went on to confirm, under Hastings' questioning, that the Moika Palace was known as the Youssoupov Palace; that no other palace in St. Petersburg was called the Moika Palace; and that on watching the film, he had believed that Princess Natasha was a representation of Princess Irina Youssoupov.[8]

Sablin was dismissed from the witness box, and Hastings called Prince Felix Youssoupov to the stand. The *Daily Express* characterized him as "tall, slim and aesthetic-looking, but dressed in conventional English morning clothes."[9] In spite of the case being Irina's, this was to prove the highlight of the trial for most of the observers.

Hastings began his questioning by asking Felix if he had seen the film. When Felix replied in the affirmative, Hastings asked the prince who, in his opinion, had been portrayed by the character of Prince Chegodieff; without a moment's hesitation, Felix answered, "Myself."[10]

Jowitt's cross-examination was once again long and thorough. He opened his line of questioning by inquiring about the Moika Palace. Felix informed him that there were only two palaces on the Moika Canal, the Youssoupov Palace and the palace of Grand Duchess Xenia, his mother-in-law. When Jowitt mentioned that the Orlov family had a palace there as well, Felix corrected him, saying, somewhat airily, that it was not an important palace, as his had been.

After a few more questions, the trial was adjourned for the day. The London press used banner headlines to promote the trial to its readers, screaming the most sensational details of each day's proceedings. With each day of the trial, the lines to enter the courtroom grew longer. On Friday, 3 March, the lines wrapped around the building, for on that day the court would hear, in detail, Prince Felix Youssoupov's own account of Rasputin's murder. The *Daily Express* reported:

> Blonde, thin and flushed, wearing a collar that shone conspicuously whiter than any in court, Prince Youssoupov was made to relive the death-throes of Imperial Russia, by confirming, step by step, the story of his many efforts to murder Rasputin. No such detailed description of a murder has ever been given from a witness box. The Prince's reiterated "Yes, I did" punctuated Sir William Jowitt's measured readings of his own accounts of the Rasputin death struggle. Over and over again, these made the Prince wince. He cast agonized glances at the back of the court, where such women as Lady Diana Cooper and oth-

ers stood, jammed for three hours, to listen to his evidence. The janitor's remonstrances with those at the door, who were still trying to force a way in, twice interrupted both Counsel and witness. Princess Youssoupov sat with head bowed throughout the cross-examination.[11]

The detail invested in Jowitt's questioning seemed lost on everyone, including the judge, Mr. Justice Avery, who, after listening to this at some length, asked curiously if all of the detail was leading somewhere.

Jowitt hoped that by leading Felix point by point through the murder as described in his published version and comparing it with the film's depiction of the same crime, he would show that there was no resemblance between the two, thus strengthening his case for M-G-M. "All he was really succeeding in doing," writes Sir David Napley, "was to further demonstrate that, despite the caption shown at the beginning, much of the film was historically inaccurate."[12]

Jowitt began by reminding Felix that in his account both the cakes and wine had been poisoned, whereas in the film only the cakes had been tainted. Felix agreed with this fact, and Jowitt, seeming happy, moved on, asking if the prince thought it was reasonable that people viewing the film might come away from it thinking that the character of Prince Chegodieff had been a depiction of Grand Duke Dimitri.

"I think," Felix answered, "in some parts of the film people admit it is the Grand Duke Dimitri, but in the part of killing Rasputin certainly not. Because the public opinion all round the world is that Youssoupov killed Rasputin and not the Grand Duke Dimitri."[13]

Felix was dismissed from the witness box, and Hastings then called his other witnesses—all attesting to their belief that Prince Chegodieff and Princess Nastasha represented the Youssoupovs. First up was Gen. Sir John Hanbury-Williams, who had served in the British Military Mission with the Russian army. He confirmed that he believed Prince Felix Youssoupov had been the principal assassin of Rasputin; that the Youssoupovs had lived in the Moika Palace, where the murder took place, and, that after viewing the film, he had believed it portrayed both Felix and Irina Youssoupov.

The other five witnesses—Adm. Sir Aubrey Smith; Alba Gordon; Prince Nikita Alexandrovich, Irina's brother; Elsie Marie Budd; and Frederick Gade—all took the stand to testify. Two of the five—Smith and Prince Nikita—had intimate knowledge of the last days of imperial Russia and confirmed that they believed Chegodieff and Princess Natasha represented Felix and Irina Youssoupov. The other three were British subjects. Having viewed the film, they felt that the two characters were the plantiff and her husband. The witnesses were finally dismissed, and Hastings announced, "My Lord, that is the Plantiff's case."[14]

25

Triumph

IT TOOK ONLY TWO HOURS for the jury to return a verdict in favor of the plaintiff; the financial award was fixed by them at £25,000. It was an enormous sum; when the award was announced, a gasp went around the courtroom. Then, realizing that they had won, Felix and Irina broke into smiles, and their friends crowded around them to extend their congratulations. Immediately, Mr. Justice Avery issued a restraining order against further public showings of the film *Rasputin and the Empress*.

"The Prince and Princess were hurried away to one of the private rooms in the Law Courts," reported the *Daily Express*. "The Princess sank wearily into a chair and smoked a cigarette. 'What a relief!' she exclaimed. 'I am so tired—so very tired.' They made their way to a motorcar in the courtyard. A crowd gathered as soon as they appeared. Strangers came up to the prince and slapped him on the back. The princess smiled and bowed to those who crowded around her, and as she drove away, she waved her hand in acknowledgment of a burst of cheering."[1]

M-G-M announced that it planned to appeal the verdict. In their complaint, they stated that there had been insufficient evidence to find that the character of Princess Natasha represented Princess Youssoupov; that the film did not depict Princess Natasha as having been either seduced or having become Rasputin's mistress; that if Natasha was depicted as having been raped, rape was not actionable on a libel; that the film, if in error, had only slandered Princess Youssoupov, not libeled her, and therefore special damages such as those awarded by the jury were unreasonable; and that Mr. Justice Avery had prejudiced the jury during his instructions to them.

On 17 July 1934, the court of Appeals ruled in favor of the plaintiff. Lord Justice Scrutton, after reviewing the evidence, announced, "There is obviously evidence, in my opinion, on which a jury might come to the conclusion that the Princess Natasha of the film is the Princess Irina Youssoupov."[2] The court of appeals, in addition, ordered M-G-M to pay costs for the trial, along with an extra £5,000 to the plaintiff.

This was not the end of the case. Action was still pending in the United States. However, because a judgement had already been rendered, it was unlikely that the results there would be much different. In addition, with an issued judgment, the plaintiff had the further right to sue the exhibitors for further damages. If, for example, a theater had shown the film five times a day, that meant that they could be sued five separate times and held accountable for the established libel judgment of £25,000. Since the movie had been shown in over a hundred theaters at the time of the ruling, the potential costs to M-G-M's legal firm, Lowe's, Inc., were incalculable.

Realizing that such judgments could put them out of business, M-G-M contacted Fanny Holtzmann. Less than a month after the court of appeals ruling in London, M-G-M released a statement to the effect that all of the litigation had been ended and that in return for payment of an undisclosed sum, all further action being contemplated by Princess Youssoupov in the United States and the rest of the world would be dropped.

It has never been entirely clear just how much money Irina received from M-G-M. The initial judgment of £25,000, with the additional £5,000, would today equal somewhere between $1 and $1.5 million. The M-G-M books show that a total of about $125,000 went to the princess in return for her agreement to drop all further action; today the same amount would be equal to roughly $2 million. Fanny Holtzmann received an additional $60,000 from the settlement made by M-G-M. Thus, the known total of Irina's financial award was somewhere between $200,000 and $250,000; in today's figures, the award would amount to between $2.5 and $3 million. There were also reports, confirmed by Fanny Holtzmann, that the undisclosed sum was closer to $900,000. Out of this, Miss Holtzmann is alleged to have received approximately $250,000, while Irina walked away with about $750,000, or, in today's figures, just over $15 million.[3] It was an astronomical sum of money and might have been expected to keep the Youssoupovs out of financial trouble for the rest of their lives.

The case of *Youssoupov v. M-G-M* remains a classic example of the legal process; it is still studied today by students of the profession because it established an important number of legal precedents: that it was in fact defamatory to say that a woman had been raped and that films were subject to action as libel and not only as slander. The judgment was the largest single award ever made up until that point in legal history. The verdict also accounts for the disclaimer, seen to this day at the end of every appropriate film, that any resemblance between the characters in the work and any actual living persons is purely coincidental.

In celebration of the victory, Fanny Holtzmann threw a victory party at her flat. Along with the Youssoupovs, over a hundred others attended—members of the aristocracy, the legal profession, and those involved in the arts. Among those present were Gertrude Lawrence, Douglas Fairbanks Jr., Count and Countess Kleinmichel, Sophie Tucker, and Rebecca West. The party went on for the duration of the night. In the morning, one of the guests was shocked when he opened the door to the bathroom and found Felix there, standing before the mirror and carefully applying mascara to his eyelashes.[4]

The long legal battle ended, and the Youssoupovs were financially secure. Felix would no longer have to worry about creditors seizing their property or being hauled off to prison for his debts. With some of the award, Irina repurchased from Cartier a few of the pieces of jewelry which they had pawned during the late 1920s; the remainder went into a trust fund for Bebé and into investments which would provide a steady income. It is a curious irony that just when there seemed to be no hope at all for Felix, he was saved by a film about Rasputin's assassination.

In 1935, Felix returned to the business world. He opened a new shop, under the old name of Irfe, in London. Located at 45

Dover Street, the second incarnation of Irfe sold exotic perfumes at extravagant prices. Felix claimed to blend some of the fragrances himself from formulas dating back to the beginning of the eighteenth century. He introduced two different scents, one for blondes and the other for brunets, which he regarded as something of a joke. Princess Irene Paley, who had married Irina's brother Prince Feodor, designed much of the artwork and packaging for the products. At the opening, many of the Youssoupovs' friends, including the duchess of Grafton and Lady Greville, browsed through the shop, inspecting the various offerings.[5]

On 19 June 1938, the Youssoupovs' daughter Bebé married Count Nicholas Sheremetiev. She had lived a rather peculiar and unsettled life. Four years old at the time of the evacuation from the Crimea, she had never really known the extravagant luxury of the Youssoupovs' lives in pre-Revolutionary Russia. In the first years of exile she lived with her grandparents Felix and Zenaide at their villa outside of Rome rather than with her parents, who were trying to settle their affairs. When, eventually, she went to live with Felix and Irina in Paris, she became by all accounts a thoroughly unruly child, spoiled by her grandparents. Felix later complained in his memoirs that the years she had spent with his parents had left his daughter "capricious" and stubborn.[6]

She was sent to school at the Cours Dupanloup in the Parc des Princes, which had, by chance, belonged to Felix's great-grandmother, the countess de Chaveuax. In 1924, when the Youssoupovs opened the Paris branch of Irfe, they had arranged for a baby-sitter to watch their nine-year-old daughter. When she failed to arrive, they reluctantly took her along with them to the opening-night party. Irina responded to this somewhat boring affair by hiding beneath a table and biting the legs of her parents' important guests.

Felix and Irina were not very attentive parents. They themselves had both been raised by nannies, governesses, and tutors, and they saw no reason why they should concern themselves with the day to day progress of their daughter. She was shuffled from school to school, sometimes out of necessity owing to both her difficult attitude and her parents' inability to pay the fees.

Her childhood was not a very stable one, because of the Youssoupovs' financial hardships and the frequent changes of residence. She was closest to her grandparents; when Count Felix suffered a stroke and Zenaide was unable to continue to care for both her husband and her granddaughter, Bebé finally went to live with her parents. She adored Felix, but relations with her mother seem to have been distant and formal.

After the M-G-M settlement, Irina used part of the award to set up a trust fund for her daughter. By 1938 the younger Irina was twenty-three, finished with school, and leading the pleasant, aimless life of a princess in exile. She had inherited much of her mother's ethereal beauty, along with her father's aristocratic bearing and manner. Irina first met Nicholas Sheremetiev in 1936. He came from one of the wealthiest and most distinguished families of imperial Russia; Sheremetievs had served at the court of the Romanovs for three hundred years. The son of Count Dimitri Sergeievich Sheremetiev and his wife, Countess Irina Vorontzov-Dashkov, Nicholas was thirty-two years old, somewhat stocky, with a dark mustache and a jovial sense of humor. Nevertheless, Felix objected to the marriage. Count Nicholas suffered from tuberculosis, and the prince insisted that he go to Switzerland to recover—the standard cure in those days being plenty of fresh air and a long stay in a sanatorium. Count Nicholas duly went off and remained in Switzerland for two years, until he was fully recovered. Although Felix was no happier with his daughter's choice of husband, he reluctantly gave his consent.

The marriage eventually took place in the Russian Orthodox Church in Rome. It was a grand occasion, with many of the Romanovs in attendance. Again, the ghosts of imperial Russia were evoked in the pomp and pageantry, the famous names of many of the guests and the crowds which surrounded the church hoping to catch a glimpse of the bride and her well-known father.

A year later, on 24 November 1939, Felix's mother, Zenaide, died in her apartment in a retirement home for Russian exiles in Sevres. She had been ill for some time, and Felix had carefully nursed her during her last days. She was buried in the Russian cemetery of Ste.-Geneviève des Bois at Essone, outside Paris, next to her husband. "She had been my friend, my confidant and my support for the whole of my life," Felix recalled.[7]

The marriage of their daughter and the death of his mother left Felix and Irina alone for the first time in their lives. They had now been married for twenty-five years. Despite the many difficulties which they had endured, the problems which continued to follow them, and the adjustments each had to make for the other, Felix and Irina continued to enjoy a happy, secure marriage, based on mutual friendship and need.

They were clearly devoted to each other, even though, at times Felix's behavior must have sorely tried Irina's patience. He never abandoned his taste for handsome men, and Irina's acceptance of her husband's sexuality surprised many of their friends. But she knew that in his own way Felix loved her and that she could provide him with the understanding, loyalty, and friendship he would never find elsewhere. Throughout the turbulent years of their exile, they managed to maintain their optimism, humor and mutual respect for each other's needs.

The years had not been kind to either of them, and the strains of their many trials showed. Felix was no longer the young, handsome prince who had captivated those who knew him before the Revolution, but a balding, stooped, slightly bitter looking man of fifty-two; Irina, too, had lost her subtle beauty and developed into a frail, chain-smoking middle-aged woman with prematurely gray hair. She continued to indulge her husband's curious tastes and caprices: Every day, when he arose, Felix spent hours before his dressing-table mirror, carefully combing his thinning hair, applying eyeliner, mascara, and rouge to shield the effects of aging. He refused to grow old gracefully. He desperately clung to the illusion that he was still young and beautiful. His friend Noël Coward, after dining with the Youssoupovs, found the act sad and described Felix as "a little macabre." During the dinner, whenever Felix smiled or laughed, the heavy makeup which he wore cracked and kept dropping to the table and into the food.[8]

On 3 September 1939, England and France, following the Nazi invasion of Poland two days earlier, declared war on Germany. For the second time in their lives, Felix and Irina were threatened by the turmoil of war.

Throughout the 1920s and early 1930s many Russian exiles actively supported Hitler's rise to power. They saw him as a champion against communism who would eventually drive Stalin from the Kremlin. Hitler's rabid anti-Semitism also struck a familiar chord in many of the exiles, who blamed many of Russia's problems on the Jews. Felix himself, more than once, expressed the belief that the Jews had been responsible for the Revolution and the murder of the imperial family. Much of this émigré support, however, ceased when, in August 1939, the German-Soviet non-aggression treaty was signed in Moscow. Suddenly the same Germans who had promised to destroy communism were now partners with the despised Stalin. Few of the exiles were willing to fight alongside the Germans knowing that doing so, in effect, supported the Soviet Union.

For exiles living in France, the case was certainly more clear-cut: Many Russians had lived in the country since the Revolution. Even before 1917 they had vacationed, owned real estate, villas, and stables, and frequented the fashionable couture houses in Paris. They felt a sense of place there and for the most part had been accepted by the French.

The German occupation of Paris in June 1940 sent many émigrés scrambling. While Felix and Irina may have wished to remain in the city, it involved numerous risks. First and foremost, they had absolutely no guarantee that they would not be arrested or, worse, forcibly repatriated to the Soviet Union. If the Germans got hold of them, there also remained the possibility that they would be used for propaganda purposes. Felix was still notorious as ever, and Irina, as the niece of the last tsar of Russia, held a certain prestige in the eyes of their fellow exiles. If they could be persuaded to collaborate with the Nazis, their very names might draw others in as well. Fearing the worst, the Youssoupovs fled Paris for the relative safety of their summer villa in Sarcelles, a tumbledown one-and-a-half-story dairy cottage hidden in an overgrown garden at the end of the village of Yveline.

Their apprehension was justified, for Hitler had issued orders that the Youssoupovs be located and questioned. A number of German officers tracked them down to their Sarcelles villa. But rather than arrest them, the officers treated the Youssoupovs with the greatest of respect. They immediately offered Felix all of the food and fuel he needed; although suspicious, the prince reluctantly accepted, fearing the consequences but desperately in need of the supplies.

Soon enough, he learned what they wanted in return: An officer informed him that the prince and princess could return to Paris, where they would be lodged in any mansion of their choosing. Whatever money he needed would be placed at Felix's disposal, and Irina would be provided with new dresses and jewelry from Cartier. In return, the Youssoupovs would act as official hosts for important guests, throwing parties and dinners. It must have been a tempting offer. Food was scarce, and most of the Youssoupovs' money was unavailable to them for the duration of the war. Yet Felix turned the Germans down. He explained that Paris was his home; that the French government had allowed him to live there and had always treated him fairly; and that he felt a moral obligation to the country.[9]

The Germans accepted this refusal—for the time being. But their real intentions became clear when Hitler dispatched his personal envoy to meet with the prince. Following the launch of Operation Barbarossa in 1941, Hitler made it clear that he planned to destroy the Soviet Union by force. Once again, this raised the hopes of many émigrés that the monarchy might be restored in Russia. Slyly, Hitler's envoy suggested to Felix that, under such circumstances, the prince might prove to be the best candidate for the throne.

It was not only the restoration and subjugation of the Russian throne under the Nazis that Hitler had in mind. It is clear, from the evidence which has come to light, that Hitler seriously entertained the idea of restoring the former King Edward VIII to the British throne in the event that England was defeated. He would replace his brother, King George VI, who had assumed the throne following Edward's abdication to marry Mrs. Wallis Simpson. The duke and duchess of Windsor had actually met Hitler following the abdication, and the Führer seemed impressed with their deference. If the Germans had succeeded in conquering Europe and Russia, puppet governments headed by popular figureheads would have been a natural evolution of the war.

To his honor and credit, however, Felix refused to cooperate, undoubtedly saving himself from the fate which awaited many collaborators after the liberation of Paris.[10] When the Nazis fled, Felix and Irina returned to the capital to live. They could not move back into their flat; with some of the proceeds from the M-G-M settlement again at their disposal, the Youssoupovs bought what was to become their final residence— a rundown mews in Auteuil. The money also enabled them to buy food on the black market. When the war finally came to an end in May 1945, the Youssoupovs joined the jubilant Parisians in the streets, linking arms and singing to celebrate the victory.

26

Twilight

THE END OF WORLD WAR II marked the beginning of a curiously peaceful period in Felix's life. In 1947 he celebrated his sixtieth birthday. Although he continued to apply eye makeup and daub his cheeks with rouge each morning, he had long ago lost his youthful beauty. He was now almost completely bald, his skin covered with tiny brown age spots. He walked with a stoop and looked desperately thin. By this time, he was also a grandfather: During the war, on 1 March 1942, his daughter Irina had given birth to a girl, whom she and her husband Nicholas called Xenia, after her great-grandmother.

Felix and Irina spent much of their time and money decorating their new home in Auteuil. Located at no. 38 rue Pierre Guerin, it had originally been a mews, converted at the beginning of the twentieth century into a residence. It was hidden from the street, surrounded by a high iron fence hung with a sign which read: "Savage Dog." Set in the middle of a wild, overgrown garden, the house was a far cry from the opulence of the Moika Palace.

The service wing enclosed a small terrace covered with lattice work; from Felix's study on the first floor, a precariously perched wooden balcony overlooked the scene below. The entrance hall of the house was decorated with icons, porcelain, and prints of imperial Russia. The large dining room, decorated with French Provincial furnishings, held cabinets filled with Felix's horrific monster etchings, which Irina refused to put on display. A steep, narrow staircase led to the first floor. The walls of the drawing room were covered in prints, family photographs, and icons. A large painting of Nicholas Youssoupov greeted visitors at the head of the staircase, and over the mantel stood a life-sized bust of Felix as a young man. The bedroom was hung in floral prints, with a large painting of Nicholas Youssoupov directly above the bed; everywhere—piled on small tables, on the headboard of the bed, and in stacks on the floor—were hundreds of books. It was all a bit incongruous for the visitor: On a table there might be a signed photograph of Tsar Nicholas II in a solid silver frame decorated with the imperial crest, while the table itself was chipped and precariously balanced on unsure legs. True, there were expensive ornaments to remind one of the Youssoupovs' great wealth in former days, but the upholstery on the sofas and chairs might be patched and the Oriental carpets threadbare. The overall impression was one of shabby gentility, of a decaying country house filled with precious memories of an era long since passed.

The experience of war reawakened Felix's spiritual side. Following his brother Nicholas's death in 1907, Felix underwent a conversion of sorts, during which time he abandoned his hedonistic lifestyle in favor of working for the poor. His transformation was only temporary. For the next forty years he had wandered without thought, living his life for pleasure. But, at sixty, with the onset of age and possibly the thought of having to repent for the years gone by, Felix returned to the center of the Russian soul, the Orthodox Church.

His rediscovered devotion may have been an attempt to expiate the ghosts of the past. Although he never expressed regret over the murder of Rasputin, Felix almost certainly believed that in some fashion he had to atone for his act. In one interview, he expressed the opinion that Rasputin had served some kind of mystical, divine purpose. In killing Rasputin, Felix said, he had also participated in this divine plan. Belief in this peculiar role may have helped ease Felix's mind about the murder, but it also clearly led him to conclude that he himself was meant to play some larger part in spiritual matters.

Felix's faith remains something of an enigma. Raised in the Orthodox Church, he devoutly followed the liturgical calendar, marking feast and fast days, praying before icons, observing the rules and customs of the faithful. Yet his lifestyle, with its hedonistic pleasures and homosexual affairs, was clearly in conflict with the teachings of the church. It is difficult to gauge Felix's own inner reaction to his homosexuality, yet it was a force which dominated his life. While he appears to have made several attempts to "cure" himself, he always returned to his old habits. Eventually, he drifted away from the Orthodox Church, although his belief in the supernatural and in a supreme deity remained intact. "I believe in God," he once explained to a friend. "I belong to the Orthodox Faith. But I don't attach much importance to it over any other. One could reach the same truth by various paths. All appear to me equally valid as long as one loves God. . . . I am guided more by my heart than by my reason. I take life as it comes, without seeking to penetrate the mystery which surrounds us. Of all philosophers, I most admire Socrates when he said, 'I only know that I know nothing.' "[1]

His attempts to reconcile these two diverse natures, very reminiscent of Rasputin's character, eventually took the form of an adventure in faith healing. This attempt is a curious parallel to Rasputin's activities in St. Petersburg. Like Rasputin, Felix apparently thought himself capable of curing the sick through prayer. It was an astonishing reversal of roles. The thought that he could truly help the sick transformed Felix. Formerly he had lounged in his bed until late morning, reading and writing letters. Now, energized with a sense of purpose, he regularly rose at six in the morning to embark on his rounds. He spent hours at hospitals and sanatoriums, holding patients' hands and praying with them. In time, Felix's enthusiasm for this activity waned. There is no evidence that any of his "cures" ever worked; however, he himself took great comfort from the experience. He clearly felt that he had a duty to fulfill. "I'm very tired," he once complained to a friend. "I have to work so hard with sick people."[2] Clearly, the factor motivating the prince in his work was a sense of devotion and unspoken obligation.

At the beginning of the 1950s, Felix decided to write his memoirs. Other Russian exiles and even members of the Romanov family had previously recorded their lives, and Felix, with his historic role in Rasputin's murder, saw no reason why he, too, should not profit from the story. He wrote in bed, Irina carefully editing the lengthy chapters as he handed them over. The book, published in 1952, was called *Lost Splendour* and was an instant success. But once again, Felix carefully presented the truth as he wished it to be remembered. Understandably, he devoted a large section of the book to Rasputin's murder, but he merely repeated—sometimes verbatim—the story as given in his 1927 book. In general, however, Felix proved candid, discussing his lifestyle, his transvestite activities, and his attraction to Grand Duke Dimitri with wit and honesty. Two years later, Felix published his second volume of memoirs, *En Exil*, dealing exclusively with the period of his life after the Revolution. While numerous Russian exiles wrote books detailing their lives set against the crumbling Romanov regime, Felix went one step further, recording his life in exile. The book did not do nearly as well as *Lost Splendour*; for most people, Felix's life began and ended with Rasputin. There was little interest in his later years.

The books brought some financial benefits for the Youssoupovs; they were still relatively poor by their own standards, though in no danger of financial hardship. They regularly received a generous interest check on the money which Irina had set aside in a trust fund, and since she had taken control of the majority of their finances, they never suffered the humiliation of their earlier years in exile. At this point, an extraordinary overture on behalf of the Soviet government came Felix's way. In the years following the devastation of World War II, Moscow began a lengthy process of restoring the former palaces of the aristocracy. Some of these residences—such as the imperial palaces of Pavlovsk and Peterhof—had been virtually destroyed by the German army. Other estates, farther in the heart of the country, were victims only of neglect. Arkhangelskoe, the Youssoupov estate just outside Moscow, had long been abandoned. In undertaking the restoration of the palace, the Soviets needed someone familiar with the history of the house and its treasures. They offered Felix the post of curator, with the promise of a wing of the house in which to reside and whatever he needed in the way of living expenses. Felix longed to return to Russia and to his childhood home. When she learned that he was considering taking the post, however, Irina exploded with anger. The Soviets had been responsible for the murders of her uncles, aunts, cousins, servants—how could Felix even consider working with these killers? Whatever Felix's wishes may have been, he bowed to Irina's refusal to even discuss the matter. It would indeed have been another peculiar twist in a life filled with violent contrasts.

The Youssoupovs traveled occasionally, visiting Irina and Nicholas Sheremetiev and their granddaughter, Xenia, or taking the sun on the Riviera. In Paris, they dined out, visited antique shops, and walked their dogs. They entertained infrequently—not having the necessary facilities to accommodate overnight guests—but this did not preclude them from accepting the numerous invitations which came their way. Felix became a well-known figure in the émigré clubs and restaurants of Paris; his entrance was inevitably marked with much bowing, applause, and enthusiastic cries of "Prince! Prince!"[3]

Felix and Irina moved in a dazzling circle of friends, including the Philippe de Rothschilds; Count and Countess von Bismarck; J. Paul Getty; Sir Oswald and Lady Mosley; and the duke and duchess of Windsor. The Youssoupovs frequently dined at the Windsors' house in the Bois de Boulogne, celebrating a peculiar and ironic friendship. There were striking similarities between Felix and the former King Edward VIII. Both were destined to be remembered for only one thing, Felix for his role in killing Rasputin and the duke of Windsor for abdicating the throne to marry Mrs. Simpson. After these events, both of their lives essentially stopped. They lived in a timeless void, celebrated for acts long since passed. The two men got on well together, which is something of a surprise, considering the duke's well-known attitude toward homosexuals. He once referred to some of his wife's friends as "those fellers who fly in over the transom," adding, "I won't have 'em in my house."[4] Irina and the duchess, likewise, seem to have had little in common. The princess, out of courtesy, always addressed the former Mrs. Simpson as "Your Royal Highness" even though King George VI had denied his sister-in-law her rightful use of this address. Irina found the situation amusing, but Wallis appreciated the gesture and fawned over "Your Imperial Highness" when Irina was present.

The peculiar friendship blossomed throughout the 1950s. Each couple used the other for their own advantage. The Windsor mansion in the Bois de Boulogne was the one place where Felix and Irina could sink luxuriously back into the grandeur of a royal household. The duchess ran the house like a miniature kingdom for her dispossessed husband; every detail smacked of rigid, royal etiquette. Liveried footmen handed around drinks, drawing-room tables overflowed with jeweled snuffboxes and trinkets, and the best French chefs carefully prepared the lavish dinners for the guests. It was the closest to the Moika Palace that Felix and Irina could now come. In turn, the Windsors gloried in entertaining such prestigious guests. They had been virtually cut off by the British royal family and grasped at any figure to give the appearance of holding court, even a court in exile.

In the last years of the 1950s the Youssoupovs received an unexpected windfall. Felix's great-grandmother, the countess de Chaveau, had left a large house in Brittany, the Château Keriolet, to the French government upon her death. In her will the countess had carefully spelled out the conditions of the gift: The government could have the property as long as the house and grounds were maintained. On a visit, Felix discovered that paneling had been removed from the mansion, some of the art treasures had been lost, and the gardens were falling into disrepair. He lodged a complaint against the government, alleging that the stipulations of the will had been violated and asking that the house and grounds be returned to his family.

The lawsuit took several years to resolve. As luck would have it, the courts eventually ruled in Felix's favor, and the property was returned to the Youssoupovs on 13 February 1956. Felix had no use for the house or its contents and arranged to have them auctioned off. Sotheby's estimated that the house and its contents were worth nearly $1 million. The proceeds from the sale once again filled the Youssoupov coffers with an overflow of funds.

A picture has often been painted of Felix and Irina as penniless exiles struggling to survive. This is completely inaccurate. It is true that they did not live in splendor and at times were certainly short of cash. But never assets. It had been only twenty years since Irina's judgment against M-G-M. Most of this money had been invested or placed in trust for their daughter, Irina. This move on Irina's part automatically limited her husband's access to the funds—a shrewd decision on her part. The greater part of this award was still intact, providing the Youssoupovs with a comfortable regular income. Royalties from books, as well as the sale of the château, allowed them to indulge in some of the luxuries which, of necessity, Irina had made Felix eliminate.

With his new funds, Felix began once again to subsidize many of the Russian exiles. Certainly his help was appreciated; in one case, it virtually kept one of the exiles alive. Nathalia Cheremetievskaia, Countess Brassova, was the widow of the murdered Grand Duke Michael Alexandrovich, brother of the last tsar. Nathalia and Michael married in 1912, illegally and against the wishes of Nicholas II. She was a twice-divorced commoner, while he stood second in line to the throne after Tsarevich Alexei. Theirs was a true love story, but the Revolution destroyed their brief happiness. Following Michael's murder by the Bolsheviks, the countess, along with her son by the grand duke—George, Count Brassov—managed to get out of Russia. In exile, none of the Romanovs would receive her. Nathalia had no income and relied on the generosity of friends in order to survive. When her son was killed in an automobile accident in the 1930s, Nathalia spent what little funds she had on two cemetery plots at Passy, one for her son and the other for herself. She lived in a small room in Paris, eating when she had the money to buy food and wrapping herself in numerous garments to keep warm. Felix, alone among members of the imperial family, often visited her, bringing gifts of food and cash.[5]

In his last years Felix gained a sterling reputation among the Russian exiles as a generous benefactor. He freely gave his money away, even when he himself was short of funds. Throughout his life in exile, Felix was an impassioned model of noblesse oblige , constantly seeking out new projects to help the émigré cause. It may have been an effort to redeem himself, but it would be too cynical to dismiss Felix's dedication to others as a simple effort to rehabilitate his image. It is one of the few threads running through his life, from the work with Grand Duchess Elizabeth Feodorovna in Moscow and his hospitals at the Moika Palace to the charity balls and organizations he founded in London and Paris. In his old age, the image of the carefree, decadent young prince who murdered Rasputin was replaced with that of a beloved, compassionate, and caring philanthropist.

The last two years of Felix's life were once again dominated by the shadow of Rasputin. In 1963 the CBS Television Network in the United States broadcast a thirty-minute teleplay called "If I Should Die," based on the murder of Rasputin. The play, written by two Chicago women, closely followed the story as related in both of Felix's books. Once again, American lawyer Fanny Holtzmann came to the Youssoupovs' aid. Felix, after consulting with her, decided to sue CBS for invasion of privacy. He contended that the teleplay had depicted him without his authorization, that the script contained many factual errors, and that the "sexual atmosphere" of the drama was offensive both to himself and his wife.

From the outset, Youssoupov's chances of victory were slim; the teleplay had so closely followed his own accounts that in order to claim inaccuracy he would himself have to admit that his version had been incorrect. CBS countered his arguments by alleging that Rasputin's murder, forty-nine years earlier, was now clearly in the public domain and that as far as accuracy, the script adhered to the prince's own story as told in two of his books.

Felix and Irina went to New York in 1965 to plead their case. The trial took place in a brightly lit, third-floor courtroom in Manhattan's Foley Square. Both Felix and Irina testified. There was minimal publicity at this, their second trial. A few reporters hovered outside the courtroom doors, waiting to speak with the prince, but in an America where the escalating war in Vietnam and the civil rights movement were making daily headlines, the Youssoupov trial amounted to little more than a historical footnote.

One of Felix's contentions was that it had misused the name of Irina in a sexual way and suggested that she had been the bait used to lure Rasputin to his death in the Moika Palace. This had always been Felix's own version of events for public consumption, and in saying that it was false, he had, in effect, to acknowledge that he had lied about what caused Rasputin to visit him that night. In the teleplay the character of Prince Youssoupov had said of his wife that she was young, beautiful, wealthy—all that Rasputin desired.

To fight against this, Irina took the witness stand. She wore a plain black dress, her white hair still coiffured in a 1920s bob. Her only jewelry was her wedding ring and a pair of pearl stud earrings. In a hushed tone she told the court that the teleplay was completely inaccurate, saying in flawless English that she had been in the Crimea during the murder and that in no way had her name ever been mentioned in connection with inviting Rasputin to the Moika Palace.

The majority of the trial, however, focused on Felix. He took the witness stand for five days of testimony. He was now completely bald, dark sunglasses protecting his failing eyesight against the harsh lighting. He sat bolt upright in the witness chair, occasionally twisting the rings he wore on his left hand.

Felix's testimony led the court through the details of the murder and events leading up to it. This time, however, he changed his story substantially. He denied that he had used Irina's name to lure Rasputin to the Moika Palace but refused to say why the peasant had come. He also contradicted his own version by claiming to have shot Rasputin twice, not once, as his books alleged. All of this was important, for here Felix appeared to be coming closer to the truth of what really happened that night. But the press ignored it.

His age and the excitement of the trial left Felix nervous and confused. At one point in the trial proceedings, when the judge asked the prince his age, Felix replied that he had forgotten. During cross-examination centering on Irina's role as bait to lure Rasputin to the Moika Palace, Felix collapsed on the witness stand and had to be rushed to a doctor, suffering from exhaustion.

Felix had sued for nearly $3 million. It took the jury of nine men and three women only four hours to find in favor of CBS. Felix and Irina returned to Paris following the verdict; it is doubtful whether Felix expected to win the suit or even if it was brought out of indignation. What seems likely is that, bored, Felix had latched on to a new trial as a way of occupying his spare time and also of seeing his name once again in print. He had relished the attention. Now that it was gone, the Youssoupovs sank back into obscurity.

There was one bright spot that year: the wedding of Felix's granddaughter, Xenia, on 20 June 1965, to Ilias Sfiris, in Athens.

Otherwise, Felix once again returned to Rasputin. The television writer Kiernan Tunney contacted the prince about a documentary he was working on called *In Search of Rasputin*. The proposed program dealt with the relationship between the peasant and his assassin. Tunney apparently believed that Felix had lied about the reasons for Rasputin coming to see him that night and also about the manner of the murder itself. When confronted with this, Felix apparently agreed that Rasputin had come to see him that evening and not his wife.

At the same time Tunney was working on his project, Felix signed a deal with Epinal Studios, a French film company, to cooperate on a film version of the murder. This time, Felix happily believed that his story would be portrayed in a favorable light.

December of that year marked the fiftieth anniversary of the murder. To commemorate the occasion, Felix gave several interviews. The first, given to Peter Lennon of the *Guardian*, was innocuous enough:

> We drove up to a small private house. The railings were blocked by a black fence, a sign over the bell said, "Savage Dog." But when the gate swung open to the buzzer, we stepped into the decor of a Russian aristocratic comedy. A dinky, two-storied house; a housekeeper leaning far out of the door smiling a welcome; greetings in Russian and the dog Gugusse IV, a cross between a good-natured slack-jawed bulldog and a terrier, waddled out to meet us.
>
> A Swedish secretary led us into the salon whose walls were resplendent with souvenirs—photos, engravings, a guitar.
>
> I was presented to the Prince: a polished head, refined features, his knees covered up by a rug in an armchair, his withered right arm lying across his lap. But his eyes seemed very much alive and intelligent and smiles of amused anticipation shivered continually across his mouth. . . .
>
> The Princess made an appearance; walking with the aid of a stick. She is tall, thin, with bobbed white hair,

dressed in a cardigan, a plain skirt and sensible shoes—
very much the style of an English lady. She took up a
watchful position in a far corner. . . .

The bulk of the interview concerned Rasputin's murder. Felix
merely repeated his carefully crafted tale as given through the
years, uninterrupted by Lennon. When asked if, given the
chance, he would murder Rasputin again, Felix shouted, "Yes!
And how!"[6]

The second, more revealing interview—with American
journalist E. M. Halliday, appeared in the quarterly journal *Horizon*. Halliday wrote an article called "Rasputin Reconsidered"
in which he questioned several aspects of the case as presented
by Felix. In a preface to the article Halliday directly challenged
the prince's veracity. "I don't know of an instance in modern
history where so many reputable as well as disreputable historians have solemnly repeated such a patently improbable story
as if it were gospel." Halliday argued that the prince had deliberately lied on two counts: first, that Rasputin was lured to the
Moika Palace hoping to meet Irina, and second, Felix's expressed
motive for the murder. According to Halliday, the interview
"was interesting but unproductive. . . . On the question of how
Rasputin was lured to the palace, the prince came close to admitting that there are indeed aspects of the famous story that are
still wrapped in mystery." Felix casually told Halliday *"On ne
peut pas dire pourqoui?"*— the closest he ever came to admitting
that he had deliberately lied about Rasputin's murder.[7] But Felix
refused to express remorse over his role in Rasputin's death to
the very end of his life. Once, when asked if he regretted killing
the peasant, Felix smiled and replied, "No, I shot a dog."[8]

Felix died on 27 September 1967, at the age of eighty. His
end was peaceful: He died in his bed, surrounded by Irina and
his servants. A servant washed the body, dressed him in a white
nightshirt, and laid him in a freshly made bed, Felix's hands
folded across his stomach. In one hand he held a long votive
candle; in the other, a cross. Throughout the afternoon, friends
and relatives filed past the bed and knelt to pray for his soul.

His funeral at the Russian Orthodox Cathedral of Alexander

Nevsky in Paris was attended by hundreds of mourners. Irina, looking frail and hopelessly lost, was escorted by her daughter, Irina, son-in-law Nicholas Sheremetiev, and granddaughter, Xenia. Her grief was genuine, for throughout the difficult years and many trials and turns which their lives had taken, she loved her husband. At the cemetery of Ste.-Genevieve des Bois, outside of Paris, Father Nicholas Obolensky prayed over the simple wooden coffin before it was lowered into the family tomb. His death was duly noted in newspapers around the world, all mentioning his role as Rasputin's murderer. In the end, Felix Youssoupov was unable to escape the shadow of the man whom he had murdered so many years before.

Epilogue

AFTER FELIX'S DEATH, Irina continued to live in their crumbling mews house, surrounded by the powerful reminders of their momentous lives together. The death of her husband left the princess shattered. For all of Felix's alleged homosexual promiscuity both before and after their wedding, he had remained devoted to Irina, regarding his wife as his greatest friend and confidante. Her unconditional acceptance and understanding of her husband's desires, however hard it may have been, demonstrated over and over again her great strength of character. As much as Felix relied on his wife, Irina loved and needed her husband, and his death plunged her into a grief from which she would never emerge. Three years after Felix's death, on 26 February 1970, Irina died of a heart attack. She was buried beside her husband and mother-in-law.

Irina had lived long enough to see the birth of her great-granddaughter, Tatiana Sfiris, in 1968. When Irina died, the Youssoupov name passed from existence. Felix and Irina's only daughter, Irina Sheremetiev, died in 1983. Today her daughter, Xenia Sfiris, divides her time between Athens and her grandparents' old Mews house in Paris. Recently, she visited the Moika Palace in St. Petersburg for the first time, marveling at her grandparents' lavish house and lifestyle.

Except for Felix and Purishkevich, none of those involved in the events of 16 December 1916 left accounts. The fragmented story of what possibly occurred is known through the brief revelations of others. Feodor and Nikita, Irina's brothers, never acknowledged that they themselves might have participated in the murder, as indicated by both Felix's cousin Vera Korelli and Rasputin's secretary, Aaron Simanovich, although Felix's cousin Vladimir did admit in exile that he had been present. History has diligently, and blindly, recorded Felix Youssoupov and Vladimir Purishkevich as Rasputin's assassins.

Purishkevich himself managed to escape the turmoil of the Revolution, only to later be caught and tried by the Bolsheviks for his involvement with the White Army. His reputation in having killed Rasputin was still such that even a Bolshevik court dared not condemn him to death; instead, he was sentenced to nearly a year of public work. But Purishkevich, fiery and unrepentant as ever, fled to Novorossiik, where he came down with typhus. He died in a Jewish hospital there in 1920. Lazovert eventually made his way to Romania, where he lived for many years as an oil trader.[1] As for Lt. Ivan Sukhotin, he, like so many other former tsarist officers, vanished into one of Stalin's infamous Gulags in the 1930s.

Exile was hard for Grand Duke Dimitri Pavlovich. He had entered England and been appointed a captain in the British army. But when he tried to enlist in the Scots Greys Regiment, he was told that he could not do so, and he bitterly left England for France.

Until 1927, his friendship with Felix had continued. But with the publication of *Rasputin* by the prince, Dimitri deliberately cut off all contact with his friend, angry that Felix had broken their pledge of secrecy about Rasputin's murder. Alone, Dimitri threw himself into an empty life filled with parties and women; he was the frequent escort, and eventually live-in lover, of the famous Coco Chanel. She seems to have been the great love of his life; but her interest in him faded, and once again Dimitri was alone.

In 1926 he married Audrey Emery of Cleveland, Ohio. Miss Emery came from a wealthy real-estate family. She was young, beautiful, and perhaps more important to Dimitri, very rich. Their engagement lasted barely two weeks before they were married in a civil ceremony at Boulogne-sur-Seine. On 21 November, they were married in the Russian Orthodox Church in Biarritz, surrounded by many Romanovs, as well as Felix and Irina.

Audrey had converted to Russian Orthodoxy before the

service and received the title of Princess Ilinsky, after Dimitri's childhood home of Ilinskoe, Grand Duke Serge's country estate near Moscow. They had one child, Paul, in 1928. The marriage lasted just ten years. Dimitri was too dissolute, too emotionally unstable, to make a good husband, and Audrey officially sued for divorce. She took their son, Prince Paul, to live in England. Dimitri's final years compared sadly with his former glamorous life in Russia before the Revolution. He lived alone in Switzerland, seeing neither family nor friends. In September 1942, he died suddenly of a kidney ailment at Devos.

Maria Rasputin survived the chaos of the Revolution. In exile she wrote three books, each defending her famous father. Her last, *Rasputin, The Man Behind the Myth*, related for the first time her controversial account of her father's murder. Like Felix, Maria capitalized on the Rasputin name. She worked briefly as a cabaret singer in Paris, then joined a circus as a lion tamer. Curiously, she named her two pet dogs Youssou and Pov. She died in Los Angeles in September 1977.

It is difficult to assess the precise impact which Rasputin's murder may have had in precipitating the Revolution. Felix, like Rasputin himself, was often blamed for having contributed to the fall of the Romanovs. Certainly, when Felix acted, he did so in the belief that others in more powerful positions would follow his lead and forestall the impending crisis. His very motivation in killing Rasputin rested almost entirely on an erroneous conception of the peasant's influence. Felix was close enough to the imperial family to know the reasons why Rasputin was at court. But he never realized the true nature of Rasputin's power over the imperial couple; listening to the peasant, it was easy enough to believe his exaggerated tales of influence and ministerial power. The prince did not understand Alexandra's hold over both her husband and the peasant; Rasputin's death still left the tsarina at the helm of the Russian government, exerting her naïve and ultimately destructive influence over her husband. Rasputin's death did nothing to alter the fateful dynamics of the imperial couple's relationship.

Nor would it be correct to say that Rasputin's death accelerated the Revolution. The forces which drove workers and students into Petrograd's streets existed prior to Rasputin's first appearance in the capital. The Revolution of 1905, the humiliating Russo-Japanese War, and the devastating effects of the European conflict simply added to generations of misery, frustration, and revolt. Rasputin's nefarious influence and scandalous reputation simply added to years of discontent. His murder did nothing to quicken the Revolution.

Felix's real responsibility lay in the rift which developed among the Romanovs. The immediate effect of Rasputin's death was a complete break between Nicholas and Alexandra and the rest of the Russian imperial family. This loss of family support had been growing for many years. But with the tsar's refusal of his family's petition on Dimitri's behalf, even the previously cold and formal relations between him and his kinsmen were irreparably shattered. Dissatisfaction and lust for power erupted into open revolt. By the time of the Revolution in March, Nicholas II's aunts, uncles, and cousins not only conspired in his removal from the throne but publicly called for his abdication.

The Youssoupov name retains a potent interest in the Russia of today. The former houses and palaces of this family attract the curious attention of visitors from around the world. Arkhangelskoe, outside of Moscow, was once the most brilliant, flawless in its setting, a perfect example of the delights of the country estate in turn-of-the-century Russia. Unfortunately, the chronic shortage of government funding, coupled with the chaotic state of Russian internal affairs, has led to a tragic disintegration of this once-beautiful estate. Plasterwork is now pocked and falling, fountains are choked with weeds, lawns reaching down to the Moscow River are overgrown. Until the Russian government intervenes and appropriates the necessary funds, the house will remain closed, slowly and silently crumbling into history.

The Moscow house, lost at the end of a long-forgotten avenue overgrown with trees, still retains something of its former splendor. Although it housed the offices of the Academy of Agricultural Sciences for many years, with the collapse of the Communist state, they were directed to find a new home so that the restoration of this great medieval house could begin. Work is already under way, although it is expected to take many years. Meanwhile, the slow process of moving years of files and records from the narrow, vaulted chambers continues amid the political uncertainty. The future of the Moscow house, unlike that of Arkhangelskoe, appears secure.

The Rococo villa at Tsarskoe Selo is now boarded up, its once-graceful lines and elegant cornices marked with holes and missing pieces. It still bears some sign of the terrible ordeal which this town suffered under the Nazi occupation, when Hitler's troops purposely destroyed the imperial palaces and much of the surrounding villas. There has been some discussion about possible restoration; but it remains a lonely, abandoned structure, decayed and almost lost in its wild garden. The Youssoupovs' Crimean properties fared much better. The Soviet government appropriated them after the Revolution, turning their villas into sanatoria for tubercular patients. It was at Koriez, the ugly stone house perched at the edge of the Black Sea, that Joseph Stalin stayed during the famous Yalta Conference at the nearby Livadia Palace.

Rasputin's old apartment in St. Petersburg has been divided up and is now shared by several families. On the wall of the landing outside the main door someone has scrawled an arrow and a legend declaring that here, in these five rooms, Gregory Rasputin had lived until 16 December 1916.

Of all the former Youssoupov possessions, the most famous, the Moika Palace, alone retains its pre-Revolutionary splendor. During the nine-hundred-day seige of Leningrad, the Moika Palace, like so many of the former capital's great buildings, was hit by Nazi shells. One of these bombs devastated the private theater; another remained unexploded, and was carefully retrieved when the German troops were driven from the city. Restoration work on the palace began immediately after the war and continues to this day. It now houses the offices of a teachers association. Although it is a private building, occasional exceptions are allowed, and prearranged tour groups are led through the opulent rooms, admiring the silk wall coverings and exquisite parquet floors.

The basement room where Felix killed Rasputin still exists, deep down in the catacomb of rooms making up the ground floor. For several years it was left untouched, the same table and chairs and ebony cabinet sitting in the same spots they occupied on the fateful night of 16 December 1916. Sometime in the 1920s, the Soviets divided the room up, making it into toilet stalls. Thus it remained for nearly three-quarters of a century, hidden from the inquisitive eyes of the curious visitors. With the spirit of glasnost and the dramatic changes in the former Soviet Union, however, the owners of the Moika Palace decided it was time to cash in on the Youssoupov-Rasputin connection. The basement room was faithfully restored, and the setting of Rasputin's murder, as it was on the night of the crime, has been re-created with stunning accuracy. Adding to the lurid effect are the two very lifelike wax figures of Felix and his victim which some enterprising authority has ordered placed in the murder room. Tours of the palace lead the visitor through the state rooms to Felix's study—now decorated with photographs of Felix and Irina, the imperial family, and Rasputin himself—and from there through the hidden doorway in the eight-sided hallway and down the narrow staircase to the cellar below, the same staircase which Felix ran up and down so many times that night as he waited for his victim to die. Beyond these historic rooms, the Moika cleaves its way through the city. Now St. Petersburg once again, the splendor of imperial Russia—of which Felix Youssoupov was one of the last privileged participants—lies across this flat city, recalling the days when the Romanovs ruled an empire, scandal flourished in the private clubs, and a wealthy prince could murder a peasant and escape to an exile of celebrity.

Acknowledgments

THIS BOOK WOULD HAVE BEEN impossible without the generous contributions of family, friends, colleagues, and fellow writers. Many were involved in the production of my first book, *The Last Empress,* but once again deserve my grateful thanks for their persistent support.

I count it a privilege to thank Grand Duchess Marie Vladimirovna of Russia, the head of the House of Romanov, for allowing me access to certain materials relating to the imperial succession. Nicholas Romanoff also supplied me with numerous dates, titles, and other important information which helped to complete my picture of Felix Youssoupov's life.

Those individuals who assisted my efforts in Russia during researches for *The Last Empress* also lent their valuable support to this project. In Moscow, Ms. Irene Fochkina, Mr. Mikhail Kupriyanov, and his wife, Milan, all helped arrange for visits to the Youssoupov properties, a miraculous accomplishment in view of the many obstacles they encountered. In St. Petersburg, Mr. Roman Vartanov arranged for my visits to the Moika and Fontanka palaces and the Youssoupov Villa at nearby Pushkin, formerly Tsarskoe Selo. Ms. Tamara Dubko and Mr. Ivan Scubichev likewise worked wonders, ensuring that I did not miss any important bit of information available in that city. Finally, to the present-day inhabitants of Rasputin's former flat, I express my gratitude at their willingness to open the doors of their homes to me so that I could explore the rooms in which the peasant had lived.

I am lucky indeed to have had the assistance of so many individuals who offered their own valuable comments. Most es-

281

pecially, I would like to thank Robert Achinson, Patte Barham, Princess M. Cantacuzéne, Nils Hanson, Pauline Grey Holdrup, Brien Horan, the late James Blair Lovell, Robert K. Massie, Marilyn Pfeifer Swezey, the late G. Nicholas Tantzos, Father Konstantin Tivetsky, and Dr. Idris Traylor for the information which they provided relevant to the life of Felix Youssoupov and imperial Russia.

My patient coworkers have, over the last five years, always supported me in this endeavor and allowed me a degree of freedom which has made the completion of the book possible. Kathryn Glennie, Jennifer Judd, Dan Kaufman, Cynthia Melin, Julie Miller, Jason Pickering, Marion San Clemente, Julian Riepe, Ryan Sharp, Viki Sinex, Edd Vick, and Courtni White ran errands, accommodated schedule changes, and assisted in many other ways. All of them have my thanks.

Being a writer isolates one, and my friends have shown a remarkable understanding of the difficulties I have encountered. The support of Sharlene Aadland, Wendy Collins, Andrea Cuddy, Angela Manning, Cecelia Manning, Mark Manning, Denis Meslans, and especially Russell Minugh has sustained me and allowed me to continue on with the frequently lonely tasks of researching and writing a book. And, once again, the deep and consistant support of my parents has allowed me to continue my writing unhindered by many other troubling considerations.

I feel immensely lucky to be able to thank my editor at Carol Publishing Group, Allan J. Wilson. His interest in, and enthusiasm for, this project and for imperial Russia has allowed me to fully explore many divergent areas without the necessity of justification. Everyone at Carol has, once again, been of exceptional support, especially the ever-friendly and helpful Hillary Schupf.

Again, I have the good fortune to thank my friend and fellow writer Marlene Eilers for her generous assistance and unconditional support. Her intricate knowledge of royal genealogy, titles, and dates has often been put to the test by my repeated requests for information. I particularly thank her for her advice and suggestions on this book; nevertheless, any errors which may exist are entirely my own responsibility.

This book owes a great deal to my friend Laura Enstone, whose financial and personal sacrifices have allowed me to continue my researchs throughout Europe and Russia. With little thought as to her own interests or agendas, Laura has repeatedly joined me with enthusiasm and good humor in the many curious and sometimes frightening adventures which accompanied my research. Happily, I can once again express my humble thanks for her valued friendship.

Susanne Meslans proves over and over again that any project I undertake would be sorely incomplete without her important and unfailingly gracious advice. Her enthusiasm for, and great understanding of, the eras and people of which I write shows in her comments and suggestions. Her unselfish contributions are spread across page after page of this book, a testament to her unique and invaluable insights.

Finally, I have to thank Gabriel Glennie. He generously read the manuscript, offering critical suggestions and responding with enthusiasm to the project. His sacrifices allowed me to complete research and meet deadlines, while his unfailing assistance made my task far easier. Above all, his great friendship and personal support sustained me through many uncertain times and troubling moments. No amount of thanks can express my appreciation for his concern, comfort, and continued presence, through undoubtedly trying circumstances, as an example of what a best friend can truly be.

Source Notes

Prologue
1. *Rasputin*, 45.
2. Ibid., 46.
3. Ibid., 48.
4. Ibid., 48.
5. Ibid., 49.
6. Ibid., 49.
7. Ibid., 50–1.

Chapter 1
1. Paléologue, 3:26.
2. Marie Pavlovna, 248–49.
3. Rasputin's apartment is now subdivided among several families.
4. Fulop-Miller, 236.
5. Mossolov, 153.
6. Paléologue, 1:292.
7. Fulop-Miller, 271.
8. Pares, 140.
9. Quoted in De Jonge, 213–14.
10. Fulop-Miller, 207.
11. Ibid., 215.
12. Ibid., 183.
13. Ibid., 185.
14. Ibid., 185.
15. Ibid., 187.
16. Ibid., 199.
17. Ibid., 199.
18. Ibid., 200.
19. Ibid., 185.
20. Ibid., 188.
21. Ibid., 199.
22. Ibid., 189.
23. Ibid., 190.
24. Mayre, 446.
25. Marie Pavlovna, 248–49.

Chapter 2
1. De Jonge, 14.
2. Fulop-Miller, 14–15.
3. Ibid., 16.
4. Wilson, 38.
5. De Jonge, 35.
6. Wilson, 31.
7. Pares, 145.
8. Wilson, 33.
9. De Jonge, 48.
10. Ibid., 13.
11. De Jonge, 94.
12. Paléologue, 1:141–42.
13. Nicholas II, Dnevnik, 229.

Chapter 3
1. LS, 62.
2. Pares, 133.
3. Alexander, 183.
4. Nicholas II's diary, quoted in Radziwill, 181.
5. Tisdall, 243.
6. Alexander, 182.
7. Ibid., 181.
8. Vorres, 142.
9. Mossolov, 148.
10. Spiridovich, 2:202.
11. Vyrubova, 92.
12. Gilliard, 29.

13. Vyrubova, 29.
14. N to ME 276.
15. Buxhoeveden, 132.
16. Ibid., 132.
17. Vyrubova, 93.
18. N to ME 276.
19. Vyrubova, 93.
20. Ibid., 94.
21. Mossolov, 150–51.
22. Vorres, 143.
23. Massie, *Nicholas and Alexandra*, 190–91.
24. Buxhoeveden, 142.
25. Iliodor, 181–82.
26. De Jonge, 141.
27. Fuhrmann, 29.
28. Buxhoeveden, *Before the Storm*, 116–19.
29. Cited, De Jonge, 139.

Chapter 4

1. Iliodor, 202.
2. Rodzianko, 27–28.
3. LS, 146.
4. Botkin, 123.
5. Vyrubova, 162.
6. Fuhrmann, 53.
7. Rodzianko, 33–34.
8. Iliodor, 108.
9. Cited, De Jonge, 169.
10. Iliodor, 111.
11. Moorehead, 72.
12. Maria Rasputin, *My Father*, 88.
13. Lockhart, 125–26.
14. Paléologue, 1:321.
15. Lockhart, 126.
16. Pares, 225.
17. Cited, Salisbury, 271.
18. AF to N, 105–06.
19. Shulgin, 266–67.

Chapter 5

1. AF to N, 86.
2. Ibid., 87.
3. Ibid., 186.
4. Ibid., 94.
5. Ibid., 291.
6. Ibid., 117.

7. Kilcoyne, 279.
8. Cited, De Jonge, 287.
9. AF to N, 394.
10. Billington, 500.
11. Kerensky, *Crucifixion*, 218.
12. AF to N, 428.
13. Alexander, 271.
14. Kerensky, *Crucifixion*, 244.
15. Salisbury, 296.
16. Alexander, 275.
17. Cited, Salisbury, 297.
18. Cited, Alexandrov, 119–20.
19. AF to N, 433

Chapter 6

1. LS, 22.
2. Massie, *Pavlovsk*, 127.
3. Ferrand, 85–99.
4. Lieven, 47.
5. Kochan, 35.
6. Vorres, 98.
7. LS, 55.
8. Stephan, 5.
9. Nadelhoffer, 286–87.
10. Ibid., 132.
11. Obolensky, 48.

Chapter 7

1. Obolensky, 4–5.
2. LS, 19.
3. Russell, in Kennett, 21–22.
4. This description of the Moika Palace is drawn from Gaynor, 122; Kennett, 73–74; Harris, 121–26; and from information gathered on a private tour of the structure.
5. Williams, 235.
6. Harris, 126.
7. Freeman, 69–70; Berton, 91.
8. LS, 30.
9. Brumfield, 310.
10. Ibid., 576 note.
11. Gaynor, 61–2.
12. LS, 34.
13. LS, 117.
14. Ibid., 90.
15. Ibid., 90.

Chapter 8

1. LS, 40.
2. Ibid., 45–46.
3. Ibid., 61.
4. Ibid., 94–95.
5. Ibid., 78.
6. Buchanan, *Dissolution*, 24.
7. Kleinmichel, 132–33.
8. LS, 64–66.
9. Ibid., 80.
10. Ibid., 81–82.
11. Ibid., 82–84.
12. Ibid., 81.
13. Maud, 44.
14. Dorr, 104.
15. Izvolsky, 86.
16. LS, 110.
17. Ibid., 42–43.
18. Ibid., 84.
19. Taylor, 8.

Chapter 9

1. Obolensky, 66.
2. LS, 113.
3. Ibid., 113.
4. LS, 114. See Obolensky, 66, for further information.
5. LS, 115.
6. Ibid., 123.
7. Ibid., 125.
8. Ibid., 126.
9. Obolensky, 66.
10. LS, 108–9.
11. Lincoln, *In War's Dark Shadow*, 126.
12. Salisbury, 101–2.
13. LS, 124.
14. Ibid., 126.
15. Ibid., 127.
16. Ibid., 133.
17. Ibid., 134–35.

Chapter 10

1. This information is drawn from Morris.
2. Dobson, 40.
3. LS, 139.
4. Ibid., 142.

5. Obolensky, 89–90.
6. LS, 157.
7. Williams, 79.
8. LS, 149.
9. Cooper, 97.
10. Ibid., 98.
11. Ziegler, 26.
12. LS, 86.
13. Buchanan, *Victorian Gallery*, 152.
14. Stopford, 43. Stopford's book *The Russian Diary of an Englishman* was published anonymously; I have referenced citations to Stopford to avoid confusion.
15. AF to N, 294.
16. Ibid., 259.
17. Ibid., 128.
18. Ibid., 237.
19. AF to N, 496.
20. LS, 88.

Chapter 11

1. LS, 162.
2. Ibid., 170; Dobson, 43.
3. LS, 172.
4. Ibid., 163.
5. Ibid., 170.
6. Buchanan, *Victorian Gallery*, 149.
7. Ferrand, 246–57 .
8. Izvolsky, 86.
9. Buchanan, *Victorian Gallery*, 184.
10. Radzhinskii, 141.
11. Quoted in Bokhanov, 240.
12. Almedingen, 137.

Chapter 12

1. For more information on these plots, see Fuhrmann, chapters 19–20; Minney, 149, chapters 28, 30; and Fulop-Miller, 311–31.
2. Almedingen, 143.
3. LS, 193.
4. Cited, Salisbury, 299.

5. Paléologue, 3:159.
6. LS, 194.
7. *Rasputin*, 67.
8. LS, 222.
9. *Rasputin*, 102, 115.
10. N to AF, editor's notes, 203.
11. LS, 221.
12. Fulop-Miller, 339.
13. Rasputin and Barham, 239.
14. Dobson, 31.
15. Berkman, 151.
16. De Jonge, 62.
17. Coward, 656.

Chapter 13

1. *Rasputin*, 61–65.
2. Ibid., 68.
3. Ibid., 69–70.
4. Ibid., 74.
5. Ibid., 75–76.
6. Rasputin and Barham, 239.
7. *Rasputin*, 90–91.
8. LS, 103–5.
9. De Jonge, 300.
10. *Rasputin*, 92–93.
11. Ibid., 93.
12. Ibid., 112.
13. Ibid., 106.
14. Ibid., 87.
15. Salisbury, 304.
16. *Rasputin*, 99.
17. Pares, 396–97; Paléologue, 3:111.
18. Paléologue, 3:153.
19. Purishkevich, 73.
20. Ibid., 73.
21. Ibid., 74–75.
22. *Krasni Arkhiv*, 1926, no. 14, 235.
23. Ibid., 123–24.

Chapter 14

1. *Soviet Zap.*, 1927–18, no. 34, 269–75.
2. Ibid., 269–75.
3. *Rasputin*, 124.
4. *Soviet Zap.*, 1927–28, no. 34, 269–75.
5. Purishkevich, 81.

6. *Rasputin*, 121.
7. Shulgin, 268–69.
8. Purishkevich, 93.
9. *Rasputin*, 129.
10. *Krasni Arkhiv*, 1926, no. 14, 231.
11. Stopford, 73.
12. Vyrubova, 174.
13. Pares, 399.
14. AF to N, 458.
15. Simanovich, 161.
16. Vyrubova, 178–79.

Chapter 15

1. LS, 231.
2. *Rasputin*, 133.
3. LS, 232.
4. LS, 233.
5. Ibid., 233.
6. Rasputin, *My Father*, 12.
7. LS, 234.
8. Ibid., 235.
9. Ibid., 235.
10. Ibid., 235.
11. Ibid., 236.
12. Purishkevich, 135.
13. LS, 236.
14. *Rasputin*, 145.
15. LS, 237.
16. Ibid., 237.
17. *Rasputin*, 147.
18. Ibid., 147.
19. LS, 237–38.
20. Purishkevich, 137.
21. Ibid., 137.
22. *Rasputin*, 148.
23. Purishkevich, 139–40.
24. Ibid., 140.
25. Ibid., 140–41.
26. *Rasputin*, 150.
27. Ibid., 151–52.
28. *Soviet Zap.*, 1927–28, no. 34, 281.
29. LS, 240.
30. Purishkevich, 142.
31. LS, 241.
32. Ibid., 243.
33. Ibid., 242.
34. Purishkevich, 146.
35. Ibid., 149–50.
36. *Rasputin*, 160.

37. Purishkevich, 150.
38. Ibid., 152.
39. Ibid., 152–54.
40. Ibid., 160.
41. Ibid., 162.

Chapter 16

1. *Rasputin*, 165.
2. Official report of the Petrograd police, Kazan District, filed 17 December 1917. Published in *"Ubiistvo Rasputina: ofitsial'noe dozanie."* Also printed in Stopford, 218–22, in a slightly different form.
3. Stopford, 215–17.
4. Ibid., 83.
5. Vyrubova, 132.
6. Obolensky, 155.
7. Ibid., 230.
8. Simanovich, 162.
9. Rasputin and Barham, 234–35.
10. For more information on this, see Rasputin and Barham, *Rasputin, The Man Behind the Myth*, afterword.
11. De Jonge, 315–16.
12. Rasputin, *My Father*, 111.
13. Wilson, 192.
14. Purishkevich, 150.
15. De Jonge, 321.

Chapter 17

1. *Ubiistvo Rasputina*, 66–68.
2. *Rasputin*, 170–71.
3. Ibid., 173.
4. Ibid., 182.
5. AF to N, 461.
6. N to AF, 312.
7. Gilliard, 183.
8. Cited, De Jonge, 325-26.
9. *Arkhiv Russ. Rev.*, 1927, no. XXII, 352.
10. Ibid., 352.
11. Quoted, Fuhrmann, 208.
12. Rasputin, *My Father*, 16.
13. Minney, 201.
14. Dehn, 121; *Padenie*, 4:107; Fuhrmann, 210; De Jonge, 324.

15. Dehn, 123.
16. Kerensky, *The Murder of the Romanovs*, 106.
17. Paléologue, 3:136.
18. See Fuhrmann, 214.

Chapter 18

1. Hanbury-Williams, 145–46.
2. Paléologue, 3:189.
3. Alexander, 277.
4. Vorres, 145.
5. Quoted, Dobson, 92.
6. Marie Pavlovna, 265.
7. Quoted, Fuhrmann, 209.
8. Paléologue, 3:171.
9. Marie Pavlovna, 264.
10. Shulgin, 109.
11. Marie Pavlovna, 253.
12. Vyrubova, 183.
13. Paléologue, 3:164.
14. Alexander, 279.
15. Quoted in Bokhanov, 237.
16. Stopford, 213–14.
17. Ibid., 93.

Chapter 19

1. Paléologue, 3:191.
2. Alexander, 283–84.
3. Paléologue, 3:157.
4. Pares, 442.
5. Cited, Salisbury, 361.
6. Pares, 443.
7. Botkin, 139.
8. Kschessinska, 169.
9. Stopford, 141.
10. Marie Pavlovna, *A Princess in Exile*, 103.
11. LS, 271.
12. Alexander, 298, 301.
13. Glenny, 160.
14. LS, 277.
15. Ibid., 275–76, Stopford, 189–90.
16. Marie Pavlovna, *A Princess in Exile*, 103.
17. Dorr, 103–5.
18. Glenny, 103–4.
19. Von Meck, 179.
20. Curator of Moika Palace to Author, 19 May 1992.

21. Nadelhoffer, 286.
22. LS, 278.

Chapter 20

1. LS, 282.
2. Prideham, 50.
3. Ibid., 67.
4. Ibid., 91.

Chapter 21

1. Clarke, 219.
2. Obolensky, 264.
3. Marie Pavlovna, *A Princess in Exile*, 105.
4. Ibid., 120.
5. Obolensky, 231.
6. Ibid., 231.
7. Ibid., 231.
8. *En Exil*, 12–13.
9. *Star*, 26 November 1919.
10. Alexander, *Always a Grand Duke*, 35–36.
11. Ibid., 68.
12. Marie Pavlovna, *A Princess in Exile*, 131.
13. Glenny, 269–70.
14. Ibid., 267.
15. Ibid., 269.
16. Ibid., 184–85.
17. Ibid., 175.
18. Alexander, *Always a Grand Duke*, 123–24.
19. Ibid., 54–55.
20. Marie Pavlovna, *A Princess in Exile*, 67.
21. Alexander, *Always a Grand Duke*, 113.
22. *En Exil*, 102.
23. Nadelhoffer, 132.
24. Ibid., 286–87.
25. Obolensky, 276.
26. *En Exil*, 37–38.
27. Ibid., 39.

Chapter 22

1. *En Exil*, 68.
2. Ibid., 69.

3. Shoumatoff, 138.
4. *En Exil*, 70–71.
5. Nadelhoffer, 132.
6. *En Exil*, 85–86.
7. Marie Pavlovna, *A Princess in Exile*, 270.
8. Izvolsky, 161–62.
9. Marie Pavlovna, *A Princess in Exile*, 103.
10. Rasputin, *My Father*, 11, 20.
11. *En Exil*, 143–44.
12. Ibid., 122–25.
13. Dobson, 145.
14. Ibid., 133–35.
15. Ibid., 90–91.

Chapter 23

1. *En Exil*, 114.
2. Ibid., 114.
3. Cited, Kurth, 186.
4. Lovell, 130–31.
5. Lovell admitted to me shortly before his death that he himself did not believe Mrs. Anderson on this account.
6. Cited, Kurth, 186.
7. *I, Anastasia*, 227–28.
8. Lovell, 252–53.
9. Dobson, 162.
10. *En Exil*, 62.
11. Napley, 62.
12. Ibid., 62–64.
13. Ibid., 66.
14. Ibid., 67.
15. Berkman, 139.
16. Ibid., 142.
17. Ibid., 143.
18. Ibid., 144.
19. Ibid., 144–45.

Chapter 24

1. Berkman, 151.
2. Napley, 85.
3. Ibid., 86–90.
4. Ibid., 90–91.
5. Ibid., 92–93.
6. *En Exil*, 179–80.
7. Napley, 94–98.

8. Ibid., 123–24.
9. *Daily Express*, 1 March 1934.
10. Napley, 128.
11. *Daily Express*, 2 March 1934.
12. Napley, 132.
13. Ibid., 133.
14. Ibid., 144.

Chapter 25

1. *Daily Express*, 6 March 1934.
2. Napley, 198.
3. See Napley, 202, and Berkman, 161, for further information on the financial settlement.
4. Berkman, 168.
5. *En Exil*, 172.
6. Ibid., 59.
7. Ibid., 198.
8. Coward, 61.

9. *En Exil*, 203.
10. Ibid., 205

Chapter 26

1. *En Exil*, 53.
2. Information from Dr. Idris Traylor to author.
3. Ibid.
4. Quoted, Bryan and Murphey, 558.
5. Information from Pauline Holdrup to author.
6. *Guardian*, 29 December 1966.
7. *Horizon*, Autumn, 1967, vol. IX, no. 4.
8. Melnik, 26.

Epilogue

1. Dobson, 87

Bibliography

Alexander Michailovich. *Once a Grand Duke*. Garden City, N.Y.: Doubleday, 1932.

———. *Always A Grand Duke*. New York: Garden City Publishing, 1933.

Alexandra Feodorovna. *The Letters of the Tsarina to the Tsar, 1914–1917*. London: Duckworth, 1923.

Alexandrov, Victor. *The End of the Romanovs*. London: Hutchinson, 1966.

Almedingen, Edith Martha von. *The Empress Alexandra*. London: Hutchinson, 1961.

Berkman, Ted. *The Lady and The Law: The Remarkable Life of Fanny Holtzmann*. Boston: Little, Brown, 1976.

Berton, Kathleen. *Moscow, An Architectural History*. London: I. B. Tauris & Co., 1990.

Billington, James. *The Icon and the Axe*. New York: Knopf, 1966.

Bokhanov, Alexander. *The Romanovs: Love, Power and Tragedy*. London: Leppi Publications, 1993.

Botkin, Gleb. *The Real Romanovs*. New York, Revell, 1931.

Brumfield, William Craft. *A History of Russian Architecture*. Cambridge, Eng.: Cambridge University Press, 1993.

Bryan III, J., and Charles Murphey. *The Windsor Story*. New York: William Morrow, 1979.

Buchanan, Meriel. *Dissolution of an Empire*. London: Murray, 1932.

———. *Victorian Gallery*. London: Cassell, 1956.

Buxhoeveden, Sophie. *The Life and Tragedy of Alexandra Feodorovna, Empress of Russia*. New York: Longmans, Green, 1928.

———. *Before The Storm*. London: Macmillan, 1938.

Clarke, William. *The Lost Fortune of the Tsars*. London: Weidenfeld & Nicolson, 1994.

Cooper, Lady Diana. *Autobiography*. New York: Carroll & Graf, 1985.

Coward, Nöel. *The Nöel Coward Diaries*. Edited by Graham Payn and Sheridan Morley. Boston: Little, Brown, 1982.

Dehn, Lili. *The Real Tsaritsa*. London: Thornton Butterworth, 1922.

De Jonge, Alex. *The Life and Times of Gregorii Rasputin*. New York: Dorset Press, 1982.

Dobson, Christopher. *Prince Felix Yusupov, The Man Who Killed Rasputin*. London: Harrap, 1989.

Dorr, Rheta Childe. *Inside the Russian Revolution*. New York: Macmillan, 1918.

Ferrand, Jacques. *Les princes Youssoupoff & les comtes Soumarokoff-Elston, Chronique et Photographies*. Paris: Jacques Ferrand, 1991.

Freeman, John, and Kathleen Berton. *Moscow Revealed*. New York: Abbeville Press, 1991.

Fuhrmann, Joseph T. *Rasputin: A Life*. New York: Praeger, 1990.

Fulop-Miller, René. *Rasputin, The Holy Devil*. Garden City, N.Y.: Doubleday, 1928.

Gaynor, Elizabeth, and Kari Haavisto. *Russian Houses*. New York: Stewart, Tabori & Chang, 1991.

Gilliard, Pierre. *Thirteen Years at the Russian Imperial Court*. New York: Doran, 1921.

Glenny, Michael, and Norman Stone. *The Other Russia: The Experience of Exile*. New York: Viking, 1991.

Hanbury-Williams, Sir John. *The Emperor Nicholas II as I Knew Him*. London: Humphreys, 1922.

Iliodor [Sergei Trufanov]. *The Mad Monk of Russia*. New York: Century, 1928.

Izvolsky, Helene. *No Time to Grieve*. Philadelphia: Winchell Co., 1985.

Kennett, Victor and Audrey. *The Palaces of Leningrad*. New York: Putnam's, 1973.

Kerensky, Alexander. *The Crucifixion of Liberty*. New York: Appleton, 1927.

——. *The Murder of the Romanovs*. London: Hutchinson, 1935.

Kilcoyne, Martin. *The Political Influence of Rasputin*. Unpublished Ph.D. diss. Seattle: University of Washington, 1961.

Kleinmichel, Countess Marie. *Memories of a Shipwrecked World*. London: Brentano's, 1923.

Knox, Alfred. *With the Russian Army*. New York: Dutton, 1921.

Kochan, Miriam. *The Last Days of Imperial Russia*. New York: Macmillan, 1976.

Krug von Nidda, Roland, ed. *I, Anastasia*. London: Michael Joseph, 1958.

Kschessinska, Mathilde. *Dancing in Petersburg*. Garden City, N.Y.: Doubleday, 1961.

Kurth, Peter. *Anastasia: The Riddle of Anna Anderson.* Boston: Little, Brown, 1983.

Lievan, Dominic. *Russia's Rulers Under the Old Regime.* New Haven, Conn.: Yale University Press, 1989.

Lincoln, W. Bruce. *In War's Dark Shadow.* New York: Dial, 1983.

Lockhart, Robert Bruce. *British Agent.* New York: Putnam's, 1933.

Lovell, James Blair. *Anastasia: The Lost Princess.* Washington, D.C.: Regnery Gateway, 1991

Marie Pavlovna. *Education of a Princess.* New York: Viking, 1934.

———. *A Princess in Exile.* New York: Viking, 1932.

Massie, Robert K. *Nicholas and Alexandra.* New York: Atheneum, 1967.

Massie, Suzanne. *Pavlovsk: The Life of a Russian Palace.* Boston: Little, Brown, 1990.

Maud, Rene Elton. *One Year at The Russian Court.* New York: John Lane, 1907.

Mayre, George Thomas. *Nearing the End in Imperial Russia.* Philadelphia: Dorrance, 1929.

Minney, R. J. *Rasputin.* London: Cassell & Co., 1972.

Moorehead, Alan. *The Russian Revolution.* New York: Harper & Row, 1958.

Morris, James. *Oxford.* New York: Harcourt, Brace & World, 1965.

Mossolov, Alexander. *At the Court of the Last Tsar.* London: Methuen, 1935.

Nadelhoffer, Hans. *Cartier: Jewellers Extraordinary.* London: Thames & Hudson, 1984.

Napley, Sir David. *Rasputin in Hollywood.* London: Weidenfeld & Nicolson, 1989.

Nicholas II. *Dnevnik Imperatora Nikolaia vtorago.* Berlin: Slovo, 1923.

———. *The Secret Letters of the Last Tsar: Being The Confidential Correspondence Between Nicholas II and His Mother Dowager Empress Marie Feodorovna.* Edited by Edward J. Bing. New York: Longmans, Green, 1938.

———. *The Letters of the Tsar to the Tsarina, 1914–1917.* London: Bodley Head, 1929.

Obolensky, Prince Serge. *One Man in His Time.* New York: McDowell, 1958.

Padenie tsarskogo rezhima: Stenografisheskie otchety doprosov i pokazanii, dannikh v 1917 q. v Chrezvychaino: Sledstvennoi Komissii Vremenaogo Pravitel'stva. Edited by P. E. Shchegolev. 7 Volumes. Moscow and Leningrad, 1924–27.

Paléologue, Maurice. *An Ambassador's Memoirs.* New York: Doran, 1925.

Pares, Sir Bernard. *The Fall of the Russian Monarchy*. New York: Vintage, 1961.

Prideham, Sir Francis. *Close of a Dynasty*. London: Wingate, 1959.

Purishkevich, Vladimir. *The End of Rasputin*. Ann Arbor, Mich.: Ardis Press, 1985.

Radzhinskii, Edvard. *The Last Tsar: The Life and Death of Nicholas II*. New York: Doubleday, 1992.

Radziwill, Princess Catherine. *Nicholas II, The Last of the Tsars*. London: Cassell, 1931.

Rasputin, Maria. *My Father*. London: Cassell, 1934.

Rasputin, Maria, with Patte Barham. *Rasputin: The Man Behind the Myth*. Englewood Cliffs, N.J.: Prentice Hall, 1977.

Rodzianko, Michael. *The Reign of Rasputin*. London: Philpot, 1927.

Salisbury, Harrison. *Black Night, White Snow*. New York: Doubleday, 1977.

Shoumatoff, Alex. *Russian Blood*. New York: Vantage, 1990.

Shulgin, Vassili. *The Years: Memoirs of a Member of the Russian Duma*. New York: Hippocrene Books, 1984.

Simanovich, Aaron. *Rasputin i evre; vospominaiia lichnago sekretaria Grigorii Rasputin*. Riga: no publisher, no date.

Spiridovich, Alexander. *Les dernieres annees de la cour de Tsarskoie Selo*. Paris: Payot, 1928.

Stephan, John J. *The Russian Fascists*. New York: Harper & Row, 1978.

Stopford, The Hon. Bertie. *The Russian Diary of An Englishman*. London: William Heinemann, 1919.

Taylor, Katrina. *Faberge at Hillwood*. Washington, D.C.: The Museum Press, 1983.

Tisdall, E. E. P. *The Dowager Empress*. London: Paul, 1957.

"Ubiistvo Rasputina: ofitsial'noe dozanie." *Byloe*. 1 n.s. (1917)

Von Meck, Galina. *As I Remember Them*. London: Denis Dobson, 1973.

Vorres, Ian. *The Last Grand Duchess*. New York: Scribners, 1965.

Vyrubova, Anna. *Memories of the Russian Court*. New York: Macmillan, 1923.

Williams, Mrs. Hwfa. *It Was Such Fun*. London: Hutchinson & Co., 1935.

Wilson, Colin. *Rasputin and the Fall of the Romanovs*. New York: Farrar, Strauss, 1964.

Youssoupov, Prince Felix. *Rasputin: His Malignant Influence and Assassination*. New York: Dial, 1927.

———. *Lost Splendour*. London: Cape, 1953.

———. *En Exil*. Paris: Plon, 1954.

Ziegler, Philip. *Diana Cooper*. New York: Knopf, 1982.

Periodicals

Halliday, E. M. "Rasputin Reconsidered." *Horizon*. Vol. IX, No. 4 (Autumn 1967).

Harris, Dale. "Inside Yusupov Palace." *Architecural Digest*. Vol. 47, No. 11 (October 1990).

Arkhiv Russ. Revolution (issue and date referenced in source notes).

Krasnii Arkhiv (issues and dates referenced in source notes).

Sovremennye Zapiski (Sov. Zap) (issues and dates referenced in source notes).

Newspapers

(dates referenced in source notes)
Star (London)
Daily Express (London)
Guardian (London)

Index